# The Rise and Fall of the Italian Film Industry

Italian cinema triumphed globally in the 1960, with directors such as Rossellini, Fellini and Leone, and actors like Sophia Loren and Marcello Mastroianni, known to audiences around the world. But by the end of the 1980s, the Italian film industry was all but dead. *The Rise and Fall of the Italian Film Industry* traces the rise of the industry from its origins in the nineteenth century to its worldwide success in the 1960s and its rapid decline in the subsequent decades. It does so by looking at cinema as an institution—subject to the interplay between the spheres of art, business and politics at the national and international level.

By examining the roles of a wide range of stakeholders (including film directors, producers, exhibitors, the public and the critics) as well as the system of funding and the influence of governments, author Marina Nicoli demonstrates that the Italian film industry succeeded when all three spheres were aligned, but suffered and ultimately failed when they each pursued contradictory objectives. This in-depth case study makes an important contribution to the long-standing debate about promoting and protecting domestic cultures, particularly in the face of culturally dominant and politically and economically powerful creative industries from the United States. *The Rise and Fall of the Italian Film Industry* will be of particular interest to business and economic historians, cinema historians, media specialists and cultural economists.

**Marina Nicoli** is a Post-Doctoral Research Fellow in the Department of Policy Analysis and Public Management at Bocconi University, Italy.

# Routledge International Studies in Business History

Series editors: Jeffrey Fear and Christina Lubinski

For a full list of titles in this series, please visit www.routledge.com

# The Rise and Fall of the Italian Film Industry

Marina Nicoli

Routledge
Taylor & Francis Group

NEW YORK AND LONDON

First published 2017
by Routledge
711 Third Avenue, New York, NY 10017

and by Routledge
2 Park Square, Milton Park, Abingdon, Oxon OX14 4RN

First issued in paperback 2018

*Routledge is an imprint of the Taylor & Francis Group, an informa business*

*Library of Congress Cataloging in Publication Data*
A catalog record for this book has been requested

ISBN 13: 978-1-138-34078-7 (pbk)
ISBN 13: 978-1-138-79005-6 (hbk)

Typeset in Sabon
by Apex CoVantage, LLC

This book is dedicated to Armando, my husband, for being by my side and for having always cheered me up, and to Alberto, my son, for his unconditional love.

# Contents

# Tables and Graphs

# Abbreviations

| | |
|---|---|
| ASI-BCI | Archivio Storico Intesa-Banca Commerciale Italiana |
| ANICA | Associazione Nazionale Industrie Cinematografiche e Affini |
| B.N.L. | Archivio Storico Banca Nazionale del Lavoro |
| S.A.C.C. | Sezione Autonoma di Credito Cinematografico |
| SASP | Società Anonima Stefano Pittaluga |
| SIAE | Società Italiana Autori Editori |

# Acknowledgments

The roots of this book have to be found during the preparation of my PhD dissertation at Bocconi University in Milan. Some years later, in 2011, I had the opportunity of being a visiting fellow at the Leslie Center for the Humanities, Dartmouth College. My grateful thanks go to Adrian Randolph, former director of the Center, and Isabel Weatherdon for their hospitality and generous support. Spring in Hanover has been really productive: I had access to some of the finest libraries in the United States and had the opportunity to visit the wonderful National Archive and Record Administration (N.A.R.A.) archive in Washington D.C. During this fruitful period, I further developed the idea of the book and decided to dig into new archival sources.

During the research and writing phase, I accumulated countless debts. Heartfelt thanks go to Franco Amatori and Andrea Colli, who had faith in my research and granted me a post-doc at Bocconi University. I am also grateful to Matthias Kipping and Ray Stokes for having supported the book project. I have to thank David Varley and Brianna Ascher at Routledge for their patience and support. In addition, the external readers encouraged me, giving useful and important suggestions.

Barbara Corsi, Daniela Manetti, Peter Miskell, John Sedgwick and Daniela Treveri-Gennari are academic colleagues who share my passion for Italian cinema: I discussed with them relevant topics of my research, and they helped with comments and advice. I am particularly grateful to Peter Miskell for his sharp suggestions on how to improve the book and for his capacity to accurately raise historical and economic issues connected to the film industry.

A special thank goes to John Sedgwick: he constantly inspires challenging themes and questions on the Italian film industry. Moreover, the study of Italian cinema gave me the opportunity to meet two excellent scholars like Stephen Gundle and Christopher Wagstaff.

Elements of the book have been exposed and debated during academic seminars at Bocconi and the EBHA (European Business History Association) and BHC (Business History Conference) international conferences.

I have benefited enormously from advice given by several colleagues, mentors and friends: Stefano Baia Curioni, Michela Barbot, Giuseppe Berta, Giorgio Bigatti, Michele D'Alessandro, Laura Forti (she is the wizard of Excel), Walter Friedman, Guido Guerzoni and Geoffrey Jones. Veronica Binda, Matteo Di Tullio and Mario Perugini are friends and colleagues who daily share the academic roller-coaster: they have supported me during this journey. A special thank goes to Francesco Boldizzoni for his precious advices. Fabrizio Perretti, a colleague who studies creative industries in the management department at Bocconi, reminded me to never lose the complexity and richness of the historical approach. Naturally, the responsibility for what has been written is entirely mine.

I am also indebted to the staff of the archives and libraries for their kindness and availability. Special thanks go to Valeria Venditti and Maurizio Di Russo that opened the doors of the historical archives of Banca Nazionale del Lavoro. I am more than grateful to Gaetano Martino and Pierluigi Raffaelli for having opened their private archives and shared many precious documents that I used for my research. Their daily effort to preserve the archival memory of the Italian film industry deserves mention. I sincerely hope that, in the future, public and private institutions will be able to invest more in the preservation and accessibility of archival sources. I would also like to thank the staff of ANICA and of the AGIS library in Milan for constant help and support with the Borsa Film.

Last but not least, many thanks to Sarah Jane Christopher: she has turned my prose into English.

I am grateful to my parents for their love and support: they have shared joy and pain of film industry datasets.

# Introduction

Film is an art and the cinema is an industry.[1]

> In a capitalist economy, a film is an intellectual product
> because it has all the requisites of a work of art,
> but it is also a type of merchandise
> because its production and consumption require
> industrial and commercial operations.[2]

One fine day Zavattini came to me with Vittorio De Sica and said, "Dino, we have a project here that is a work of art". "What is it?" "*Il giudizio universale/The Last Judgement*". I was doubtful about the project, but there was Zavattini, De Sica as the director, and an outstanding cast, so we made this picture, intending to make a work of art. It was a flop at Venice and it was a flop with the public. You can't define a work of art from the outset. When I made films with Fellini, I said to him, "What does this film mean?" "I don't know, Dino, I'm waiting for its release and then the critics will tell me what this film means". A work of art is something that in a certain sense we can't decipher. We can't start off saying, "I'm going to create a work of art". We, American producers, think of ourselves as showmen, and we try to make a good quality product for audiences all over the world, not just in America.[3]

This anecdote illustrates some of the criticalities that have characterised the Italian cinema from the start. This conversation between producer Dino De Laurentiis and screenwriter Cesare Zavattini, (the film was released in 1961) highlights the constant tension between the dictates of art and of economics, in a sector whose industrial and artistic components are bound together. It shows that film production is a risky business even with an outstanding cast, and that a film's success always depends on the public's reaction. This is also the story of an Italian producer, Dino De Laurentiis, who left for Hollywood in the 1960s because he felt that Italy was no longer a suitable place for cinema production ventures. Finally, it helps us to understand the fundamental difference between the American and Italian models.

The aim of the US model was to produce a technically valid film for an international public, while the Italian model was constantly uncertain about the nature of film as a product: was a film art, or was it a product made for entertainment purposes?

This book traces the evolution of the Italian industry across a series of quite distinct institutional environments. The aim is to examine which forces, political, economic, cultural and technological, were most important in shaping the development of the Italian cinema industry over the past 120 years. Clearly some of the forces shaping Italian cinema were international ones, also faced by other film industries, like the international expansion of the American companies from the 1910s or the transition to sound. These global trends were both threats to be resisted and opportunities to be exploited. Against these global industry-wide trends, we also see changes in the national political environment, with the shift from a liberal state to fascism and then to democracy after WWII. This perspective will allow the interpretation of the patterns in the industry both as a phenomenon of cooperation or competition with Hollywood and as the result of changing strategies, domestic and international policies, economic and political ideologies, and social and cultural practices.

The complex interactions among forces mentioned above (art, business and politics) explain how Italian cinema became an institution (Burch 2001, Casetti 2005): its transformation into an independent and qualified field, the formation of its productive structures and its own specific language, and the ways in which production practices, artistic aspirations and movie consumption are interconnected. The processes of institutionalization affect why and how Italian cinema determines for itself specificity and legitimacy, its own personality and identity.

Among the three broad "forces", the business one will occupy a special place in the book, since it has been rather neglected by the literature but is essential in understanding the movie industry. In fact, every movie is a "product" and, like any other business, the industry exists to make money (Squire 1993). For this reason, the history of Italian cinema will be examined considering issues such as the evolution of its industrial organization; the working of the movie value chain; the impact of technological innovation; the characteristics of demand; the importance of international trade and its influence on industry dynamics; government intervention, including the reasons behind movie industry regulation; and the impact of the various trade and regulatory regimes on the development of the industry. The overall aim is to identify how these factors shape the industry's trajectory and to understand how the Italian case differs from that of other countries.

## Cinema as a Creative Industry

Cinema, as well as museums, archives, festival, theatres, broadcasting, publishing, videogames and the music industry, is part of the broad family of "cultural and creative industries".[4] These are usually defined as those institutions that "employ the characteristic modes of production and organisation of industrial corporations to produce and disseminate symbols in the forms of cultural goods and services, generally, although not exclusively, as commodities" (Garnham 1990). In a more recent reconceptualization (Peltoniemi 2015) cultural and creative industries are defined as "those that produce experience goods with considerable elements and aim these at the consumer market via mass distribution".

The balance between economics and culture can be a slippery slope and involves a constant tension. Hirsch (1972) has noted that production shapes artistic expression because artists and creative people have different standards. Other researchers point out that cultural managers need to find a balance and reconcile artistic ambitions and the economics of mass entertainment. Nowadays, there is still controversy over whether art and profit are mutually exclusive or complementary.

Cultural and creative industries are usually set apart from conventional conceptions of an industry due to their specificities: they supply products and goods that serve more aesthetic, broadly educational or entertainment purposes rather than any immediate "technical" function (Throsby 2001) and for this reason it is usually difficult to assess the value they create through purely quantitative measurement. The social and cultural significance is unarguable, but these industries have also started to account for a significant and growing share of economic activity.

Insofar as cultural and creative industries are becoming more and more important as a source of innovation and economic dynamism, the development of these sectors is a relevant issue in the current political agenda of national governments. According to the UNCTAD Creative Economy Report, cultural and creative industries are among the most dynamic emerging sectors in world trade: world exports of cultural and creative goods and services are increasing at an average annual rate of 8.7%. The contribution of these industries to the economy is, however, not limited to their direct and quantifiable impact. Cultural and creative industries are also an innovation driver in non-cultural sectors (Throsby 2001), indirectly contributing to industrial development (by influencing product developments), local and regional regeneration (by attracting investments, talent and tourism) and social ties (Mccarthy 2005, Brown 2004). For all these reasons, cultural and creative industries represent a strategic sector in the knowledge-based economy (Marcus 2005). The definition boundaries around these industries remain somewhat fuzzy, but in the last years, cultural and creative industries have been taken to include arts, heritage, film, television, radio, press, publishing, etc. In the last decades, creative industries have become part of the political agenda, and over the past 30 or 40 years several scientific communities[5]—Economics, Sociology, Anthropology, and, to a minor extent, Political Sciences and Law, Urban Studies and Geography—have all identified specific research fields intersecting the broadly intended world of art

and culture. These studies directly or indirectly affect the way in which these
industries are defined, thought, perceived and represented. The inclusion of
cultural industries as topics of interest within the different social sciences
has been, almost obviously, characterized and limited by the dominance
of the epistemological premises of each discipline. Social sciences are, of
course, not monolithic and in many cases (like economics, sociology and
anthropology), the confrontation with the subject of cultural and creative
industries spangled all along their intellectual history, providing a set of
different solutions and approaches. "Cultural economics" or "the economics of the arts and culture" represent an appealing research field both on
the theoretical and methodological level because of the challenge defining
whether and how cultural goods and services are different from the other
economic and market goods, and how they give birth to different practices of cultural consumption, production and exchange. This research area
developed from the late 1970s, when a group of economists—William Baumol, Mark Blaug, Bruno Frey, David Thorsby—analysed the art and entertainment market using the tools of economic theory. Cultural economics
is a field whose borders are not always well defined, and problems arise in
the first place because of the difficulty of defining the concept of "culture";
Borofsky compared the task to "trying to cage the wind". Ginsburgh has
observed that the cultural economy "is located at the crossroads of several
disciplines: art history, art philosophy, sociology, law, management, economics", and this explains the methodological difficulties in identifying the
most suitable analytical tools for understanding the functional dynamics of
the cultural goods and industries sector.

One of the key challenges faced by the study of cultural and creative
industries is the relationship between culture and the economy. Books, fashion, films, music, paintings and so on are simultaneously cultural products
and commodities. As cultural products, they reflect, and in turn shape, the
prevalent cultural values and norms of (particular sectors of) particular societies. As commodities, they are imagined, designed, produced, publicized,
circulated and finally read, worn, seen, listened to and looked at by particular groups of targeted consumers. Thus, despite increasing popularity in
this field of research, there is no comprehensive view on the subject. Some
researchers have emphasized the selection process through which cultural
and creative goods have to pass in order to get to their audience (Hirsch
1972). Others stress the inherent uncertainty of any cultural goods because
consumers do not have complete information about the product (De Vany
2004; Towse 2003b) or their non-utilitarian value (Lampel et al. 2000).
Many researchers have dealt with the conflicts that arise between economic
and artistic motives (Eikhof and Haunschild 2007). Artistic motives concern
stories and styles and they respond to the purposes of entertainment and
identity building. On the other hand, economic motives regard the management of production and distribution processes, where economies of scale
play a very important role. Given the uncertain boundaries and features of

cultural products, research on this topic has followed different paths that can be summarised as follows: by focusing on the product, researchers have tried to explain why certain products reach the market and others fail; on the organisational level, the aim is to understand the way organisation can affect the end product and, finally, at the industry level, researchers study the consequences of industry structures on creative outcomes. Even though cultural and creative industries research is vast, several areas remain for future research.

## There Is No Business Like the Movie Business

Cinema represents the emblematic art of modernity, one of the most pervasive "factories" creating the myths, collective consciousness and identity of the twentieth century. If we accept the hypothesis that every period of history has its own "eyes", i.e. its own particular way of looking at the world, and that this can reflect in the visual texts that a society produces, then we can say that cinema was the "eye" of the 1900s. It was a collective way of seeing, a visual depository for the spirit of the time. "The cinema is not only complex in the present and potentially fertile, but is also typical of this mankind to which we belong. It is a product of the times and sign of the times; a product because it is created by present day skills, but it is also a sign, because its widespread distribution shows its adaptation to the current psychology, to the point that it not only receives a colossal impulse, but also confirms, moulds and inspires the tastes of modern man".[6]

Cinema, movie theatre, film industry, film: this wide number of meanings seems to reflect its complexity. Cinema: art or industry? Cinema as a phenomenon or cinema as a production method? Cinema, like the other cultural industries—live entertainment, music, publishing—is a specific sector, influenced by economic and intangible factors[7] that require an investigative methodology capable of taking account of its peculiar features.

Even use of the words "film industry" is in itself problematic, since it immediately introduces what for many years was perceived as a contradictory relationship between art and industry. "We must remember that film production is not just an art, but also industry". There are many variants, but these words appear in every discussion regarding cinema. The office of Will Hays, the American film industry censor, achieved a compromise by talking about an art-industry. Industry certainly appears to be much more necessary for the art of the cinema than for the theatre; it would be difficult for the art of the cinema to exist without the triple structure of production, distribution and exhibition.

In the words of Morin, "a cultural industry must continually overcome a fundamental contradiction between its own bureaucratic-standardised structures and the originality (individuality and novelty) of the product it provides".[8] So, can cultural creation be integrated into an industrial production system?

The cinema's products are primarily artistic, but they have a great deal of industrial value. The conflict between the industrial and cultural aspect of the cinema is the conflict between the exchange value of the product and its intrinsic value, which affects all artistic products. Exchange value is connected with the artistic product's position on the market, while intrinsic value derives from its use. According to Benjamin, reiterated by Adorno and Horkeimer, a work of art loses authenticity in the age of mass media and technical reproducibility: reproducibility gives an exchange value to a work of art, which then goes onto the market as merchandise.

The fact that a film is both an artistic product and an economic product makes it difficult to find a parameter for indicating the performance of a film. A film may be evaluated according to its box-office success, and, on the other hand, it may be evaluated according to its innovative capacity and cultural content.

A film's performance can be measured by its box-office achievement, or by the opinions of film critics. Alfred Hitchcock, interviewed by Francois Truffaut, famously declared: "when a director is disappointed by critics because he realises that they do not accurately analyse his movies, oh well, the only thing he can do is to make commercial movies. If a director shoots only for box office, he will be soon influenced by routine and this is bad. Critics are often to be blamed for this situation, because a director is induced to be worried by box office and to declare I don't mind critics because my movies are commercially successful".[9] Therefore, economic performance seems to require the repetition of successful formulas, whereas cultural performance, i.e. art, seems to require new approaches, innovation and creativity, but could inevitably disappoints the public.

We also know that film production entails a high level of risk. There appears to be no entrepreneurial formula for guaranteeing that a film will be a box-office success or acclaimed by the critics. There are plenty of examples of unexpected flops and unexpected successes (Hesmondhalgh 2002). The cinema is the "nobody knows" industry, because nobody can predict what will happen at the box office (Goldman 1983). Moreover, in the history of the film industry there are very few films that have been both box-office successes and artistically outstanding. Besides this, the film industry is a context in which economic and artistic performances depend on physical/material capital, human capital and social capital. Physical capital is extremely important for the commercial success of a film. The budget determines the technical input and the quality of the human capital involved in production. Famous actors, the possibility of shooting in different and exotic locations, and the use of special effects are important for the film's chances of success. Human capital means acquired skills and knowhow, while social capital is even less tangible than human capital and is related to interpersonal relations. All three forms of capital can have an effect on production and on box-office results.

In the late nineteenth century and early twentieth century, an intensification of the circulation of technologies, cultural texts and cultural workers was registered. The waves of internationalization of cultural products came mainly from the United States (Tunstall, 1994): the speedy capture of the world movie market by Hollywood from the end of WWI, the coming of sound movies in the '30s, the spread of American entertainment newspapers are some of the example of the progressive dissemination of American culture.

The economic features of film-making (high fixed and sunk costs, high risk and uncertainty) created powerful incentives to export worldwide and international competition started since the beginning of cinema invention (Bakker 2008). The search for market share control reached its peak during the '20s with the rise of Hollywood that was able to set worldwide organizational, artistic and technological standards (Balio 1985). In order to be appreciated by the international audience, a movie had to respect a specific set of artistic and technological standards and Hollywood had deeply influenced these standards as well. More than other economic sectors, the film industry produces goods that require creativity and innovativeness. Both are the strategic resources of creative industries, and they have to be constantly maintained since they rapidly get old. This is in line with one of the characteristics of cultural and creative goods: the capabilities of offering experience, fun and pleasure. Innovation does not mean that the primary goal is the improvement of performance of functionality, but that creation of different types of goods is useful to please different and fickle tastes (Power and Scott 2004, Hirschman and Holbrook 1982). A way to feed creativity and innovativeness could be to foster cultural exchanges and contaminations. If this is true, public policies should constantly stimulate and feed exchanges between native culture and foreign ones for strengthening and developing the first. This is one of the reason why during the twentieth century, policy makers worked to promote and regulate the movie industry not only to gain economic goals but also to suit broader national purposes, like the defence of national cultural sovereignty against the overwhelming American imperialism.

Given the above features, film production has been usually seen in relation to two great models. One is the American model, where Hollywood means the vertically integrated major studios, and the other is the European model, with only a few large vertically integrated film companies and a greater number of small-medium companies. Another important actor also characterises the European model: the state, seen as both a producer and a regulator. The idea of the American studio system is overburdened with connotations. In addition to its original meaning, i.e. an integrated system of production, distribution and exhibition, it has taken on other meanings that relate more to its results than to the specific nature of the system. Thus, the studio system denotes a structure that actually existed in a certain form, and has come to include more or less implicitly an artistic ideal, an ideology of the cinema and a communicative style. Over time, the studio system has become increasingly identified with the classical Hollywood as it was from the late 1920s to late 1940s, with the star system and codified film genres, a distinction between the roles of director and screenwriter, the Hays Code of self-imposed censorship, hugely influential producers, etc. The European film industries had always hoped to copy the American model; harshly criticised because of its association with the idea of a standard production, it was at the same time admired for its earning power.

Within this framework, it is undoubtable that cinema represents a complex research field embedded with economic, cultural and even ideological concerns (Sojcher 2002), where the hegemony of distributors and US producers has greatly affected the rules the game, by influencing industry structures and strategies and government policies in many other countries. In the past century, the movie industry lived its successful parable, and the analysis of this sector can offer interesting and meaningful insights in order to better understand how a specific historical, cultural and economic context can shape the development of creative industries. Much of the current research on the cinema industry has been done within the framework of cultural studies, even if some European, especially French, authors have stressed the duality between art and industry (e.g. Frodon 1998, Benghozi and Delage 1997, Creton 1997, 1994). On the other hand, more recently economic and business historians have contributed significantly to the understanding of the movie industry. However, these scholars have focused primarily on an analysis of the Hollywood model and the way it became dominant (Bakker 2012, 2008, 2005, Miskell 2009, 2006) and on the determinants of movie revenues (Sedgwick and Pokorny, 2005a, 2005b, 2001, 2002). By contrast, an examination of the relationship between cinema policies and industrial dynamics is currently missing from this literature. This book therefore aims to provide a more comprehensive approach, examining how culture, economics and politics (including state institutions overseeing the movie sector) have interacted to influence industry dynamics and frame policy measures.

## Italian Cinema: An "In Between" Film Industry

> The Italian film industry today is in the same identical situation as it was at its beginning: above all, it lacks intelligent industrial and commercial organisation, and it also lacks a general and specific artistic direction; in other words, it has no clear idea of its objectives, what it is, or where it is going. It lacks everything it needs for our production companies to be world leaders in the film industry and become solid organisations.[10]
>
> (Turin, December 1918)

> The serious problem is that everybody wants to do something for the Italian cinema. If they knew what it was, it would practically be the Italian cinema of tomorrow. Unfortunately, however, the huge majority of those who want to do something do not know exactly what they want. Cinema taste has to develop [. . .]. I do not see this as an industrial problem. It is a problem of taste and climate, i.e. the involvement of Italian intelligence. Then, at the same time, work is required on the technical aspects.
>
> (Milan, February 1933)

No economic factor can replace or compensate for the lack or deficit of the creative forces of intelligence and fantasy. A healthy financial and technical organisation is effectively only a prerequisite, but it is an essential prerequisite for the artistic success of the production.

(Rome, November 1941)

Editors of "*La Vita Cinematografica*" magazine in the 1920s, Ettore Margadonna[11] in the 1930s and Eitel Monaco[12] in 1941 maintained that the Italian cinema of tomorrow should invest in global consolidation of all the elements that form this complex "industry": its artistic, cultural, economic, financial and technical factors. A competent industrial and commercial organisation combined with a precise artistic direction would be the base on which to build solid production companies.

During the twentieth century, Italian cinema experienced a vast array of structural, technical and organisational changes, cyclical crises and production revivals. The fascist regime attempted to apply a capitalistic approach and industrial structure to Italian film production in the 1930s and early 1940s, and this approach was then repeated with the policy of co-production and international collaboration.

Italian cinema reached its height of expansion in 1957. This new stage saw large production and technical organisations, wider distribution networks and large cinema chains. The transformation also changed the relations between production and technical systems. The service structure, i.e. distribution, cinemas and technical industries, became the load-bearing structure of the Italian film industry and influenced production models. In any case, Italian film production started up again at full speed, thanks to the system of state funding for films, the easy credit offered by the Banca Nazionale del Lavoro, and the expansion of export markets. Italian cinema became competitive once again, and was appreciated by the international public and critics alike.

On the eve of the 1970s, the film market was a sector controlled by the economically stronger industrial organisations, whose strategy was very much conditioned by the market. Italian producers did not understand the changes taking place and continued to repeat the same strategies as before, convinced that the public went to the cinema out of habit—an artificially created habit—rather than out of free choice. Italian cinema began to find itself facing competition from television, and went from being a form of mass entertainment to being an elitist form of entertainment similar to the theatre. What happened to Italian cinema during the 1970s is not very different from what happened at the same time to Italian industry in general. After achieving excellence in the 20 years following World War II, just when Italian cinema needed to make a new qualitative leap forward, it stopped dead. It attempted to guarantee its own easy survival under protection from the market, which continued and went ahead with successful foreign films that were mostly American. Italian cinema disappeared from domestic and

international cinemas, and Italian films were considered to be both technically (picture and sound quality) and artistically obsolete. Was this the end?
It certainly seemed so.

The overall economic situation of the Italian film industry is well illustrated by Libero Solaroli: "The reasons for its backwardness and inferiority
lie in its lack of industrialisation, the absence of a solid base (industrial and
above all commercial), a state of constant crisis and survival guaranteed
by protective legislation".[13] However, this view is incomplete and does not
explain why industrialisation failed to take place and why solid bases were
not built.

A detached look at the Italian film industry immediately reveals its fragmentation and the smallness of the production companies. As for all national
film industries, the first years of the twentieth century were a period of rapid
growth, but then the sector settled down into a structure that included only
a few solid organisations (e.g. Cines, Ambrosio, Itala Film and Pasquali)
alongside dozens of small production companies, which sprang up to make
just one film and then disappeared within a year, or even after just a few
months. The multitude of production companies meant that a certain variety of experimentation and experience was guaranteed, but these companies
sprang up and then died without leaving behind any lasting legacy of skills
or knowledge, and the big investors and industrialists stayed well away
from a sector that was consequently seen as having unstable foundations.

Of course, there were exceptions: Italian cinema also included production
companies with a serious entrepreneurial approach, which made technically
and artistically valid films that were internationally acclaimed and left a
lasting impression on the public. These defects, limits or omissions seem to
continue into the present day. The future of the cinema is always a topic of
discussion, since its health swings back and forth between crises and good
times.

The history of the Italian film industry has often been marked by improvised business ventures. Film-makers have often been suspicious of the management methods used in other sectors, convinced as they were that art
and culture should not necessarily converge with the interests and the tastes
of the public. These film-makers have always proudly asserted their own
autonomy and independence from the market, asking the state to take on
the problems of financing their ventures, based on the principle of "art for
art's sake".

It has been said many times that Italian cinema's weaknesses were caused
firstly by the failure to industrialise production processes in the period up to
the 1960s, and then by the failure to implement a flexible model in the last
30 years. These weaknesses are mainly due to the lack of entrepreneurial
culture, to the small size of the Italian market, and to the tireless idealistic
defence of an excessively elitist conception of the art of cinema. Although
this can explain why the Italian cinema system failed to grow and to become
internationally competitive, it does not justify the absence of any efforts to

change this trajectory. Nowadays, although it is clear that a film is an intellectual product, there is also a consensus that even creative sectors have to deal with the market, based on Rossellini's far-sighted opinion that "you need to make useful films that produce useful returns".

In a film production system like Italy's, which is very fragmented, producers and distributors realise that the complexity of the entertainment business and the near impossibility of predicting successful films means that improvised entrepreneurs can no longer remain on the market for long. The difficulty of taking a more sophisticated entrepreneurial approach could be explained with the very nature of film-making. Every film can be considered the unique result of a production process with high value added, i.e. it is a product requiring a high level of specialised work and is not easy to standardise, while its success depends not only on specific skills, but also on the trust and respect between those involved in the various stages of production. The tasks required are complex, difficult to standardise, and highly independent. This is why the film industry is often called an industry of prototypes: it is difficult to make forecasts about production costs and eventual box-office takings and earnings from subsequent exploitation of the film.

The film industry develops in a series of stages—creative, productive and distributive—that are sequentially interdependent. Italian cinema as a production sector has always lacked the strong points of vertical integration that were the hallmark of the US majors. This is compensated by forms of aggregation between the various specialists, which are sometimes favoured by the market and sometimes by stronger operators who bring the others together. However, this loose organisation does not help to strengthen the entrepreneurial structure of the different production stages. The single components need to become stronger, to have better control over the interdependence of production phases, and to develop virtuous collaboration mechanisms. The specialised and fragmented structure of the Italian film industry does not correspond to the demands of the market, which drive towards greater aggregation in the industry. For example, distribution is very much connected with production, since channels (cinema, home video, TV, etc.) and film promotion are often decided while the film is still being made. Interdependence is equally intense in the creative stage, when director, actors and screenwriters are a real team. The creative and artistic stages cannot avoid evaluating the public and the market.

This all shows that a film-maker who wants to compete at the international level needs a more integrated/coordinated production system. In the Italian case, one primary cause of insufficient integration is the lack of an industrial culture in the film industry, because the cinema was for many years viewed as a small-scale artistic activity that was not subject to market influences. This eventually limited the willingness to take risks and invest, with a preference for situations offering more guarantees, such as working for others (the state, television), rather than more courageous and really entrepreneurial decisions. This has prevented the growth of medium-large companies and led to the multiplication of small organisations, unable to make internationally competitive films. This doesn't necessarily mean that vertical integration is the only answer. In fact, different studies have shown that in creative sectors, highly differentiated inputs can influence vertical disintegration (Gil and Spiller, 2007; Storper 1993; Christopherson and Storper 1989). Independent production is not cheaper than studio films, but independent movies can offer, on average, superior, yet volatile, financial results. Majors are usually better equipped to pursue a portfolio strategy, and they are able to recoup investments through sale in large markets. Independents have less financial capital, and they need to rely on their selection capabilities. This distinction between majors and independents opens up some interesting debate about concentration and diversity, which means the way industry structure can affect a variety of products. The pioneering study of Peterson and Berger (1975) concluded that high levels of concentration correspond to low levels of diversity and vice versa. More recent research has shown that product standardisation is not simply a matter of ownership structure but the result of large markets (Ahlkvist and Fisher, 2000), which are usually better controlled by large corporations. Italian cinema history is extremely useful for exploring these features and dynamics.

## Learning from Italian cinema History

There are many reasons why Italy is an interesting case, and Italian cinema epitomises a very different model of development from the US model. In the 1960s, Italian cinema triumphed globally. Directors such as Rossellini, Fellini and Leone and actors and actresses like Sophia Loren and Marcello Mastroianni were known to audiences around the world. However, by the end of the 1980s, the Italian movie industry was all but dead. This book traces the rise of the industry from its origins in the nineteenth century to its worldwide success in the 1960s and its rapid decline in the subsequent decades. It does so by looking at cinema as an institution subject to the interplay between the spheres of art, business and politics both at the national and international level. By examining the role of a wide range of stakeholders (including the film directors, producers, exhibitors, the public and the critics) as well as the system of funding and the influence of governments, the book shows that the Italian movie industry succeeded when all three spheres were aligned but suffered and ultimately failed when they pulled in different directions. This in-depth case study makes an important contribution to the long-standing debate about promoting and protecting domestic culture(s), namely in the face of the culturally dominant and politically as well as economically powerful creative industries from the United States.

At the same time, the Italian case is interesting because it is the history of a prestigious post-World War II cinema with international ambitions: admired by critics, envied abroad and outstandingly successful at the box office. Again, it is the history of cinema in a nation that experienced the transition from a liberal state to dictatorship and then to democracy. During these three periods, Italian cinema was forced to define its role and engaged in continual negotiation with governmental structures. It began at the turn of the century as a form of entertainment, became a powerful propaganda vehicle under the fascist regime, and was then a factor in the renaissance of a country that had lost World War II but was anxious to be included in Europe's new post-war political structure. *Roma città aperta* (1945), *Paisà* (1946), *Il bandito* (1946), *Aquila Nera* (1946), and *Vivere in pace* (1947) symbolise the rebirth of the Italian film industry.

In Italy, the film making of production companies has often been based on intuition, or at least has not followed the organizational models typical of the Hollywood -style vertically integrated companies. At the system level, the lack of sure and solid references, the uncertainty in determining production policies and in defining the most suitable legislation, meant that the Italian film industry experienced times of crisis. Despite this uncertainty, it is undeniable that, nonetheless, it managed to make films that have become part of collective imagery.

Finally, it is also the history of an industry pervaded by ideological dogmatisms, in which it seemed impossible to reconcile the producer's needs with the director's needs. When it was a question of defending art, the only impartial arbiter seemed to be the state, although state intervention was not without its ambiguous aspects: "For twenty years the State was the worst of all the producers. But in the present situation I still have hopes in the State, because it has the power to do exactly the opposite of what the previous State did".[14]

Contemporary historical research on Italian cinema is inspired by the need to propose a model of "integrated history"[15] or, as defined by Barbara Klinger with a metaphor inspired by French historian Braudel, a model of "total history". "Total history" does not really mean a totally exhaustive historical narrative, but rather the possibility of achieving the most complete understanding of production methods and the social and historical context surrounding the cinema as it interacts with other "institutions" (legislation, religion, politics, dominant ideologies), and of the symbolic meanings and collective consciousness that films create. Given the complexity of this kind of study, historical reconstruction of the "cinema phenomenon" would be "terminable and interminable",[16] producing potentially incomplete results, although these can satisfactorily explain a certain event at a certain point in history: "this remains a coherent and total horizon for the researcher, although often, unfortunately, only ideal".[17] Obviously, there are certain risks involved in attempts to write "general histories" of the cinema, especially the risk of excessive fragmentation. The cinema is often seen as the sum of separate parts, and each is analysed using the specific tools of the different disciplines to which it belongs. As Ortoleva stressed in an interview on the relationship between historiography and cinema research:[18] "one consequence of this approach is that when the cinema is analysed as an industry, the categories of economic history are applied; the cinema is studied as a social institution using the tools of social history. The cinema as an artistic form is studied as one of the visual arts; and the cinema as a technological production system is approached by applying theories and principles relating to organisational and business systems". If the truth of these statements is accepted, Ortoleva states that what is lacking is the definition of variables and explanation of the interrelations between the different "spheres"; these remain isolated from each other, and each one offers "its own truth, as if they were recounting their own different histories".[19]

Given its importance even in a global context, Italian cinema, unsurprisingly, has been studied extensively by both Italian and foreign scholars. In terms of its historical development, there are many publications regarding the silent period (Brunetta 1982, Bernardini 1980) the fascist regime (Ricci 2008, Zagarrio 2004, Reich and Garofalo 2002, Stone 1998, De Grazia 1981) and, equally if not numerous, the post-WWII rise to worldwide glory (Brunetta 2009, Corsi 2001, Brunetta, Ellwood and Kroes, 1991, Quaglietti 1980). Moreover, Italian cinema has been studied for its aesthetical evolution (Wagstaff 2008, Mosconi 2006, Landy 2000, Zagarrio 1988, Redi 1986), for its social role as a new form of entertainment (Brancato 2003, Fanchi and Mosconi 2002, Casetti, 2000, Brunetta 1982) and as a powerful means of mass communication (Zinni 2010, Eugeni 1999, Colombo 1998, Abruzzese 1992).

These studies are generally well researched and offer valuable contributions to the field with approaches based on auteur theory, literary or art history. Yet they tend to be inward looking and do not address the industry from an economic and business point of view, reflecting the focus on cinema as an art form rather than as a creative good. Furthermore, linkages among factors that impact on industry dynamics are missing or not rendered explicit. For instance, government policy choices are embedded in the narrative but are not included in the critical analysis. In this respect, many of these studies start from an a priori idea of what the industry needed in order to determine to what extent governments were able to meet those needs. In addition, this literature usually pays more attention to the national dimension of the industry rather than considering it part of a global entertainment market. There are two books where Italian cinema is examined as a "market good" (Quaglietti 1980, Bizzari and Solaroli, 1958), but they are somewhat out of date and, more importantly, biased by the authors' direct involvement and sympathies with communist ideology and politics. There are at least two recent exceptions. One is the economic history of Italian cinema by Barbara Corsi (2001). This work is well informed, even though, here and there, more evidence based on primary sources would be desirable. The other book is the study by Manetti (2012), who has made an important contribution to our understanding of the adoption and role of cinema laws—albeit with an exclusive focus on the fascist period. The difficulty of finding sources and data have made the study of industrial and, more specifically, economic phenomena more difficult.

This book accepts Ortoleva's invitation and attempts to examine the relationships between economics and culture more closely, beginning with the premise that "it is no longer possible to separate economics and production from ideology and culture, since cultural artefacts, images and representations have become a part of the economy".[20] The cinema offers a privileged observation point, where the relations between culture and economics are particularly evident because of its classification as a creative industry. What are the relations between artistic and industrial/economic requirements? How do these affect each other? How can these in turn influence cultural policy decisions in the film industry?

Many factors have prevented Italian cinema from defining a long-lasting industrial and artistic project. These have involved the difficulties of finding capital, together with an initial underestimation of this new form of entertainment (and possible art form) seen merely as a show for the masses, and the absence of suitable models for interpreting and evaluating artistic worth for investment purposes. There was a failure to understand the central importance of cinema's intangible assets, i.e. that content, style, screenplay, artistic skills and stylistic innovation are a source of competitive advantage. Besides, there was no development of an entrepreneurial/industrial structure capable of adapting to changes in the industry and of dealing with competition from other countries: not only the United States, but also the most important European countries, France, Germany and Great Britain.

The obstacles to industrialisation originate in some deep-rooted sociological characteristics that took shape in Italy starting in the eighteenth century. For example, the lack of venture capital is not due to Italy being a poor country, as is sometimes stated or written, but is the paradoxical consequence of a national system that achieved record levels of economic modernisation and wealth throughout the 17th century. After Italian Unification in 1861, this system created an articulated social structure around some fundamentally important institutions: the family, corporations and the state.

In Italy, there was an extraordinary development of small businesses that were usually family-owned, and of professional organisations, together with a proliferation of national and local legislation unequalled in other countries. This legislation favoured the establishment of a political and administrative system in which mediation and cronyism played a central role. In every chapter of Italian economic history, the principal social actors involved in defining strategic decisions have included families and corporations on one side, and political organisations on the other.

The fact that a film is a prototype product encourages the formation of flexible production companies, whose development can be very volatile. These companies have been a central element in the history of the Italian cinema and have conditioned the long-term development of the sector.

How much does the film industry have in common with Italian capitalism, characterised by the coexistence of artisanal and industrial models, state interventions and family ventures? The prevalence of the family model, an artisanal approach, scarce attention to international changes, and delays in updating business and production systems, have been elements of success and have also slowed down the processes of updating and growth. Although the "craftsman's touch" could provide a high quality product, Italian film companies did not have the strength needed for investing in new technology and opening up to international trade, where product quality had become a fundamentally important factor of competitiveness.

Analysis of the reasons why the Italian film industry did not become industrialised does not mean supporting the theory of delayed development, that certain industries are like certain countries, i.e. they are further behind. In reality, in certain times, places and situations, strong traditions resist and actually take over. The cinema includes the work of the craftsman and the work of the industrialist, the individual's craft and the work of the professional organisation, the hidden economy of small opportunities, and the economy of concentration and investment. The history of industrial development in Italy includes passive heritage alongside modern movements, and this is the same for the cinema. This is not simply a case of delayed development, but is a specific story that must be examined in order to understand: how the cinema was institutionalised, its transformation into an independent field, the definition of its production structures and its specific language, and how production methods interconnect with artistic and cultural specificities.

Analysis of the Italian film industry as it developed in the 1900s means attempting to understand the scope of a statement by Margadonna that, "Our nation accepts the cinema as merchandise, but doesn't yet feel that this is a problem, i.e. a will of art. What is the obstacle separating us from the cinema?"[21]

The book is structured into three parts. Part I covers the period from the birth of the industry (1895) to the rise of fascism (1922), when the Italian movie industry attempted to make the most of the opportunities presented by an emerging technology and experienced a period of international acclaim—quickly cut short by technological and organizational changes in the industry as well as WWI. The analysis of the original productive structures and the functioning of the value chain serves as the starting point for the subsequent study of the sector. This also explores the social and cultural environment and shows how the perception of cinema as an art or as a business influenced its cultural legitimacy and its subsequent development. Part II is dedicated to an analysis of Italian cinema industry under fascism from 1922 to 1943. This section examines the intervention of the fascist regime in the movie industry and reconstructs the debate about the policies designed for its protection and promotion. It shows the contentious relations between the state and cinema entrepreneurs and highlights how political forces and the pressures from international competition, mainly emanating from Hollywood, impacted the economic and organizational features of the industry. Part III analyses Italian cinema after WWII, from 1945 until the end of the 1960s. It explores how Italian cinema managed to reach second place in the world market, identifying continuities and discontinuities with respect to industry structures and relations with the state. It shows how forces shaping industry patterns are more numerous, including alongside government, professional lobbies and American capital. The detailed analysis reveals the role of a changed political and cultural environment under democracy, leading to different public policy choices. Development patterns of Italian cinema will then appear as the result of strong interactions between different forces whose relations have changed over time and in their intensity. For instance, cultural forces have influenced both political forces—in formulating theories of the role of the cinema within the state—and economic forces, in propounding theories on the cinema as an economic sector. For many years, the cinema was seen as an exclusively speculative sector: this influenced any inclination the financial system or private operators might have to invest in the cinema, limiting the amount of capital invested. Economic forces, here seen as operators of the value chain, mainly interacted with political forces especially by lobbying associations connected to the category. The political forces on their part acted on the economic forces by carefully regulating the sector and by opting for protectionist/free trade policies.

The intricate plot among these different forces has determined the numerous crises and the rebirth of Italian cinema. This complicated and intriguing story reached its apex after the end of WWII, when Italian movies were internationally acclaimed.

If Italian cinema of the '50s and '60s was second only to American cinema, why is this no longer the case today?

## Notes

1  Chiarini, Luigi 1938, "Bianco e Nero", *Anno II*, n. 7.
2  Bachlin, Peter 1958, *Il cinema come industria: storia economica del film*, Milan: Feltrinelli.
3  Interview with Dino De Laurentiis in Della Casa, Stefano et al. 2003, *Capitani Coraggiosi. Produttori Italiani 1945–1975*, Milan: Mondadori Electa.
4  Many authors use these terms interchangeably (Peterson and Anand 2004, Thompson et al. 2007).
5  "Hesmondhalgh and Baker make a distinction between three approaches: (1) the political economy of culture, concerned with how cultural production is financed and organized, and the effects of this on power and social justice; (2) organization, business and management studies on the specifics of cultural production including innovation, organizational structures and the management of creative labour; and (3) cultural studies aiming to study popular culture as a social phenomenon", in Peltoniemi, Mirca 2015, "Cultural Industries: Product-Market Characteristics, Management Challenges and Industry Dynamics," *International Journal of Management Review*, 17: 41–68.
6  Gedda, Luigi 1941, "Conclusione", in Basari, Enrico et al., *Il volto del cinema*, Rome: Editrice AVE, p. 325.

7  Benhamou, Francoise 2001, *L'economia della cultura*, Bologna: Il Mulino.
8  Morin, Edgar 1963, *I divi*, Milan: Mondadori, p. 29.
9  Quoted in Carlini, Fabio 1974, *Hitchcock*, Florence: La nuova Italia.
10  "Many newspapers write about what the Italian film industry lacks in order to be perfect. What does it lack? A great deal: first of all a precise idea of what the film industry is as an artistic industry. Nowadays the cinema has exceptional artistic and commercial requirements. We used to have real cinema industrialists, but now the few survivors have not evolved mentally beyond 1924 and have not been able to keep up with the decade that has finally eliminated them from the contest. Maybe everybody is ignorant about how complex it must be to organise a production company. According to some of our industrialists, films can be sold almost like boxes of shoe polish. They start to make a film just as they would set off on a trip tomorrow." "Battute d'aspetto", in *La Vita Cinematografica*, December 1918.
11  "Everybody wants to take a short-cut, but the only possibility is the longest road of all. We are only interested in real Italian film-makers: people who have the same noble and serious feelings about the cinema that people have had and cultivated for poetry, architecture, music, painting etc. since time immemorial." Ettore Margadonna, *Lettera aperta sul cinema italiano*, "Cineconvegno", 25 February 1933. Margadonna, writer and screenwriter, wrote one of the first books about the Italian cinema in 1932, *Cinema italiano ieri e oggi*. Ettore Margadonna began his career as a journalist for *La Rivista della Cooperazione* (1922–1925) and later worked as a screenwriter for the cinema.
12  Monaco, Eitel 1941, "Maturità", in *Cinema Italiano. Anno XIX*, Rome: Arti Grafiche Tuminelli Eitel Monaco was head of the *Federazione nazionale fascista degli industriali dello spettacolo*, and then in 1940 replaced Luigi Freddi at the *Direzione Generale per la Cinematografia*; after World War II he was nominated president of ANICA. Eitel Monaco was in favour of a cinema directed at the market and of consolidation of the film industry, unlike Luigi Freddi (nominated head of the *Direzione Generale per la Cinematografia* in 1934), who had always advocated a totalitarian and propagandistic cinema at the service of the regime, totally controlled by the state.
13  Libero, Bizzarri and Solaroli, Libero 1958, *L'industria cinematografica italiana*, Florence: Parenti.
14  Zavattini, Cesare 25 August 1945, "Poesia solo affare del cinema italiano", in *Film d'oggi*, 10.
15  Casetti, Francesco 2005, *L'occhio del Novecento. Cinema, esperienza, modernità*, Milan: Bompiani.
16  Klinger, Barbara 1997, "Film History Terminable and Interminable: Recovering the Past in Reception Studies", *Screen*, 38 (2): 107–128.
17  Mosconi, Elena 2006, *L'impressione del film. Contributi per una stori culturale del cinema italiano. 1895–1945*, Milan: Vita & Pensiero, p. 21.
18  Ortoleva, Peppino 1988, "Sulla categoria modi di produzione. Note sullo stato attuale dei rapporti tra storiografia e ricerca sul cinema", in *Dietro lo schermo. Ragionamenti sui modi di produzione cinematografici in Italia*, Pesaro: Quaderni della Mostra Internazionale del Nuovo Cinema Pesaro, p. 149–165.
19  Ibid. p. 153.
20  Connor, Samuel 1997, *Postmodernist Culture: An Introduction to Theories of the Contemporary*, Oxford: Blackwell, p. 51.
21  Margadonna, Ettore 1932, *Cinema ieri e oggi*, Milan: Domus.

# Bibliography

ABRUZZESE, Alberto 1992, *Forme estetiche e società di massa. Arte e pubblico nell'età del capitalismo*, Venice: Marsilio

AHLKVIST, Jarl, FISHER, Gene 2000, "And the hits just keep on coming: music programming standardization in commercial radio", *Poetics*, 27: pp. 301–325

BACHLIN, Peter 1958, *Il cinema come industria: storia economica del film*, Milan: Feltrinelli

Bakker, Gerben 2012, "How Motion Pictures Industrialized Entertainment", *Journal of Economic History*, 72, 4 (Dec.): 1036–1063.

_____. 2011, *Entertainment Industrialised*, Cambridge: Cambridge University Press

_____. 2008, *Entertainment Industrialised*, Cambridge: Cambridge University Press

_____. 2005, "The decline and fall of the European film industry: sunk costs, market size, and market structure, 1890–1927", *Economic History Review*, 58, 2: pp. 310–351

_____. 2004, "How Films Became Branded Products", in Sedgwick, John and Pokorny, Mike (eds.), *An Economic History of Film*, London: Routledge, p. 48–85

BALIO, Tino 1985, *The American Film Industry*, Madison: University of Wisconsin Press

BASARI, Enrico et al. 1941, *Il volto del cinema*, Rome: Editrice AVE

BENGHOZI, Pierre-Jean, DELAGE, Christian (eds.) 1997, *Une histoire économique du cinema francais (1895–1995): Regards croisés franco-américains*, Paris: L'Harmattan

BENHAMOU, Francoise 2001, *L'economia della cultura*, Bologna: Il Mulino

BERNARDINI, Aldo 1980, *Cinema italiano: arte, divismo e mercato 1910–1914*, Rome-Bari: Laterza

BIZZARRI, Libero, SOLAROLI, Libero 1958, *L'industria cinematografica italiana*, Florence: Parenti

BRANCATO, Sergio 2003, *La città delle luci. Itinerari per una storia sociale del cinema*, Rome: Carocci

BROWN, Adam et al. 2000, "Local music policies within a global music industry: cultural quarters in Manchester and Sheffield", *Geoforum*, 31 (4): 437–451

BROWN, Alan 2006, "An Architecture of Value", *GIA Reader*, 17, 1

BRUNETTA, Gian Piero 2009, *Il cinema neorealista italiano: storia economica, politica e culturale*, Rome: Editori Laterza

_____. 1982, *Storia del cinema italiano 1945–1982*, Rome: Editori Riuniti

BRUNETTA, Gian Piero, ELLWOOD, David and KROES, Rob (eds.) 1994, *Hollywood in Europe: Experiences of a Cultural Hegemony*, Amsterdam: VU University Press

BRUNETTA, Gian Pierro, ELLWOOD, David and KROES, Rob 1991, *Hollywood in Europa industria politica, pubblico del cinema, 1945–1960*, Florence: Ponte alle Grazie

BURCH, Noel 2001, *Il lucernario dell'infinito. Nascita del linguaggio cinematografico*, Milan: Il Castoro

CASETTI, Francesco 2005, *L'occhio del Novecento. Cinema, esperienza, modernità*, Milan: Bompiani

_____. 2000, *L'occhio dello spettatore*, Milan: Università Cattolica

CHRISTOPHERSON, Susan, STORPER, Michael 1989, "The Effects of Flexible Specialization on Industrial Politics and the Labor Market: The Motion Picture Industry", *Industrial & Labor Relation Review*, 42 (3): 331–347

COLOMBO, Fausto 1997, *L'industria culturale italiana dal 1900 alla seconda Guerra mondiale. Tendenze della produzione e del consumo*, Milan: Università Cattolica

COLOMBO, Furio 1998, *La cultura sottile*, Milan: Bompiani

CONNOR, Samuel 1997, *Postmodernist Culture: An Introduction to Theories of the Contemporary*, Oxford: Blackwell

CORSI, Barbara 2001, *Con qualche dollaro in meno. Storia economica del cinema italiano*, Rome: Editori Riuniti

CRETON, Laurent 1997, *Cinéma et marché*, Paris: Armand Colin

_____. 1994, *Economie du Cinéma: perspectives stratégiques*, Paris: Nathan Collection

DE GRAZIA, Victoria 1981, *Consenso e cultura di massa nell'Italia fascista. L'organizzazione del dopolavoro*, Rome-Bari: Editori Laterza

DELLA CASA, Stefano et al. 2003, *Capitani Coraggiosi. Produttori Italiani 1945–1975*, Milan: Mondadori Electa

DE VANY, Arthur 2004, *Hollywood economics: how extreme uncertainty shapes the film industry*, London-New York: Routledge

EIKHOF, Doris, HAUNSCHILD, Alex 2007, "For art's sake! Artistic and economic logics in creative production", *Journal of Organization Behavior*, 28 (5): 523–538

EUGENI, Ruggero 1999, *Film, sapere, società. Per un'analisi sociosemiotica del testo cinematografico*, Milan: Vita & Pensiero

FANCHI, Maria Grazia, MOSCONI, Elena (eds.) 2002, *Spettatori italiani. Riti e ambienti del consumo cinematografico*, Rome: Vita & Pensiero

FRODON, Jean-Michel 1998, *La projection nationale: cinema et nation*, Paris: Odile Jacob

GARNHAM, Nicholas 1990, *Capitalism and Communication: Global Culture and the Economics of Information*, London: Sage

GIL, Richard, SPILLER, Pablo 2007, "The Organizational Implications of Creativity: The US Film Industry in Mid-XXth Century", *National Nureau of Economic Research Paper*, No. 13253

Ginsburgh, Victor 2001, "Economics of Art and Culture", in SMELSER, Neil, BALTES, Paul (ed.), *International Encyclopaedia of the Social and Behavioural Sciences*, Amsterdam: Elsevier, p. 758–764

GOLDMAN, William 1983, *Adventures in Screen Trade*, New York: Grand Central Publishing

HESMONDHALGH, David 2002, *The cultural industries*, London: Sage

HIRSCH, Paul 1972, "Processing Fads and Fashions: An Organization-Set Analysis of Cultural Industry Systems", *American Journal of Sociology*, 77 (4): 639–659

HIRSCHMAN, Elizabeth C., MORRIS, B. Holbrook 1982, "Hedonic Consumption: Emerging Concepts, Methods, and Propositions", *Journal of Marketing*, 46 (Summer): 92–101

JONES, Candace 2001, "Co-Evolution of Entrepreneurial Careers, Institutional Rules and Competitive Dynamics in American Film, 1895–1920", *Organization Studies*, 22 (6): 911–944

KLINGER, Barbara 1997, "Film History Terminable and Interminable: Recovering the Past in Reception Studies", *Screen*, 38 (2): 107–128

Lampel, et al. 2000, "Balancing act: Learning from organizing practice in cultural industries", *Organization Science*, 11 (3): 263–269

Landy, Marcia 2000, *Italian Film*, Cambridge: Cambridge University Press

Manetti, Daniela 2012, *Un'arma poderosissima. Industria cinematografica e Stato durante il fascismo 1922–1943*, Milan: FrancoAngeli

Marcus, Carmen 2005, *Future of Creative Industries: Implications for Research Policy*, Working Document EUR 21471, Brussels: European Commission

Margadonna, Ettore 1932, *Cinema ieri e oggi*, Milan: Domus

McCarthy, Kevin et al. 2005, *Gifts of the Muse: Reframing the Debate about the Benefits of the Arts*, Santa Monica, CA: Rand Corporation

Miskell, Peter 2009, "Resolving the Global Efficiency versus Local Adaptability Dilemma: US Film Multinationals in Their Largest Foreign Market in the 1930s and 1940s", *Business History*, 51 (3): 426–444

_____. 2006, "Selling America to the World"? The Rise and Fall of an International Film Distributor in Its Largest Foreign Market: United Artists in Britain, 1927–1947", *Enterprise and Society*, 7 (4): 740–776

Morin, Edgar 1963, *I divi*, Milan: Mondadori

Mosconi, Elena 2006, *L'impressione del film. Contributi oer una stori culturale del cinema italiano. 1895–1945*, Milan: Vita & Pensiero

Ortoleva, Peppino 1988, "Sulla categoria modi di produzione. Note sullo stato attuale dei rapporti tra storiografia e ricerca sul cinema", in *Dietro lo schermo. Ragionamenti sui modi di produzione cinematografici in Italia"*, Pesaro: Quaderni della Mostra Internazionale del Nuovo Cinema Pesaro, n. 32

Peltoniemi, Mirva 2015, "Cultural Industries: Product–Market Characteristics, Management Challenges, and Industry Dynamics", *International Journal of Management Reviews*, 17 (1): 41–68

Peterson, Richard, Anand. Barhat, 2004, "The production of culture perspective", *Annual Review of Sociology*, 30: 311–334

Peterson, Richard, Berger, Dave 1975, "Cycles in symbol production: the case of popular music", *American Sociological Review*, 40: 158–173

Power, Dominic, Scott, Allen 2004, *Cultural industries and the production of culture*, London: Routledge

Quaglietti, Lorenzo1980, *Storia economico-politica del cinema italiano, 1945–1980*, Rome: Editori Riuniti

Redi, Riccardo 1986, *Ti parlerò . . . d'amor. Cinema italiano fra muto e sonoro*, Turin: RAI-Eri

Reich, Jacqueline, and Garofalo, Piero 2002, *Re.viewing Fascism: Italian cinema, 1922–1943*, Bloomington: Indiana University Press

Ricci, Steven 2008, *Cinema and Fascism: Italian Film and Society, 1992–1943*, London: University of California Press

Sedgwick, John, Pokorny Michael 2005a, "The film business in the U.S. and Britain during the 1930s", *Economic History Review*, 58, 1: pp. 79–112

_____. 2005b, *An Economic History of Film*, London: Routledge

_____. 2002, "Product Differentiation at the Movies: Hollywood, 1946–65", *Journal of Economic History*, 62: 676–704

_____. 2001, "Stardom and the Profitability of Filmmaking: Warner Bros. in the 1930s", *Journal of Cultural Economics*, 25: 157–184

Sojcher, Fréderic 2002, "The Economics of Cinema: History, Strategic Choices and Cultural Policy", *Contemporary European History*, 11, 02 (May): 305–316

SQUIRE, Jason (ed.) 1992, *The Movie Business Book*, New York: Simon and Schuster

SQUIRE, Jason 1993 (ed.), *The movie business book*, Upper Saddle River, NJ: Prentice Hall

STONE, Marla 1998, *The Patron State: Culture & Politics in Fascist Italy*, Princeton, NJ: Princeton University Press

STORPER, Michael 1993, "Regional 'worlds' of production: Learning and innovation in the technology districts of France, Italy, and the USA", *Regional Studies*, 27 (5): 433–455

THOMPSON, Paul et al. 2007, "From conception to consumption: creativity and the missing managerial link", *Journal of Organizational Behavior*, 28 (5)

THORSBY, David 2001, *Economics and Culture*, Cambridge, MA: Cambridge University Press

TOWSE, Ruth 2003b, "Cultural industries", in Towse, Ruth 2003 (ed.) *A Handbook of Cultural Economics*, Cheltenham, UK/Northampton, MA: Edwar Elgar

TUNSTALL, Jeremy 1994, *The media are American*, London: Constable

UNCTAD 2010, *Creative Economy Report*, Unctad

WAGSTAFF, Christopher 2008, *Italian Neorealist Cinema: An Aesthetic Approach*, Toronto: University of Toronto Press

ZAGARRIO, Vito 2004, *Cinema e fascismo: film, modelli e immaginari*, Venice: Marsilio

_____. (ed.) 1988, *Dietro lo schermo. Ragionamento sui modi di produzione cinematografici in Italia*, Venice: Marsilio

ZINNI, Maurizio 2010, *Fascisti di celluloide. La memoria del ventennio nel cinema italiano (1945–2000)*, Venice: Marsilio

# Part I
# The Early Making of an Industry

# 1 The "Thinkability" of the Cinema
## Is It Art or Is It a Business?

A new art, even though made of modest ambitions.
A simple replication of other form of entertainment has born.[1]
This art . . . which art: this celluloid industry, a dishonest daughter.
What is exactly this strong industry—aggressive as money making to our
lives?[2]

## The Cinema: The Eye of the Twentieth Century[3]

The first public film show took place at the Cinématographe Lumière
on 28 December 1895, and is usually said to mark the birth of cinema,
with brothers Louis and Auguste Lumière of Lyon taking the credit for its
invention.

Cinema appeared as a totally modern art, almost the natural outcome
of the new industrial and technical era. It was the completion of photographic objectivity, the technological convergence of a series of cultural
forms already present in modern society.[4] At first, it was a technological
and scientific experiment, seen as an investigative technique with a special
language of moving images to use in exploring fields of scientific research
that had been developed in the previous century, like the study of human
and animal movement.[5]

However, the invention of a technology for projecting images cannot be
compared with the impact of the cinema as a social and cultural institution.
This exciting novelty permeated contemporary society, affecting many of
life's economic, social, cultural, political and artistic aspects. If every historical era has its own "eye", i.e. a particular way of viewing the world that is
reflected in society's visual products, then the cinema was the "eye" of the
twentieth century.

The cinema seemed to have been created to become a mass spectacle that
was able to touch the emotions of more demanding spectators and working
classes alike. It gave every social class, linguistic group and country an activity that was a more culturally and economically accessible form of entertainment and recreation than the traditionally bourgeois spectacles like theatre

and music. The cinema became a factory of myths, symbols, illusions and identity.[6]

> The cinema is an enormous encyclopaedia written with moving images, and it can be said that there is not one single entry in this universal encyclopaedia, in other words not one single film, which does not inspire a positive or negative reaction in the spectator, no matter how bland or banal the film may be. The cinema contributes to the spectator's psychological and mental experience and to the creation of his awareness. In brief, it contributes to the spectator's interpretation of the world.[7]

The most fascinating feature of the cinema was that it could open a window on the world, revealing far-off countries, events and personalities that were outside the experience of most members of the audience.

The novelty of moving pictures was enough to attract the public, and the first improvised cine operators filmed everything around them. Lumière filmed workers coming out of a factory in Lyon, a train arriving in the station, the family having breakfast. The cinema gave everything, including images of daily life, a new communicative force. Most of the early moving images showed people and events in other countries, information previously given only by the press. Lumière cine operators travelled to the furthest corners of the world, and were soon imitated in other countries, thus paving the way for the development of national film industries.[8]

Pioneers of the new technology were uncertain about the direction for future development of this "invention" that could be a scientific instrument, a means of recording events, and a form of entertainment. No one seeing the first footage of landscapes could have imagined that this new form of expression would permeate everyday life to become a popular mass spectacle, a collective ritual of vision capable of forging a national patrimony of shared values and symbols. Gradual recognition of the cinema's communicative potential would involve not only its artistic and expressive levels, but also its political and economic potential. Films could communicate across national borders, making them one of the most effective vehicles of cultural hegemony and imperialism. Contemporary observers felt that the cinema could define the character and soul of a nation.[9] The cinema was industrialised entertainment, creating products distributed on a global scale.

In Italy—as elsewhere—there was intense expansion in the early years, with a proliferation of halls showing the first rudimentary films.[10] Newspapers portrayed the cinema as a spectacle far removed from the upper classes, a sort of poor man's theatre providing inexpensive entertainment for the urban working classes (factory workers and artisans).

> After a hard day's work, for just a few coins, the cinema offers the most imaginative illusions, sometimes projected in the workers' local café.

The cinema meets the needs of people who have little time for fun, and who want to feel strong emotions rather than intellectual pleasures.[11]

The rapid development of the cinema, the overwhelming enthusiasm of public audiences and especially the spread of permanent projection halls (changes occurring in most national film industries between 1906 and 1910) meant that the cinema became a focus of intellectual and social debate.

## The Legitimation Issue

Added to the problems of a social nature were those of a more cultural type: the cinema lacked real legitimacy. The cultural context of the time recognised no relationship between popular entertainment and the traditional arts like theatre, music and literature. The two spheres were seen as totally independent and incompatible, due to their different audiences: the educated bourgeoisie, on the one hand, and the working class, on the other.

Moreover, when the cinema first appeared at the end of the nineteenth century, the arts system was already defined. Popular shows like the circus, music hall and waxworks museums were classed as mere money-making activities, while the traditional arts had acquired full institutional status, with the legal recognition of copyright, the formation of literary, theatrical and musical writers' groups, and aesthetics as a subject of academic study. Italian theatre journals were among the cinema's most vehement opponents. In particular, *L'Argante*[12] published articles denigrating the cinema as an excessively populist form of entertainment, and created a movement strong enough to promote a conference calling on the state to curb the cinemas. The diatribe over the "artistic" merits of the cinema continued in many national film industries at least until the 1920s, and so many articles focused on the constant conflict between theatre and cinema that it seemed as though the cinema's claims to "artistic nobility" were at stake.

The first attempt to explain the cinema came from Giovanni Papini, with an article entitled *La filosofia del cinematografo* (The Philosophy of the Cinema) in *La Stampa* on 18 May 1907. After a brief review attempting to explain the miraculous expansion of cinemas, Papini invited philosophers to reflect on "these new entertainment factories", which should not be dismissed as a simple curiosity for young people, women and common people. Papini claimed that the cinema had many qualities:

In comparison with the theatre, the cinema has the advantage of that the shows are shorter, less tiring and less expensive. . . . For thirty cents, everyone can take part in this brief magic lantern show for twenty minutes, and it does not require too much culture, too much attention, or too much effort.

Although Papini recognised that the cinema had some positive qualities in comparison with the theatre, he still saw it as inferior. The cinema could reproduce vast and complex events, even real events of just a few days ago, not just a description in words or a still picture, but a succession of movements filmed from real life. In this first stage of development, the cinema had not yet managed to find its own ideals or artistic independence and was still seeking to define its own cultural status by imitating the theatre, music and literature, and drawing on their contents for its subjects and texts.

In France, Pathé launched Film d'Art in the late 1910s, a production company targeting a bourgeois audience. It drew mainly on the theatre, both for contents and for human resources, signing contracts with actors from the "*Comédie Française*" and the writers' union (Société des Gens de Lettres). Film d'Art films had literary or historical subjects and copied the typical narrative and acting models of the theatre, especially pantomime. Thus, high-level culture and the great texts of world literature became accessible to the lower classes: "Everything in the cinema's artistic field needs to be created and recreated. But the public still flocks in, so we can rejoice that in the current desire for art in the cinema as a small step towards improvement, and we can see that poetry is making progress in the cinema".[13]

For commercial reasons, the cinema preferred existent literary and theatrical works to original texts, in the same way that its acting drew on the theatre. Unfortunately, these techniques and styles were often unsuitable, because action was the principal characteristic of the cinema.

Interest in the cinema grew constantly. In 1914, the first newspaper film columns and cinema journals appeared, but this did not translate into critical and aesthetic criticism. Most of the cinema journals gave information about film showings and news about the cinema and production companies, sometimes with some critical and theoretical articles. At the European level, a 1913 article on the cinema by Lukacs laid claim to definitions and evaluations to be included in the study of aesthetics.[14]

The most significant step towards legitimating the cinema in Italy was D'Annunzio's work on *Cabiria*, previewed on the evening of 18 April 1914 at Turin's Teatro Vittorio Emanuele. Produced by Turin-based Itala, *Cabiria* was directed by Giovanni Pastrone, the real *deus ex machina* of the entire project. Although Pastrone also wrote the screenplay, it was actually attributed to D'Annunzio, who therefore became the film's leading author and promoter. Cinema first attracted intellectuals, especially writers and poets, mostly for economic reasons, since the industry could pay them much more than they could traditionally earn with literature. Intellectuals and men of letters viewed the fascinating world of cinema with a certain distaste and disquiet, seeing it as a medium that completely transformed the role of the intellectual, who was no longer the centre of the creative process, but just one of many cogs needed for the complex mechanism of film production to work. As far as cinema is concerned, intellectuals are paid for their services, and screenwriters, directors and actors adapt their work as they perform it.

This was certainly alienating for intellectuals, who now found themselves working on a form of expression reduced to an industrial product rather than being perceived as an art form. The problem with a film is that it is not a unique product, like an artistic or cultural event or a play, where the artist's contribution is a one-off event, whether the artist be a writer or an actor. A film presents the same story and the same creation *ad infinitum*; this certainly makes it immortal, but this means that film lacks the aura of uniqueness that makes a work of art.

In this respect, Pirandello's novel *I quaderni di Serafino Gubbio Operatore* (Notebooks of Serafino Gubbio, cine operator) is emblematic. The labyrinthine plot involves many characters vainly seeking their emotional and existential goals; it expresses Pirandello's particular vision of the relationship between man and machine, and the alienation caused by the increasing presence of machines. When he speaks about the invention of the cine camera and the passive role of the cine operator, Serafino Gubbio says: "They invented it. It has to act; it has to feed. It feeds on everything, any stupidity they put in front of it. I tell you, it will feed on you as well, it feeds on everything!"

Opposition to the cinema continued right through the first decade of the 1900s. In 1913, Sabatino Lopez, playwright and director of the *Società Italiana Autori* (Italian Writers' Union), wrote a letter to *La Vita Cinematografica* (Cinema Life) claiming that the cinema was "art for illiterates and deaf mutes", and inviting authors to refuse all forms of direct or indirect collaboration. Not all literary writers and intellectuals supported Lopez in his criticism. Piedmontese intellectual Nino Oxilia was a vigorous supporter of the value and dignity of the seventh art: "Is the cinema an adjunct to the theatre? No. The cinema is an art form in itself. It is absolutely different from the theatre, but has its own elegance. The opponents of this silent art say that no form of art can come into being or perish, since art and human life are bound together. . . . But the cinema is a new form of art".

Oxilia collaborated with Itala Film and Cines. He was the first and most fervent supporter of the need for an active and constructive dialogue between literary writers and the cinema. According to Oxilia, the cinema needed intellectuals to elevate it to a form of expression and communication, to a make it a true art form. On the other hand, artists needed to learn from the cinema as a place for experimenting with new forms of expression.

Actors soon began to share the alienation felt by literary writers. Most cinema actors came from the theatre, which was often the provincial dialect theatre. This created plenty of problems because they were not used to the continual interruptions involved in shooting a film. They had no contact with the public and no immediate feedback. A flesh-and-blood actor became a two-dimensional image on a screen; the actor felt robbed of his role, reduced to being a simple component in an industrial process. Nevertheless, not only bitterness and disappointment awaited actors, since film stars began to emerge in the 1910s. Performers were becoming the object of symbolic films, and it was mostly actresses who became the new cinema stars.

The problem of cinema legitimation was also linked to the fact that it did not yet have all the characteristics of an independent sector. Film was included in other forms of show and the embryonic structure of the production system was totally conditioned by the places where films were shown. There were not yet any dedicated structures, but places like cafés and dance halls were used, or else films were included in other shows like the circus or varieties.

The link with other kinds of show also involved the cinema's stylistic component, since it drew on codes, experiences and forms of popular culture that had existed for centuries. These could be traced back to traditional storytellers, the hall of wonders and magic lantern shows, all of which gave audiences the chance to travel with the imagination to distant unknown lands.

## Cinemania

The cinema was now physically present in urban centres and in society. What had initially seemed no more than a passing curiosity had become one of the most widespread forms of entertainment, but public authorities and religious institutions claimed that the cinema was immoral, blaming it for encouraging deviant behaviour.

The public authorities intervened with safety measures, since early films were highly inflammable and therefore very dangerous. Cinema audiences also had to contend with smoke, poor ventilation, sweat, uncomfortable seats, thieves and criminals. However, despite all the discomforts, the cinema was still seen as a pleasurable entertainment venue for the lower classes. In Italy, the pressures on public opinion and on the authorities to resolve the educational and moral problems raised by the cinema via repression and censorship culminated in Law no.785 of 25 June 1913, which introduced official "vigilance over cinema films". Since some members of the upper classes considered the cinema as inferior to other forms of show, more like the activity of street performers, the cinema was not seen as an investment sector. This meant that financial and human capital was diverted elsewhere: "the most important credit bodies very rarely trust cinema companies because they are unstable, and are run by disreputable persons of little conscience".[15]

> Wanted a capitalist partner prepared to use money for speculation in the film industry. Utmost reliability. Guaranteed future.[16]

This contradictory advertisement gives an immediate insight into one of the distinctive features of Italian film production as it developed in the early years of the twentieth century. The first page of *La cinematografia italiana* no. 15 of February 1908 has the following advertisement: "Do you have 8 to 10 million lire? A very modest cinema, with everything included, costs much less than this figure and gives a net return of 25,000 lire a year for an investment of half a million lire, being situated in Via Torino, Colonne di S. Lorenzo. If you have the money, get in touch. We will take care of the lease (in addition to the venue, machinery, films, furnishings, staff) and deal with all the paperwork required in order to operate legally." There were also advertisements for professional services:

> Artistic director available, very experienced in every field of knowledge, acquainted with all types of literature, an expert in different languages, with an exceptional imagination, very knowledgeable about the customs and habits of different peoples, architecture, and so on. Has written many excellent works and is a highly praised art critic, well known for staging successful plays, and as an amateur actor.

Journals gave resonance to new production companies with a guaranteed artistic and financial future; the very same production companies went on to make two or three films at most, which they were unable even to sell:

> A new film production company is about to set up in our city . . . with large amounts of capital provided by a select group of our fellow citizens, and with highly competent first-rate management and artistic personnel. . . . It is easy, therefore, to predict a guaranteed artistic and financial success. . . .[17]

The "new art" recruited its neophytes from the most disparate social classes, interested in the cinema less out of faith or enthusiasm than because they thought it was an easy way to get rich. The cinema seemed like an industrial Eldorado, and large and small businessmen were prepared to risk what were, for the times, huge amounts of capital.

Most people did not see the cinema as requiring any particular specific ability, believing it possible to improvise when it came to forming a company, directing a film, writing a screenplay, or acting.

> They flocked into the most accessible and attractive silent film theatres, from the theatre and even from the opera, from the variety halls, from literature, from the false and the true aristocracy, from politics, from cosmopolitan high society and from our own good people. People including the convinced, the deluded, the capable and the failures, the competent, the amateurs, the rich and poor, the honest and the fraudulent, were all deceived with promises of easy wealth and fame, or at least of a certain flattering notoriety, by the Publicity Fairy and the first modern advertisements.[18]

Film industry ventures were for a long time synonymous with becoming millionaires in just a month; this deeply affected how trade journals judged the quality of Italian films, and influenced the definition of suitable censorship and control procedures. The Italian film industry seemed unable to shake off its reputation for improvisation and speculation that would lead to calls for "serious work to build the bases and re-create actors and directors, but, above all, to establish the film industry on technical, artistic and financial foundations".[19]

Thus, the cinema had the dubious reputation of being improvised and ephemeral. It was a kind of heterogeneous and suspicious hybrid area for people in search of fame, including aristocrats like *Contessa Aurelia* "a personality who was very much at home in that world".[20]

Aristocrats and the bourgeoisie were dazzled by the beauty of the great female stars, who were promised leading roles in films that were created especially for them. For these new arrivals, the cinema conferred prestige, providing a combination of modernity and high society that ensured social legitimation and a confirmation of cultural superiority. This attitude was seen as provincial, and so ingenuous as to be almost laughable. Aristocrats were also joined by people from lower social classes, who hoped to improve their social status and exploit the cinema's vast potential for making money.

The cinema was seen as immoral and vacuous, with a seductive potential to corrupt all social classes. This was especially true of young people, who were fascinated by the "flickering shadows of life which appear on the screen; shadows which could be mistaken for reality".[21] The public's growing enthusiasm for film shows led religious and political authorities to talk of a real "cinema addiction"; they accused it of spreading dissolute morality, inciting criminal behaviour and disturbing the peace, especially among the working classes. Film shows were believed to endanger public hygiene and to harm citizens' physical and mental health.

This affected the definition of regulations regarding safety (films were highly inflammable) and film content. Before centralised control was entrusted to the Ministry of the Interior's Central Cinema Revision Office—Public Security Division (*Ufficio Centrale di revisione cinematografica—Direzione di Pubblica sicurezza*), the city *prefetti* (government officials) were in charge of controlling the content of Italian and foreign films. In general, the films that were banned were "deemed offensive in that they ridiculed public officials, or else contained lascivious or titillating scenes".[22] Censorship affected the film industry by slowing down the process of cultural legitimation, and thus influencing the ruling class's perception of the cinema as a possible investment opportunity. It also increased the risks involved in making a film; films were approved *ex post* by the public control authorities, making it impossible to recoup investments if the film were banned.[23]

It is interesting to note that the contemporary perception of the cinema as precarious and ephemeral also appears in the documents concerning the industry. In the 1930s, some observed that it was impossible to do serious research on the Italian film industry. Here are Antonello Gerbi's astute comments: "It is a double torture for a scrupulous researcher who is eager to obtain results, because he has to read everything but finds hardly anything. Three-quarters of cinema literature consists of studio gossip, biographies cooked up in press offices, rumours and scandals and theoretical nonsense. The big production companies who feed this literature are another disappointment. If you ask them how many lovers have satisfied Pola Negri, what jewellery Gloria Sullivan wore the day she married, or if it is true that Ramon Novarro sends a hundred dollars a month to his poor blind mamma, who knows nothing about her son's fame, then you will receive ready answers, illustrated with photographs, facsimiles and maybe even autographs. But if you ask a serious question, even just the number of films shot in a year, they will not even give you the satisfaction of a refusal: nothing at all".[24]

## The Creation of a First Rudimental "Industry Structure"

The voraciously increasing demand stimulated film production: on the one hand, the "exhibitors" carried out a process of backward vertical integration, and on the other hand, the mirage of sudden wealth encouraged the first film factories, as will be discussed in more detail in the next chapter. The structure of the film production system was beginning to take shape. Most academics agree that a film exists only when it is shown. The film industry is generally seen as having three stages that follow each other in chronological order and involve very different economic strategies. The first stage is *production*, which "consists of finding the resources needed to make every single film, for editing, creating the product, and selling distribution rights. Resources are meant as financial, physical, technological and human resources". The second stage is *distribution*, "the activity of distributing the film on the market. It involves a series of operations in addition to simply selling the product, such as making the number of copies of the original film needed for the distribution area, possible dubbing, the real advertising campaign, and of course negotiations with suppliers (producers) and retail outlets (cinemas)". The last stage is the *cinema*, which "provides a film service to the final purchaser, the cinema spectator".

The first film "products" were short documentaries, known in technical language as "live action" films, recording both international and local events; they were filmed a few days before screening, and mostly used to complete a variegated programme of screenings with low-cost products. The first cinema programmes generally consisted of eight to ten separate films, none longer than three minutes, and cinema managers usually put together a combination of films from different countries.

Product quality was not yet essential, but it was vitally important that the programme (consisting of different short scenes grouped together in a 15–20 minute show) was constantly updated with novelties in order to draw audiences in. An early twentieth-century cinema would show films of daily life ("People leaving the Church of Santissima Annunziata after mass", "The congregation leaving the Cathedral", "Women brawling in Cannaregio, Venice", "Children playing in Villa Bellini"), Italian natural and artistic beauties ("Among the eternal snowfields", "On the immaculate peaks of Mont Blanc", "Picturesque Lake Como", "Italian gardens"), sporting events ("Susa-Moncenisio race", "Cycle tour of Italy"), Italian industrial life ("Sulphur mining in Sicily", "A glass plate factory", "Decorative pottery factory"), distant countries ("The Czar's day", "Umbrella factory in Burma"), and wars ("The conquest of Zuara", "The Italo-Turkish War"). The cinema could transform the simplest gestures, habits and daily tasks into fascinating moving pictures.

In this "pioneer" phase of the cinema, however, most attention concentrated on making constant technological improvements to projection machinery and film cameras. The flickering images of the first screenings were fuzzy and unstable, and red eyes were a common irritating side effect for spectators. Experiments in this area brought important changes to film production, also affecting film content, since stable images made it possible to develop the first rudiments of film editing and produce longer films. Alongside the rather crude live action films appeared the first fiction films, thus paving the way for full-length feature films.

## Notes

1  Ferri, Giustino October 1906, "Tra le quinte del cinematografo", in *La lettura*, p. 796.
2  Gozzano, Guido 5 May 1916, "Il nastro di celluloide e I serpi di Laocoonte", in *La donna*, now in Gozzano, Guido, 1961, Poesie e prose, Milan: Garzanti, p. 1089.
3  According to Roland Barthes, the cinema is "the place where the vision of our century operates". Barthes, Roland 1994, *Sul cinema*, Genova: Il Melangolo, p. 10.
4  "The society of imagery has existed for hundreds of years. The cinema has just simply—which is plenty—brought the technological content of imagery up to date, raising the tension, the human talent for imagery, performance, showmanship, ritual, and best technological achievement", Linguiti, Francesco, Colacino, Marcello 2004, *L' inconscio cinema: lo spettatore tra cinema, film e psiche*, Torino: Effatà Editrice.
5  Tosi, Vittorio 2001, *Breve storia tecnologica del cinema*, Rome: Bulzoni Editore, p. 10.
6  Metz has defined the cinema as *a complex social institution*. The cinema constructs and depicts collective social and cultural identities and those of the single individual: "The cinema is a complex interrelation of dynamics which symbiotically determine the dimension of the cinema, as an anthropological dimension of consumption, and text building". Metz, Carl 1980, *Cinema e psicanalisi*, Venice: Marsilio.
7  Luciano de Feo in an article in "Cinema" commented on the cinema's ability to "provide visual knowledge, the fastest and most superficial form of knowledge" via which "it is possible to profoundly touch the masses, to give them a powerful stimulus towards understanding collective, individual, historical and natural

phenomena". Luciano de Feo in the editorial of the first volume of "Cinema", 10 July 1936.

8   Bernardini, Aldo 2002, *Cinema muto italiano. I film dal vero 1895–1914*, Pordenone: La Cineteca del Friuli.

9   In 1919, the English journal *Bioscope* wrote that the cinema had become the Church's main competitor in creating national identity.

10  In this first phase, the travelling cinemas played an important role in the expansion of the cinema in Italy, arriving with their vans to show films in town squares and at fairs across the country. This had a profound impact on the social image of the cinema, since the places used were seen as morally dangerous and corrupting. The travelling cinema operators were, on the other hand, seen as real industrialists, "novelty impresarios, very different from dirty thieving gypsies with brutish criminal faces; they risk large amounts of capital and lead honest lives", in Brunetta, Gian Piero 1991, *Cent'anni di cinema italiano*, Rome-Bari: Editori Laterza.

11  "Cine-journal", 67 del 1908, quoted in Burch, Noel 1994, *Il lucernario dell'infinito*, Parma: Nuova Pratiche, p. 61.

12  One of the most important theatre journals of the twentieth century.

13  Niga, Edoardo 10 September 1913, "Cinematografo e . . . teatro", in *Il Maggese Cinematografico*, a. I, 10.

14  Lukacs, György 1978, "Riflessioni per un'estetica del cinema", in Barbera, Alberto, Turigliatto, Roberto, *Leggere il cinema*, Milan: Mondadori, p. 25–31.

15  Osti, Luigi 1920, *Le industrie cinematografiche*, degree thesis, Università Commerciale L. Bocconi.

16  The advertisement appeared in *Il Cinematografo* of Naples several times in 1907.

17  The advertisement in the text comes from "La Vita cinematografica", 1912/15, quoted in Friedemann, Alberto 2002, *Le case di vetro. Stabilimenti e teatri di posa a Torino*, Turin: Biblioteca FERT, p. 61.

18  Bianconi, Luigi November 1939, *D'Annunzio e il cinema*, in "Bianco e Nero", *Anno III*, 11, XVII.

19  *Necesse est edificandi*, in "La cinematografia—Giornale d'arte e di battaglia", 15–30 May 1929.

20  Ibid.

21  This perception led to restrictions and controls; most States set up specific governmental film censorship commissions, which could impose a total or partial ban on screenings in cinemas.

22  These were often Pathé or Nordisk comedy films, accused of pornography.

23  The censorship law was retroactive: a film produced before 1914 and still in distribution was subject ministerial control. A production company could therefore incur losses in relation to potential earnings from further commercial exploitation.

24  ASI-BCI, Antonello Gerbi's personal paper and preface to Margadonna, Ettore 1932, *Cinema italiano ieri e oggi*, Milan: Domus.

## Bibliography

BARBERA, Alberto, TURIGLIATTO, Roberto 1978, *Leggere il cinema*, Milan: Mondadori

BARTHES, Roland 1994, *Sul cinema*, Genova: Il Melangolo

BERNARDINI, Aldo 2002, *Cinema muto italiano. I film dal vero 1895–1914*, Pordenone: La Cineteca del Friuli

Boschetti, Carlo 1999, *Risorse e strategie d'impresa. Il caso delle imprese cinematografiche*, Bologna: Il Mulino

Brunetta, Gian Piero 1991, *Cent'anni di cinema italiano*, Rome-Bari: Editori Laterza

Burch, Noel 1994, *Il lucernario dell'infinito*, Parma: Nuova Pratiche

Clair, René 1953, *Storia e vita del cinema: reflexion faite: appunti per servire alla storia dell'arte cinematografica dal 1920 al 1950*, Milan: Nuvoletti

Friedemann, Alberto 2002, *Le case di vetro. Stabilimenti e teatri di posa a Torino*, Turin: Biblioteca FERT

Linguiti, Francesco, Colacino, Marcello 2004, *L' inconscio cinema: lo spettatore tra cinema, film e psiche*, Torino: Effatà Editrice

Margadonna, Ettore 1932, *Cinema italiano ieri e oggi*, Milan: Domus

Metz, Carl 1980, *Cinema e psicanalisi*, Venice: Marsilio

Mosconi, Elena 2006, *L'impressione del film. Contributi per una storia culturale del cinema italiano 1895–1945*, Milan: Vita e Pensiero

Osti, Luigi 1920, *Le industrie cinematografiche*, degree thesis, Università Commerciale L. Bocconi

Pirandello, Luigi 2007, *I Quaderni di Serafino Gubbio operatore*, Milan: Mondadori, collana I Meridiani

Rosten, Leo 1941, *Hollywood: The Movie Colony, The Movie Makers*, New York: Hartcourt

sadoul, Georges 1960, *Manuale del cinema (Tecnica, industria e organizzazione del film)*, Turin: Einaudi

Soldati, Mario 2006, *Cinematografo*, Palermo: Sellerio

Tosi, Vittorio 2001, *Breve storia tecnologica del cinema*, Rome: Bulzoni Editore

# 2 Cinemania
## Entrepreneurs and Would-Be Producers

The cinema industry organization is sacred.
We need to organize capitals, directors, actors.
Cinema is a big and difficult industry.
It has to be founded on solid basis.[1]

### The Pre-Industrial Debut

At the very beginning of the twentieth century, the international film industry was in a state of relative equilibrium, although some countries' industries were just starting to emerge ahead of others.

The first name in Italy associated with the cinema was Filoteo Alberini, who patented the Kinetografo Alberini in 1895 as a "machine for shooting, printing and projecting films". Alberini knew that the Lumière Brothers had already invented a projector, but could not imagine that only two months later spectators would pay to see the first *cinématographe* show. After working as a cinema manager in Florence, Alberini moved to Rome and began film production in 1905 with *La presa di Roma* (The Conquest of Rome), thus marking the start of the Italian film industry.

The United States patent war started by Edison had launched a race towards the new industry, demonstrating its economic potential. German machinery was taking over the northern European market, and French films were exported all over the world.

Italy had not yet overcome its dependence on foreign films in general, and on France in particular, but this did not seem to have a decisively negative effect on the fortunes of the sector. The reasons for the difficulties of the early film industry are not completely different from those of other economic sectors. In the film industry, as in other new industries, investors were suspicious of a fragile economic structure very much influenced by fashions and by the tastes of the public. The Italian business class had proven to be very immature, with poor technical skills and a lack of industrial organisation and management expertise. At first, it seemed impossible to reverse this situation. Economically and technically stronger, with an increasingly vast film industry, the French made no secret of their ambitions to expand on the Italian market. Only after 1906, when the number of Italian cinemas had grown substantially, did Italian entrepreneurs begin to recognise the potential of the cinema. Not only could Italy provide a workforce at competitive prices, but the country's literary, historical and traditional heritage also offered a vast variety of subjects for screenplays. This meant that there was the potential for captivating Italian audiences with films whose cultural content was more familiar.

In addition, George Eastman had consolidated Kodak's Italy branch in 1905, so that it could now supply blank film, limiting Italy's dependence on French suppliers. However, it is important to recall that Italy always remained a net importer of blank film and was never able to manage without foreign imports of this raw material. Italy was a few years behind other nations when it began to create its own film industry; Italian film production began after the development of cinemas, whereas the two sections of the film industry developed at the same time in France, Great Britain, Germany and the United States.

Unlike Italy, the more organic development of the film industry in other countries brought it into close contact with other similar industries, of which precision mechanics was the most important. The most significant consequences were that capital became more readily available and that there was an underlying impetus towards a monopoly. This never occurred in Italy, and besides the three great production companies, Cines, Ambrosio and Itala, there were many other companies that had their origins in exhibition branch. This slowed down the concentration of film production in just a few big companies, so typical of the American film industry. In Italy, these companies were prevalently local, started up by cinema owners who then expanded into production. Often the enthusiastic owner of one or more cinemas wanted to increase the number of projections with homemade *ad hoc* films. These companies were, however, very short-lived. On the one hand, they ensured a variety of film output because they met the needs of market segments often ignored by the big producers, such as regional/dialect films, but the constant proliferation of companies lasting just one or two years confirmed the film industry's image of fragility and improvisation.

Producers and cinema owners felt the need for greater integration between the different branches of the production chain; producers saw the importance of organised marketing. Cines, Ambrosio and Itala created a network of agents and representatives across Italy and used foreign distributors for the foreign market. Cinema owners, on the other hand, needed a production structure to ensure a constant turnover of programmes on offer to the public. Despite the lack of a real commercial structure, film distributors began to appear. They worked for big Italian or foreign production companies, and began independently to create the rudiments of a film distribution network (albeit disparate and disorganised). Other important developments around the film trade, such as information bulletins, production company's catalogues and cinema journals, all had an effect on the production system.

Real rental, i.e. the evolution of the commercial network from a sales intermediary to a sector and financial partner of the producers, did not develop so rapidly, but French attempts to monopolise the Italian market encouraged the transformation of Italian film distribution. The French giant Pathé, whose films were essential for Italian cinemas, decided to organise an exclusive rental system (using agents, dealers or controlled companies) in Italy. This meant a monopoly over price control and a series of rules about the way to use the films, such as the number of consecutive days of screening.

Faced with these threats, Italian reactions were disorganised and relatively inconsistent. In 1907, however, there was a first attempt to establish a set of rules for the industry, and to organise the various professional categories in a move towards rationalising the industry. Film rental began to develop among the small cinema owners, while the owners of a larger number of cinemas continued to buy films.

The Italian market included a wide variety of distribution systems and practices, to the point that the relations of the distribution businesses with each other and with the production companies were so diversified that they were always unstable. It was rare for a rental company to have exclusive rights for one single production company, and more common for a rental agent to represent several companies, both Italian and foreign. Relations between cinema owners and the rental agent consisted of the following stages: the rental business gave instructions to the managers of individual agencies that the film had to guarantee a certain income as well as covering costs. There were two types of sale: either as a percentage of takings or at a fixed price (the sum agreed by the two parties was based on the film's estimated earning potential and took account of both the cinema and the film).

Distribution obviously started in the most important urban centres and in what were considered first-run cinemas, where tickets were more expensive, the cinema itself more comfortable and refined, and the programmes featured the best of the current season's films. These cinemas offered educated middle-class audiences something similar to the theatre in terms of ticket prices and cinema architecture and style. A film opened at the same time in the first-run cinemas, which generated around 20% of what would be the film's total earnings nationwide. The cinema system was organised according to a hierarchy of screenings; the film was launched firstly at the regional and national level in ten cities: Turin, Milan, Genoa, Trieste, Venice, Bologna, Florence, Rome, Naples and Palermo. The next stage was the distribution of 25 copies of the film in "key cities" that were provincial capitals; here the cinema tickets were cheaper and the cinemas were more basic. Second-run cinemas brought in 60% of total takings. The remaining 20% came from rentals in the small towns, in the so-called inner city neighbourhood, suburban or popular cinemas, where the film stayed on the programme for a long time and tickets were very cheap. The distribution sector worked like a chain: the rental agent who obtained the distribution rights for the film in the first-run area then granted distribution rights to a sub-dealer who took care of the second and third runs in the less important cinemas. When the sub-dealer had used the film, he passed it on to a third intermediary: in all these successive stages, the producer actually made the smallest profit. The Italian distribution system always struggled to develop more cohesive organisation strategies: film circulation was entrusted to a vast number of structures, which fragmented the national market. This problem went unnoticed until Italian films became popular, but when the invasion of Hollywood "dreams" reduced the market share for Italian producers, an already unstable situation was aggravated by the structural problem inherent in the total lack of cooperation within the production chain.

Despite the risk of using rather insidious divisions into "periods", 1909 can be considered a crucial year in the chronological history of the Italian film industry, as well as for other national cinema industries. The 1908 financial crisis had also had important consequences for the film industry, which was therefore scaled back. The crisis marked the end of the experimental period, and ushered in a new stage of real development.

The main reasons for the crisis were generally seen as the excessive number of films in circulation, caused by the eagerness of cinema owners and rental agents to maximise their profits via intensive exploitation of the films. Added to this were the technical inadequacies of the production plants and the cinema halls. Another important factor was connected with artistic expression, because producers and film-makers tended to use the same old well-worn narrative models. The public began to abandon the cinemas, apparently tiring of monotonous programmes made up of short films and variety numbers.

Italian cinema started to become independent, although the numbers of French imports remained consistent. Italian film output overtook other European countries, including Germany, Great Britain and Scandinavia. From 1910, manufacturers began making new cinema machinery, and Italian patents involved technical improvements to existing models. Film historian M. A. Prolo recalls that "until about 1908 every cine film manufacturer had his own perforation gauge and projectors had to be fitted with adaptors". Giovanni Pastrone revolutionised the systems used so far by inventing a system with maximum perforation precision in the stages of transferring the film from the negative to the positive. The first logo of Itala Film was a cartouche containing the word "Fixité", showing that a fixed image was considered an important element of film quality.

The greatest progress was made in ensuring the stability and fixity of images, with the spread of the three-blade fan (1908) and the Maltese cross system (invented in 1905). This is further confirmation that the crisis was a decisive factor in spurring entrepreneurial exploitation of achievements that had remained economic dead letters. In these early years, however, "entrepreneurial" efforts mainly focused on resolving technological problems and perfecting machinery, and this is generally seen as a "technology driven" era in the various national film industries. Production companies carried out all processes independently, from shooting the film to selling it. Every factory worked with modified cine cameras and perforation devices, sometimes made *ex novo* by their own staff. This made it even more strategically important to protect every new technique jealously in order to keep ahead of competitors. There were two main reasons why control over technology and technological development had always been important strategic variables in the competition between film companies: market control and business differentiation. In the first case, there is the example of the US patents war, leading to the formation of the Motion Picture Patent Company in an attempt to dominate the market by maintaining exclusive control over technology. The most outstanding example of differentiation strategies is the introduction of sound film in 1926, the result of an experiment by Warner Bros. supported by a team from Western Electric.

The objectives of the first Italian production company demonstrate the importance of technical and scientific aspects and of relations with similar sectors (photographic, electrical and chemical industries). *Società Anonima Ambrosio* was formed in Turin in 1907 with a share capital of 700,000 lire to "produce and sell film and photographic cameras". In 1909, *Società Italiana Cinematografica Films e Affini* (Turin) was producing, selling and marketing film, optical instruments, cameras and patents.

## The Formation of Production Companies

Following its pre-industrial debut at the turn of the century, the Italian film sector began to acquire the characteristics of an industry, creating the conditions for competition with the flourishing French film industry. Alongside the first companies—Cines, Società Anonima Ambrosio, and Fratelli Troncone—other film production ventures gradually expanded across the entire country, so that until the First World War the sector was *polycentric*.

Graph 2.1 shows the trend in the number of film production companies and the number of films produced in the silent film era. Although the silent film era conventionally covers the years between 1895 and 1926, the graph continues up to 1931 because the source used (*Archivio del cinema Italiano*) records silent film production until that year. In fact, the adoption of the new sound film technology proved to be a slow process, in particular because it required financial investments in production and in the cinemas. In the late 1920s, very few production companies were able to make this kind of investment, as will be seen below.

The number of films shown in the graph therefore includes both shorts and full-length films, since the production companies continued producing both types of film even after the industry experienced the first technological wave, i.e. the advent of full-length films, which took place in 1913 in Italy. Short films, live action films and documentaries persisted because the technological changeover was a gradual process. The production companies had to acquire new technical and artistic skills and more money, and cinema owners were not keen to accept full-length films, because this meant radical changes in the way they used films; in the first years of the cinema, earning potential depended on the rotation of shows with a programme of 10 one-or two-minute films.

Between 1905 and 1931 (the year when sound film arrived definitively) there was a total number of 570 production companies. Graph 2.2 shows

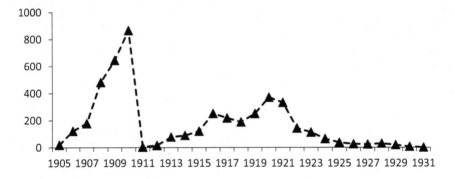

*Graph 2.1* Films Produced by Italian Companies, 1905–1931.

Source: author's elaboration on Bernardini (1911 has been represented as a break between short and full-length movies).

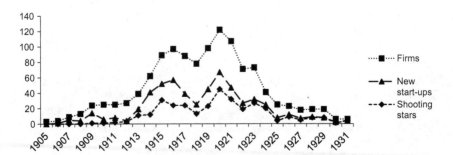

*Graph 2.2* Typologies of Firms in the Italian Film Industry, 1905–1931.

Source: author's elaboration on Bernardini *Archivio del cinema italiano.*

that the number of active companies began to grow from 1913 and that, in the same year, 49% of companies were newly formed: 39 active companies and 19 new companies. Between 1905 and 1915 new production companies sprang up at a rate of 48% (per year), with 40% of these surviving just one year. These figures were due to the limited investment required to start up a film production company: it was possible to make artisanal short films in what had once been photographers' workshops. The stories they told were not yet complex enough for actors and actresses to command high fees, and blank film was the most expensive item of the production process. The percentage of short-lived production companies shows that, although the market was open to new enterprises, their survival was limited. Graphs have been built considering effective productivity; a company formed in 1905 may not have begun film production until 1908. Productivity is used as the indicator to analyse the life cycle of the sector due to the lack of systematic studies on the general situation of the film industry (the compilation of statistical data on the industry began with fascism), and is also due to the diversity of the sources and the discrepancies that emerged during the course of research.

The availability of capital was not always synonymous with productivity and a medium- to long-term project. Companies were formed with an average social capital of 300,000 lire. There were production companies like Mediolanum Film, which formed in 1913 with a social capital of 250,000 lire and made six films in three years, of which only one was a full-length film, or Psiche Film, which formed in 1911 with a social capital of 32,000 lire and made 30 films in four years, three of which were full-length films.

## The Advent of Full-Length Films

Worn-out narrative models, falling demand and technological innovation led to a real "technological leap forward" with the changeover from shorts to full-length films. Longer films required significant changes in production methods and techniques. Films were no longer documentaries or collections of moving images, but now required a complete screenplay, more time to complete and greater levels of technical and artistic specialisation. The growing professional expertise of technicians and artists added value to their work, leading to higher pay, and this trend would really explode with the first movie idols. The "material" resources like film sets and props, technical equipment and make-up all took on a more significant role, accounting for a greater share of the production budget. While production became more of a specialised process, a full-length film was actually more of a risk. Finally, however, full-length film meant that the film industry now had the chance to acquire greater artistic status, since longer films required more complex and articulated subject matter and more fully developed characters, and were also suitable for the film versions of operas or plays.

Initially an experiment, the use of full-length film expanded mainly after 1910, and most films were narrative films rather than comedies. A full-length film consisted of three to four reels (a total of 1,000 metres) and took about an hour to show. It was not only producers who had to become accustomed to this new development, but audiences also needed to understand the novelty. Cinema owners were at first obliged to show full-length films over several evenings, and then had to change the methods they used to advertise and promote films.

With the advent of full-length films, films themselves increasingly had the characteristics of cultural products; each film was a prototype whose life cycle played out on the screen in a different way. In order to recover higher production costs, every film needed to be adequately publicised and distributed in order to attract audiences. Italy was very ready to switch to full-length film and followed the two countries that had made the biggest investments in the changeover: Germany and Denmark. Italy's Milano Films, the smallest of the big production companies—or the biggest of the small companies—immediately invested in full-length film with a very ambitious project: *L'Inferno*, inspired by Dante Alighieri's literary masterpiece. The intention was to make an epic. First shown in January 1911, *L'Inferno* was an enormous success. Cinemas in London and Paris ran it for 18 weeks, while audiences in the United States had to pay higher than usual prices for a ticket. Itala had the same success with *La caduta di Troia* (The Fall of Troy) and Cines with *La Gerusalemme Liberata* (The Relief of Jerusalem).

In 1912, the production companies who had converted half of their output to full-length films were Ambrosio, Itala, Pasquali and Aquila in Turin; Cines, Savoia, Latium, Caesar, Roma Film, and Volsca in Rome; Milano Films in Milan, and Vesuvio Film in Naples. The Italian film industry was polycentric and revolved around four cities; these were Rome, Milan, Naples and especially Turin, whose FIAT car factories were turning it into an industrial city.

There were also signs of development involving programmes and manufacturing, particularly involving organisation and product standardisation. The latter came about via catalogue classification of film genres, the so-called formula pictures. The process of differentiation into genres, especially narrative genres, was a deliberate move by the production sector, which explicitly labelled its films by classifying them in more or less important categories. One of the most difficult Italian genres, which required more effort from the production company, was the historical costume film set during the Risorgimento, and based on theatrical or literary texts. This type of film required a substantial investment in terms of money and production for the screenplay, the costumes and the sets, the work of actors and directors. The popularity of this genre is shown by the various series: Cines had the "*Serie d'arte*" and "Serie Princeps", Ambrosio Film had the "*Serie d'oro*" and Itala had the "Serie d'arte". Although equally popular with audiences, comedy was less important in Italy; modelled on French examples, Italian comedies never managed to equal or surpass the quality of French and American films.

The advent of full-length film marked the passage from a "technology driven" to a "content driven" era in which the competitive advantage now depended on the ability to create stories satisfying the needs of the public. Literature was an immense source of stories and ideas for screenplays. The works of Dante, Homer, Boccaccio, Dumas and Verdi came to life on the screen. Italian full-length historical films proved successful with the public. Theatrical action scenes and luxurious exotic costumes that recalled a glorious past now viewed with nostalgia, fascinated people. Acting styles were greatly influenced by the theatre, but the grandiose scenes and attention to detail made an exciting show for audiences.

Until the years following the First World War, the Italian film industry managed to obtain prestigious international recognition in Europe and the United States. The expansion of Italian cinema abroad was certainly helped by the great numbers of Italians emigrating to North and South America, and the Italian immigrants crowding into the cities and suburbs of the United States, Argentina and Brazil made up a vast potential market. Here was a public whose nostalgia for Italy gave a very strong incentive to the distribution of Italian films. However, the strength of the promotional campaign on foreign markets was proportional to the productive and financial capacity of Italian companies. The weaker film companies had a less systematic presence on the foreign markets, but almost all companies succeeded to some extent in exporting their films, and could often count on the solidarity and support of others who had arrived on the foreign markets before them. Full-length films like Itala's *La Caduta di Troia* (*The Fall of Troy*), *L'Inferno* (*Inferno*) by Milano Films and *Gerusalemme liberata* (*The Liberation of Jerusalem*) by Cines were a great success with foreign audiences and praised by trade journals. These films created a fashion for Italian historical films and helped to overcome the American industry's suspicion and resistance towards full-length films. Itala and Ambrosio began to concentrate on producing epics: *Gli ultimi giorni di Pompei* (The Last Days of Pompeii), *Quo Vadis?* and *Cabiria* symbolised the ambitious policy of grandeur characterising the Italian cinema of the time. With the end of 1914 and the outbreak of the First World War, all Italian film production collapsed, especially on the American market. The outstanding success of *Cabiria* was the Italian cinema's last really valid gasp, and it now began to lose important ground on both the home and foreign markets.

In some ways, the Italian cinema of these years had some definite successes, but it is important to highlight certain aspects showing the backwardness and fragility of many of its structures in comparison with the foreign competition.

This does not imply a value judgement or comparison with the American model, which was difficult to replicate in the Italian and more general European context. However, it is a case of identifying the factors that can best explain the development of Italian cinema during the twentieth century. In what has been called the Golden Age of the Italian film industry, the production system was unable to organise an industrial structure to cope with difficulties or with competition from other countries.

The switch to the production of full-length films took place very rapidly in the United States, from four films in 1911 to 610 in 1915. In addition, while the average output for a production company was 66 films a year between 1895 and 1910, from 1911 (the year American cinema history gives for projection of the first full-length film) the average fell to just five films per year. As the number of films fell, the number of production companies rose, especially between 1909 and 1914. The advent of full-length films led to the same changes in Italy; from an average of 42 films per year, the number dropped to three. The greatest difference between Italy and the USA is the exponential increase in US companies producing full-length films (from two to 170 between 1909 and 1914), while Italian production companies continued making both shorts and full-length films. Although the larger Italian companies had the technical and financial means for medium- to long-term projects, and would have been able to invest in full-length films, for years they continued to prefer short films. The moment they decided to concentrate on producing only narrative films marked the start of their progressive decline.

In terms of company numbers, the numbers of new entries rose continually and stood at 58% in 1916, when the 97 active companies included 57 newcomers. The following two years saw a slight drop in the number of films produced and therefore in the number of active companies, but in 1919 there were 98 production companies, and in 1920 the number had risen to 122, of which 55% were newcomers.

The production companies were already in financial difficulty on the eve of the War, as the result of reckless financial operations and the rising cost of hiring actors. Adding to this series of problems came the US introduction of protectionist measures to help its own film industry.

On the technical front, inadequate expansion of the most important technological innovations was a factor delaying development of the Italian film industry. However, what really impacted the industry's development processes was its failure to develop the distribution system and cinema management.

This situation requires economic analysis, also to partly rebut some recurrent theories. An original note to the text of a French-style sale contract between film purchasers and vendors reads "in order to enable the continual production of new films, they must have a guaranteed market. This was the main reason why sales were replaced by rental. To ensure a sufficient demand for new films the old films must be taken out of circulation after a certain time. This meant that there was a time limit to the use of a film. This (monopoly) was generally fixed at five years, and copies had to be withdrawn from the market and destroyed when it expired, unless a new licence had been agreed".

The time limit did not guarantee production companies a sufficient market to recover increasingly higher production costs. Their response was intensive exploitation. Faced with rising costs, the producers were obliged to reduce the amortisation period, so that they intensified and concentrated their exploitation of the film in the first months following release. Exploitation can be concentrated in two ways: the film can be launched at the same time in the greatest possible number of cinemas or else launched exclusively in a limited number of cinemas, while general release is delayed by several weeks. Although these strategies were theoretically available to producers, the anarchic conditions of the distribution sector and cinema management made it difficult to apply them in Italy.[2]

French cinema programmes changed every week, but Italian programmes often changed in an irregular way. Sometimes programmes were extended, with new films inserted among less recent films, and this had inevitable negative effects on the production sector, since "the cost of the films must be recovered over a shorter period, because the great number of novelties does not allow a film to be shown for too long in the cinema program".[3]

Continual production had to be guaranteed by a constant market, and the passage from intermittent production to constant production is a sign that the sector was developing. It is equally true that exhibition is the sector with most interest in maintaining and developing market demand. Although the sector's three-part structure of production, distribution and exhibition tends to place the greatest risks of recouping costs on the final stage, the particular situation in Italy meant that the brunt of the risk was borne by the production stage. The Italian film industry produced few films in comparison with the potential demand, and this failure to exploit the sector's potential was clearly seen by those operating in it.

The biggest production companies created their own representation and distribution systems. In the same way, wide-ranging commercial ventures were also launched; SIGLA (Società Italiana Gustavo Lombardo Anonima) was formed in 1910 to "centralise film rental for all production companies in central southern Italy, in order to prevent depression and devaluation of film production by the dubious methods of a great number of small speculators".[4]

SIGLA deserved credit for attempting to rationalise Italian film distribution by bringing together Italian production companies like Itala Film and Milano Film, French companies Eclair and Gaumont, and Americans Vitagraph and Edison. However, the venture was short-lived due to the competition it faced and because it lacked the support of the larger companies like Ambrosio and Cines, which had their own distribution networks.

What did actually lead to the creation of an effective, if rather crude, distribution network were some important changes in the production sector, the most important being the introduction of full-length film. This was a novelty not in terms of narrative, but also in the allocation of costs. Full-length films required a greater investment at the production stage, and meant that cinema owners had to invest in publicity and promotion for every film. This made it necessary to rationalise the anarchic distribution sector with its rentals, licences and sales. The "exclusive rights in separate areas" system adopted had already been tried out. The licence-holder of a certain production company became its exclusive distributor at the national level, and organised a network of rental agents in each area. These agents then granted cinema owners exclusive rights for a certain number of days, guaranteed by entries in the literary property registers to protect them from possible plagiarism and unauthorised copies.

Italian cinema reached its highest point on the eve of the War, but fell into a serious and prolonged recession just a few years later.

## The End of the Golden Age

Between 1915 and 1919, the Italian film industry became concentrated around two companies: Caesar Film and Tiber Film. The war created a situation of instability and uncertainty, but this setback was seen as a pause from which the industry recovered as soon as the war ended. What counted was to continue working, as was suggested by the journals: "we have urged our production companies to produce, produce, produce, to produce enormously now in order to avoid being empty-handed when the war ends and the world markets open up again".[5]

Underlying this recession was the loss of international competitiveness. One reason was that enemy countries closed their markets during the War, and the other was the growth of foreign film industries, especially in the USA, which introduced protectionist measures in 1907 to defend its home industry against Italian films. Reconstruction of the import-export film trade is particularly difficult in view of discrepancies in the data. The starting point has always been a table published in 1922, whose data relating to the period from 1912 to 1918 have been rebutted by more specific research published in various international specialist journals. The figures also differ from those of the United States Department of Commerce,[6] so that it is doubtful that import-export statistics are reliable enough to allow a rational analysis of the international film trade. Despite the differences between the various published data, what counts is the growth of the Italian film industry registered on the home and foreign markets. This was completely reversed during the 1920s, when the United States became the main market for films imported into Italy.[7]

The war years weakened the Italian film industry and created another imminent problem for the European film industries: the US film industry, with its *"men and facts which threaten the home cinema"*, as it was reported in many headlines at the time. It was perceived as an economic threat, weakening the position of an important Italian industry, which was a source of tax revenue, and as an artistic and cultural threat. The Italian public was gradually becoming fond of the new American model, with entertaining films depicting a young and dynamic America, the extreme opposite of the provincial Italy portrayed by the home film industry, which had used the

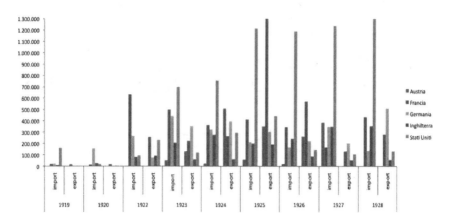

*Graph 2.3* Import-Export of Italian Films, 1919–1928.

Source: author's elaboration on *Statistica del commercio speciale di importazione ed esportazione* (values expressed in metres). Note: for 1921, data are missing.

same worn-out models for years and languished in a state of technical and expressive stagnation. The American cinema had revolutionised the traditional techniques of filming by introducing the close-up. This change in film making technique had an immediate effect on the average spectator's codes of perception: from now on there would be only close-ups, and audiences would expect only films using this new technique.

From the economic point of view, the rise in fixed and sunk production costs had made the size of the market an important factor in making profits, and American production companies began to create their own distribution agencies in European countries in order to obtain more complete control of export markets. Reviews of American films initially judged them as ingenuous and elementary from a narrative point of view, although technically sophisticated. At the end of the war, however, the adjective "American" was used to mean a society and film style that were original, lively, modern and new. At the time when the dominant production standard and object of international competition became the full-length feature film, the Italian industry had only a limited number of companies with a solid enough organisational structure to ensure the continuity of production and business projects. Alongside these few companies, the cinema continued to attract self-styled producers who tried the fascinating film industry for a year, or maybe even less, and then disappeared, leaving no trace of their production companies.

However, these short-lived production companies were not an Italian peculiarity, but a congenital feature of all national film industries. German data indicate that, as late as 1926, the percentage of production companies making just one film was 42%. In the same year, the biggest companies made an average of 12 films per year, and there were many medium and small companies with an annual output of just two or three films[8] (these accounted for 25% of the sector, therefore 67% of production companies made no more than three films).

The vertically integrated studio was not necessarily the norm even in the United States. Alongside the big companies, there were small independent production companies: "companies formed in order to carry out individual projects" (Robbins, 1993). Management of the relations between the business organisation and artists is often used to explain the advent and the success of this type of company in the United States: in the typical Hollywood studio, the artist (actor, actress, director, screen-writer, and so on) was seen as an employee and had an open-ended/permanent contract. This gave a certain security, but also meant that creative freedom might be excessively limited and controlled by a company mainly interested in ensuring that production stayed within its budget. The independent producers offered more freedom for artistic expression and were often better equipped to make innovative films than the big studios.

The presence of small production companies in Italy has been interpreted as both a strength and a weakness. Bernardini claims that Italy had an advantage over France and the United States precisely because "none of its production and distribution companies had achieved the economic and organisational strength of Pathé or Edison". This meant that there was limited intervention by the Italian film industry in the competition to control technical equipment and international markets. The result was that "the disorganisation and improvisation with which production companies formed and proliferated was, in a certain sense, a guarantee of freedom that ensured the survival of minor companies and prevented foreign companies from intruding".[9] Brunetta[10] also claims that the dominant feature of the Italian film industry was the presence of so many small production companies, which made it "fragile but also charming and different".

If a film is considered as a prototype that requires a production project, the meteoric production companies can be interpreted as a positive phenomenon, since the great number of companies meant that there was a certain variety of experience. If flexible production also has a high degree of innovation, high levels of expertise are required, in particular what Bell defines as intensive (Bell, 1973), where theoretical knowledge takes the leading role in the production process. In the cinema, theoretical knowledge corresponds to the set of technical and artistic knowledge and skills that can contribute to the complex structure of a film production. If the film industry is the result of interconnection with a high rate of transactions between individuals within which the exchanges between economic and social variables have a significant weight,[11] the tiny production companies could be considered as diffused entrepreneurship and knowledge expressed from time to time in single production projects. In other words, a film is a product whose creation requires heterogeneous skills and knowledge, and entails high levels of risk; this could make it advantageous to adopt a flexible organisational structure, able to draw on people with specific expertise as needed, involving them in production and thus sharing the risks.

If this description could have been the strength of the meteoric production companies, what actually happened in Italy was that companies were started by people without any kind of specialised knowledge of what it really meant to "produce for the cinema". Therefore, the short-lived companies were far from being the expression of production network systems, and were actually a symptom of the sector's weakness, because they were too small to create a critical mass; they were unable to set a growing strategy based on the production of goods in tune with audience tastes and competitive on international arena. Moreover, their aura of speculation served to keep capital investments away from the industry.

The constant number of ephemeral companies indicates that financial input was not enough to ensure a medium- to long-term presence on the market. Industrial production required an initial investment of substantial amounts of capital. The studios needed all the sets, spaces and equipment required for the production process: from creating and exposing films, to developing and printing the positive copies, to post-production, and in some cases also the distribution of films on the home and international markets.

Most historians of Italian cinema have underlined that it was improvised and artisanal, even to the point of suggesting that an Italian cinema industry comparable to the Hollywood model maybe never even existed. If we consider the classical definition of an industrial sector as a combination of the three elements of production, utility function, and market segments, it is impossible to deny the existence of a film industry in Italy. However, it can be said that the Italian film industry probably did not succeed in playing an important role in the national economy as in the United States.

Instead of contesting the existence of the sector, it would be more correct to analyse what was lacking in order for it to function well. For example, there was a lack of available capital to support industrialisation of the production sector. In the history of the cinema, there came a point when production costs rose as films and production times became longer and levels of specialisation and technical competence increased. Industrial structure was a consequence of greater capital investment. The big budget films that reflected the public's favourite narrative genres could not be made without solid financial backing.

## Creating a Competitive Advantage: The Importance of Intangible Components

Both the movement towards full-length film and genre specialisation required greater levels of organisation in the film production plants.

Moreover, the post-war invasion of US films had shown that the competitive advantage depended on a solid industrial and commercial organisation, but most of all on the ability to make films the public appreciated. Marketing is the "branch" of the film production system with the strongest and most direct contact with the consumer market. Given that the spectator is the ultimate judge and source of earnings for the sector, this direct contact gives the cinema owner greater power in a production system where national products are in competition with foreign films. If the cinema manager can choose between Italian and foreign films, he will choose what he knows the public prefers, and in the 1920s the public preferred Hollywood films. In these conditions, a balance of power in favour of producers can be recreated by vertically integrating all three branches of the production system (production integrates towards distribution and exhibition), by investing in film content (style) so that the public prefers films by a certain producer, and by creating loyalty marketing mechanisms like the star system.

Insufficient investment in content not only affects box-office takings but also influences the processes of the production system; a producer whose films are not popular with the public has less bargaining power with the distributor and cinema owner. The interaction of economic components (in particular, cost structures and production chain organisation) with cultural components (enhancement of intangible components and innovation in film making style) is the key to interpreting what have been described as the reasons for the backwardness and inferiority of the Italian film industry.

> The Italian film industry lacks subjects. It makes no effort to find them. . . . These subjects should no longer be sought mainly in literature. What is important, I'd say the secret, is to put a little poetry in the story or performance. Art therefore? No, not really, but sufficient technical ability to give the illusion of art. The art of pleasure. We believe that the first basic cause of this industry's problems is this mistaken concept of the Italian film industry, which separates production from rental, i.e. product manufacture from retail and recovery of the capital used. Otherwise, it might not be possible for the industry to cross oceans, but certainly for it to be self-sufficient.[12]

The product of the film industry has a dual nature: it is an *economic product* and an *artistic product*. This distinction also exists at the lexical level, where the word *cinema* indicates the means of artistic expression and *cinematography* is used to indicate the industrial aspect. As an economic product, the film can be considered a *commodity*; it is a strip of frames reproduced from a master copy and can be the object of transaction in the production chain between the producer, the distributor and the retailer. A film has common distinctive characteristics with other products: it is produced for the market via industrial activity, its manufacture requires capital investments (fixed and variable capital, industrial capital and financial capital), it is "manufactured" to be consumed, it has a *value in use* (a film is consumed for entertainment, aesthetic pleasure, and learning) and a *value in exchange* (access to a film show is via payment). Unlike other goods, every film is a *prototype* (this characteristic gives a film its economic and commercial value), and because it requires collective consumption, it also creates a kind of social ritual. In addition, it can result in rejection or even opposition between consumption and appreciation; there is a certain degree of randomness involved in choice, since only when a film (a prototype) has been "consumed" is it possible to know if it is appreciated.

A film is also an artistic product, a text, and a language. The two meanings—cinema as goods and cinema as art—are often intermingled in Italian historiography, so that cinema history is often mixed up with film history. As Luigi Chiarini said: "If film is art, the cinema is an industry". The process of making a film is not very different from the process involved in the production and marketing of any other industrial product, but the final output involves a series of intangible elements that are difficult to measure. In the first pages of his *Der Film als Ware* (*Economic History of the Cinema*), Bächlin stated that "as an intellectual product, a film has all the prerequisites of *a work of art*, but it is also necessarily a *product*, due to the different industrial and commercial operations required for its production and consumption".[13]

A film exists only on the screen, and only if spectators "consume" it. To have a full understanding of the film industry it is necessary to observe the strong interconnections and interactions between the production system, the cultural system, and the social, political and economic contexts. From the outset it was a common conviction that one of the greatest problems of managing the film industry was due to its nature as an artistic industry.[14] Although the cinema was considered "a very high art", the principal objective of production had to be "maximum economic returns".[15]

The sector's complexity therefore derives from the coexistence of economic and artistic processes; these two apparently very different areas have rules and mechanisms that are sometimes difficult to reconcile. The organisation and structure of film production is extremely articulated, since it requires the coordination and integration of very different specialised skills.

Many people had believed that starting up a film company was a simple affair, within the reach of anyone with capital to invest; the result had often been short-lived production companies that lit up the industry like a meteor for a few months, or at most a year, and then disappeared (cf. the paragraphs on film industry demographics). However, to work well in the cinema, following solid organisational principles and a medium- to long-term business project, it was necessary to coordinate the work of different well-defined professional figures. It implied coordination of the work of managers, writers, actors and actresses, and technical staff by the production manager, *the essential and principal element of the film*. The production manager needed knowledge and experience of every level of the production process in order to draw up the budget, the basic requirement for film production. The figure of the production manager did not exist in the early years of the cinema, when other figures could be in charge of coordinating production: the set manager, the industrialist (financier) or the studio manager. However, cinema's continual growth, together with technical improvements, developments in audience tastes, and rapid changes in film style, led to the definition of an organisational structure with clearly defined roles and functions. Obviously, this did not always happen for every production company.

> [The producer] is a complex figure: as the foremost exponent of the public he must be the man in the street to understand and predict "what works"; as a great industrialist and something of an artist he must know how to impose his product, meaning that he must not humbly serve the crowd but rather interpret what it wants.[16]

The subtlety of artistic creativity versus the imperious dictates of economics. Producers seemed to follow the dictates of economics and commerce, especially since they provided the capital that was the economic and operational base without which the film could not be made. At the beginning of the film industry, the producer could also be the owner or representative of the company's partners, and the specific functions of today's producer were the responsibility of the film director. As the sector grew and became more specialised, production companies adopted the following division: the person directing the entire production was known as the producer, but the actual responsibility for every project was entrusted to the "production manager".

The Italian film industry recession from 1920 to 1922 and its low output were blamed on the fact that only a very small number of people could be defined as real cinema entrepreneurs. Production was often in the hands of self-styled producers who improvised a production company for largely speculative motives. The film industry involves high sunk costs in the production of the first copy, and an equally high multiplication factor if the film manages to satisfy the changeable tastes and needs of audiences, which could encourage purely speculative investment in film production.

There was plenty of debate in the trade journals about the figure of the producer during this period: the articles seemed to propose a stylised figure, and the characteristics and skills needed to form a solid company were identified as a good technical foundation. There was talk of "industrial education" for producers, who were accused of being mere speculators with a financially and morally irresponsible approach to company management.

If the producer was a central figure, the history of the film industry has always highlighted the critical role played by the actors, actresses and film directors in defining the competitive strategies of film companies. For example, the typical Hollywood studio system gave its actors and actresses long-term contracts at the beginning of their careers, thus allowing producers to control resources with great potential value: stars are often considered able to affect a film's performance. Stars help to make the film a recognisable product and are still a widely used strategy for guaranteeing and protecting investments in film production, to differentiate films, and to guarantee a minimum box- office success.

Careful choice of the artistic components and more specifically of the subject, film director and actors, could provide stylistic and economic advantages, especially when it came to planning strategies; a good film was easier to distribute in the first-run cinemas before the process of exploitation was completed in the second- and third-run cinemas, thus increasing profits for the production company. An effective communication campaign was an equally important part of the production process; the public were very interested in their idols, their whims, and their lives on and outside the film set. Where possible (i.e. with a big budget), producers invested in promoting the name of a celebrity, whose presence in the cast could improve the fortunes of a mediocre or poor-quality film.

Therefore, film production meant being able to coordinate an extremely complex structure, precisely because the finished product was the result of the interconnecting abilities and skills of a large number of different professional figures.

Analysts who studied the shortcomings of the Italian film industry in the 1920s were convinced that the ability to manage and enhance the skills of every single profession would translate into a successful production. Italian cinema did not seem to keep abreast of the changes in industrial and artistic methods, and it was extremely difficult to exploit an artistically outdated film in Italian and foreign cinemas. Contemporary commentators felt that Italy did not possess the conditions for enhancing an industry in which intangible, especially human, capital played a vital role.

According to intellectuals, the Italian film industry needed a change of style in order to revive; it could no longer afford to be provincial, presenting stories with little appeal for foreign markets outside Italy.

The possibilities of improving the quality and cinematographic language of film production were strictly connected with the formulation of cinematographic aesthetics to achieve a definition of the so-called *cinematographic specificity*. Perhaps Italian cinema never managed to become totally independent from other cultural sectors. Maybe if the roles of the scriptwriter, screenwriter and film director had matured, this would have helped to create a place or an environment for sharing techniques and expertise; even a professional association could have been a fertile cultural terrain able to create a fully legitimating environment for the seventh art. In France, for example, this was provided by *"Les Cahiers du Mois"*, a journal founded in connection with the great *Exposition Internationale des Arts Décoratifs et Industriels Modernes*. It aimed to promote a series of conferences and debates on the subject of "Creation d'un monde par le cinéma", to address the issue of defining the cinema and its specific aesthetic code, and to find the spirit of the cinema, as L'Herbier wrote in Vol. XVI.

In order to understand how an Italian cinema production enhanced intangible assets, it is useful to analyse film production expenses, looking at the incidence of each single item in more detail to begin defining the relations between the economic and artistic factors.

The lack of primary sources, at least for the silent film era, is further accentuated when asking questions about the economic and financial aspects of the Italian film industry: How much money was spent on making a film? How much were the actors paid? How much did the film earn?

When documents are found, they provide general information, with broad indications as to the costs of each item of the film budget. In this respect, the data in the historical archive of *Banca Commerciale Italiana* (Comit) are a particularly valuable source. The bank officials who inspected film company accounts paid particular attention to the economic and financial aspects. Most reports on the COMIT-funded production companies highlighted that planned film production budgets were either non-existent or badly calculated, and usually quite different from the final balance sheets.

The most expensive items in the budget of an Italian film were the cost of blank film, rental and general expenses, and the actors. If the hard and soft components are separated, the most strictly industrial process—from the blank film to post-production and finally rental—accounted for around 66% of the total outlay. The remainder was for the intangible elements, i.e. the story, the script, author's rights and the salaries of film directors and actors. Table 2.1 shows the comparative data for an average Italian, German and American film; the Italian figures are from the text by a contemporary cinema journalist, and have been selected to highlight the different levels of investment in the film's intangible components.

The US film data are confirmed by other sources,[17] although information about the budget of American films is not always found. When available, the data show that 10 to 25% of the budget was for the actors, 0.5 to 18% for copyright, 3 to 18% for the film director, and 0.5 to 11% for film sets.

Table 2.1 shows that the artistic component (manuscript, film director, actors) accounted for ¼ of total production costs of Italian and German

*Table 2.1* Approximate Average Distribution of Production Costs per Film in Italy, Germany and the USA during the 1920s (Percentage of Total Production Costs)[a]

| Macro costs | Italy | Germany | U.S. |
|---|---|---|---|
| Theme and script | 3% | 3% | 12% |
| Directors | 6% | 5% | 18% |
| Actors | 16% | 11% | 21% |
| Sets | 7% | – | 12% |
| Celluloid | 15% | 11% | 6% |
| Licenses | – | 5% | 6% |

Source: Raffello Maggi, *Filmindustria-Riflessi economici* (Busto Arsizio, 1934).

[a]The figure totals do not equal 100% because only the most significant cost items are listed. Numbers have been rounded.

films, but about half of the total cost *of films made* in the United States. The most evident differences between the Italian/German and US film budgets are the items "manuscript" and "film director": respectively 3% vs 12%, and 6% vs 18%.

The cinema magazines of the time constantly evoke the magic of Hollywood and the way its films were able to express "the dreams we want to dream". The American cinema universalised and standardised the realism, esoticism and escapism the audiences loved, to the point that they would see the same film maybe two or three times in a week, as reported by Kines in 1931.

It is useful to emphasise that the available data about the distribution of the material and intangible factors in the budget provide information on the overall magnitude, since budget estimates could vary greatly from film to film, depending on the importance of the subject and company organisation. Companies with a medium- to long-term programme tended to reduce the incidence of artists' pay on each film by giving them exclusive medium-term contracts. In addition, the budgets of films from different countries may refer to different years, or contain more or less detailed cost items. Sometimes even the terminology used is different, but the items related to the intangible assets are easy to identify: story and script (for European films this item is usually summarised in "manuscript and authors' rights"), actors, director, technical and artistic staff. The figures may not therefore be representative *per se*, but they certainly provide a first indication regarding the enhancement of the intangible components of film production.[18]

All big Hollywood production companies had a *"Scenarios Department"*, with writers, researchers, typists and shorthand typist working on research and development. Paramount had its two *"Story* Departments" in Hollywood and New York; the New York department worked with literary circles and chose the stories best suited to the company's style or to a certain actor or director. Once a week, the department sent summaries of all its material to Paramount's managers; if the stories were approved, an "adaptor" would be asked to draught a script. Then production could begin or else the script could be catologued for future use.[19]

The problem of enhancement of the intangible components became more evident during the 1920s, although articles published in the first decade of the century had already stressed the importance of a good story and of authors and screenwriters with new ideas for constant innovation in film production.

The lack of data and the specificity of every single case do not prevent some general considerations.

If the screenplay, director and actors accounted for a large share of the total cost of an American film, this meant that their value was perceived, as was the importance of increased enhancement. The public judged the cinema's ability to create dreams and provide a few minutes of escapism with their favourite actors and actresses or an interesting story. In this case, the intangible elements made the difference: an original idea became an attractive screenplay with skilled actors. The question remains as to whether a popular star could guarantee a film's success. Plenty of research has confirmed the theory that production companies used actors/actresses like brands, repeated in different films to create customer loyalty mechanisms that did not depend on a specific film.[20]

Brand awareness was necessary for ensuring good box-office returns, but was not in itself sufficient, because a film is created by the interaction of many different creative inputs. Success was increasingly connected with the film's intrinsic quality, but the Italian film industry seemed to have given little importance to this factor.

Independently of the effective numerical value of the percentages shown above, a comparison between the European and American film industries clearly shows that the American industry gave importance to the choice of a story and screenplay based on three factors: Situation, Suspense and Climax.[21]

However, it was common for European producers to neglect any kind of artistic or aesthetic analysis, so that "producers often ordered a single person to write two or three hundred typed pages hurriedly in a couple of months. This deplorable system is the principal, if not only, reason why all our films are embarassingly empty and extenuatingly verbose, static and devoid of invention and situations"[22].

Another basis for comparison was the German film industry of the late 1920s, which successfully defined a style of its own capable of competing with Hollywood films. In addition to state intervention, what had helped the revival of the German film industry was precisely the choice of new stories and the production of films with real content. Italy's Cinecittà and Centro Sperimentale di Cinematografia were founded during the fascist era in order to address the lack of technically and artistically qualified cinema professionals.

## Business Projects and Artistic Assets

A first general summary of the Italian film industry can now be attempted, with particular attention to the production branch. The general considerations cover the period until 1931, the year of the definitive changeover to sound film, as already stated. The 1920s will be discussed in more detail in the following chapters. This final paragraph will offer a summary, with some figures that help to explain the structure underlying Italian cinema.

With regard to the structure of the industry sector, during the period studied (1905–1931) a production company made an average of eight films per year. There were of course exceptions like Cines, Itala Film or Ambrosio, which could produce up to 100 films a year. For example, the industry was highly concentrated, with just two film companies responsible for 95% of film production in 1905 and 90% in 1906: Società Ambrosio (63% in both years) and Cines (32% and 27%). The aggregate data for short and full-length films made between 1905 and 1931 give a total of 9,816 films; the maximum production period was between 1908 and 1914, when 6,303 films were made, i.e. 64% of the total. The film industry grew very rapidly, even as much as 120% from one year to the next; 646 films were made in 1909, 850 in 1910, and over 1000 in 1911. The Italian film industry's structures expanded and consolidated greatly between 1912 and 1914, its moment of greatest glory; 1,127 films were made by just 27 production companies in 1912. If the data are broken down, short and full-length films are taken separately and the policies of principal companies are observed, it can be seen for example that Società Anonima Ambrosio produced mostly short films, at least until 1917 when all films made were full-length.

To give a more adequate picture of the sector's structure between 1905 and 1931, the short film period from 1905 to 1915 and the full-length film period from 1915 onward have been considered separately, since the production of these two types of film required very different skills and different economic, financial, technical and human resources. The end of the first period has been taken as 1915, because from this year full-length film accounted for an increasingly large share of total film output, up to around 60%. Concerning construction of the groups, the following hypothesis has been formulated: the eleven years from 1905 to 1915 correspond to 132 months and 572 weeks; a production company could have made one single film in eight years, 132 films (one a month) or 572 films (one a week). This first period had 66 active companies, most of which are in the group "from 2 to 11" short films (42%), while 27% made just one film. Only 7% of companies had a more consistent output of over 100 short films, including some that made over 1,000 films: Società Anonima Ambrosio (1,027) and Cines (1,462) seem to have been working at maximum productivity.

For the following period, from 1916 to 1931, the same rule is used to construct the groups, but it must also be considered that the process of making a full-length film was quite different from that of a short film, and that a narrative film usually took about one month to make.

In the period analysed, 53% of the industry was made up of production companies with just one film; these short-lived companies will be analysed further on. Only 8% of companies were able to produce more than 16 films, and the biggest producers in this group were Cines, Società Anonima Ambrosio and Itala Film, which had already controlled market shares during the short film period. In addition, there were two new companies: Tiber and Caesar Film, which produced respectively 118 and 147 films.

Those within the industry had already spoken out against the continuing instability and speculation underlying the formation of new production companies:

[. . .] The Italian film industry has not considered that film manufacture was not and should not be an exclusively capitalist operation, but should be seen as a venture involving work and capital, and that the

financial movement/operation should have no other purpose but to support the work. Before forming, any film company should firstly have
ensured that it had the truly technical and artistic resources. It should
have considered this, because the technical and artistic element would
have guaranteed its own capital. However, avid speculators have not
seen beyond their greed for big returns, and what should have been
important has been overlooked.

Although the vertically integrated structure was a goal for many people, we
could hypothesise that the Italian context did not provide ideal conditions
for the development of an organisational structure like the "Hollywood
Studios". One reason, and possibly the most important, was the limited
size of the home market; it seemed to have achieved a sub-optimal state of
equilibrium in which a very small number of companies with medium- to
long-term projects co-existed with small and medium companies.

Even apart from every consideration of the unpredictable nature of
every cinema production, this seems to clash with the narrowness of
our home market. Our market does not seem to bear the costs of regular organisation, but it is perhaps sufficient for the intermittent activity
of the independent producers, who tend to erode the monopoly Cines
enjoyed until a while ago.[23]

## Notes

1  G. Napolitano, Luigi 10 November 1936, "Cinema italiano? Cinema italiano",
   in *Cinema*, vol. 9.
2  Bernardini recalls the so-called "bicycle system", widely used by cinema owners
   in Rome and Naples. Films were on the programmes of different cinemas at the
   same time (even those not under the same ownership) and the reels were rushed
   from one cinema to the other by bicycle couriers, so that there was no need to
   buy or rent a second copy. Cf. Bernardini, Aldo 1982, *Cinema muto italiano
   1896–1914*, 3 voll., Rome-Bari: Laterza, vol. I, p. 18.
3  "Il programma", in *Lux*, 30 October 1910, p. 1.
4  "La vita cinematografica", 20 December 1910, p. 3.
5  Bernardini, Aldo 1982, vol. I, p. 184.
6  Department of Commerce, Foreign commerce and navigation of the United
   States, Washington, 1910–1914.
7  Cf. the data reported in *Statistica del commercio speciale di importazione ed
   esportazione*, Rome: Ministero delle finanze.
8  Bachlin, Peter 1958, *Il cinema come industria. Storia economica del film*, Milan:
   Feltrinelli, p. 35.
9  Bernardini, Aldo 1982, vol. 1, pp. 183–184.
10 Brunetta, Gian Piero 2000, *Cent'anni di cinema italiano*, Bari: Laterza,
   pp. 26–27.
11 According to Storper and Christopherson (1987), the film industry could be
   compared with the model of diffused economy proposed by Sabel and Piore,
   who saw Italy as an exemplary case of a flexible specialisation system. The economic and organisational fabric of this "Third Italy" consisted of local diffused

economic systems in which production processes were oriented towards cus-
tomised production, in Storper, Michael, Christopherson, Susan 1987, "Flexible
Specialization and Regional Industrial Agglomerations: The Case of the U.S.
Motion-Picture Industry," *Annals of the Association of American Geographers*,
77: 260–282.

12 ASI-BCI, Carte di Raffaele Mattioli, Corrispondenza A-Z (CM), cart.127, fasc.
"GIORDANA Tullio", N. 5/455.

13 Bachlin 1958, p. 1.

14 Bovini, Filippo 25 March 1934, "La cinematografia come industria", *Cine-
convegno*, vol. XV.

15 Ibid.

16 Luciano de Feo in the editorial of the first volume of "Cinema", 10 July 1936.

17 See Bachlin, 1958; Kennedy, Joseph 1927, *The Story of the Films*, Chicago: A.W.
Shaw; Koszarski, Richard 1990, *History of American Cinema III: An Evening's
Entertainment. The Age of the Silent Feature Picture, 1915–1928*, New York:
Scribner; Jewell, Richard 1994, "RKO Film grosses, 1929–1951," *Historical
Journal of Film, Radio and Television*, 14 (1): 37–49; Glancy, Mark 1995,
"Warner Bros Film Grosses, 1924–1948," *Historical Journal of Film, Radio and
Television*, 15 (1): 55–73.

18 "Paying creative inputs not only for their quality but also for the market value
of their popular appeal should produce widely divergent payments rather than
convergence to an industry average", Bakker, Gerben 2001, "Stars and Stories:
How Films Became Branded Products", *Enterprise and Society*, 2 (3): 461–502.

19 Lewis, Howard 1933, *The Motion Picture Industry*, New York: Van Nostrand,
pp. 182–185. Warner Brothers and Twentieth Century Fox also had similar
departments. In general, almost all studios had a department working on new
stories and screenplays.

20 See Bakker 2001; Kindem, Gorham (ed.) 1982, *The International Movie Indus-
try*, Carbondale: Southern Illinois University Press; Simonoff, Jeffrey, Sparrow
Ilana 2000, "Predicting Movie Grosses: Winners and Losers, Blockbusters and
Sleepers", *Chance Magazine*, 13 (3), 15–24.

21 Spagnol, Tito 2008, *Hollywood Boulevard*, Turin: Nino Aragno, p. 49.

22 Ibid, p. 52.

23 *Riunione del 5 maggio 1933: verbale definitivo*, in ASI, Fondo VCD, volume 21,
f. 3.

# Bibliography

BACHLIN, Peter 1958, *Il cinema come industria. Storia economica del film*, Milan:
Feltrinelli

BAKKER, Gerben 2001, "Stars and Stories: How Films Became Branded Products",
*Enterprise and Society*, 2 (3): 461–502

BALIO, Tino 1993, *Grand Design: Hollywood as a Modern Business Enterprise
1930–1939*, Berkeley: University of California Press

BELL, Daniel 1973, *The Coming of Post-Industrial Society*, New York: Basic Books

BERNARDINI, Aldo 2002, *Cinema muto italiano. I film dal vero 1895–1914*, Pordenone: La Cineteca del Friuli

_____. 1991, *Archivio del cinema italiano. Il cinema muto. 1905–1931*, Rome:
Anica

_____. 1982, *Cinema muto italiano 1896–1914*, 3 voll., Rome-Bari: Laterza

BORDWELL, David, THOMPSON, Kristin 1994, *Film History: An Introduction*, New York: Mc Graw Hill

BRUNETTA, Gian Piero 2000, *Cent'anni di cinema italiano*, Bari: Laterza
_____. 1993, *Storia del cinema italiano*, 4 voll., Rome: Editori Riuniti

GLANCY, Mark 1995, "Warner Bros Film Grosses, 1924–1948", *Historical Journal of Film, Radio and Television*, 15 (1): 55–73

JEWELL, Richard 1994, "RKO Film grosses, 1929–1951", *Historical Journal of Film, Radio and Television*, 14 (1): 37–49

JONES, Candace 2001, "Co-evolution of Entrepreneurial Careers, Institutional Rules and Competitive Dynamics in American Film, 1895–1920", *Organization Studies* 22 (6):911–944

KINDEM, Gorham (ed.) 1982, *The International Movie Industry*, Carbondale: Southern Illinois University Press

KOSZARSKI, Richard 1990, *History of American Cinema III: An Evening's Entertainment. The Age of the Silent Feature Picture, 1915–1928*, New York: Scribner

LEWIS, Howard 1933, *The Motion Picture Industry*, New York: Van Nostrand

NEGRO, Giacomo, SORENSON, Olav 2006, "The Competitive Dynamics of Vertical Integration: Evidence from U.S. Motion Picture Producers, 1912–1970", in BAUM, Joel, DOBREV, Stanislav, VAN WITTELOOSTUIJN, Arjen (eds.), *Ecology and Strategy* (Advances in Strategic Management, Volume 23), Emerald Group Publishing Limited, pp. 363–398

NOWELL-SMITH, Ebyg 1996, *The Oxford History of World Cinema*, New York: Oxford University Press

PALACIO, Manuel, PEREZ, Julio 1998, *Historia General del Cine. Volumen III. Europa 1908–1918, Madrid:* Catedra

ROBBINS, James 1993, "Organization as a Strategy: Restructuring Production in the Film Industry", *Strategic Management Journal*, 14 (S1): 103–118

SEDGWICK, John, POKORNY, Michael 2004, *An Economic History of Film*, New York: Routledge

SIMONOFF, Jeffrey, SPARROW, Ilana 2000, "Predicting Movie Grosses: Winners and Losers, Blockbusters and Sleepers", *Chance Magazine*, 13 (3): 15–24

SPAGNOL, Tito 2008, *Hollywood Boulevard*, Turin: Nino Aragno

STORPER, Michael, CHRISTOPHERSON, Susan 1987, "Flexible Specialization and Regional Industrial Agglomerations: The Case of the U.S. Motion-Picture Industry", *Annals of the Association of American Geographers*, 77: 104–117

# Part II

# The Design of a "Powerful Weapon"

## Cinema under Fascism

# 3   The Visible Hand
## A Way to the Cinematic Renaissance

This could become a new and extremely useful
vehicle for Italian propaganda, in the highest (. . .) sense of knowledge.
In this way Italy will have a film industry that will enhance our people's daz-
zling beauty, and our invincible strength in our immortal history.[1]

## Public Intervention in the Movie Industry

Analysis of the film industry's relationship with fascism involves looking at the wider field of public intervention in the creative industries and asking questions about the rationale behind this type of intervention and how it affects industry dynamics.

The broad context of this story is the economic and cultural clash between United States and European countries, a topic that has been much debated. Several researchers have studied it by asking whether the quality of Hollywood films, international audience preferences and the overall organization of the value chain—or the three factors combined—can provide an exhaustive explanation.[2] Free trade for popular culture products is a particularly sensitive commercial and cultural issue. For the past three decades, free traders and *exceptionists* have fought over global regulation in the audio-visual industries. This conflict dates back to the 1920s, when the US began to dominate the trade in filmed entertainment, and the American movie industry soon came up against daunting barriers in many markets, especially in Europe. This particular historical moment was a time of many industrial and political changes. The motion picture industry faced a new technological shift towards sound, and the addition of dialogues raised new cultural issues, creating barriers between countries and fostering the idea of "national cinemas". International trade was also exacerbated by the rise of political nationalism and totalitarian governments. If economic historians have identified war and recession as factors that may explain why countries adopt tariffs and protectionism, in the case of cultural industries, these arguments are neither sufficient nor satisfactory. Trade in cultural goods and services is not comparable to any other type of trade. The government's ability to maintain viable, homegrown cultural industries is crucial to a sense of national identity. Films are a powerful instrument of collective conscious-ness, and they have an importance that transcends economic considerations where government policy is concerned. Since films embody national culture and values, it is necessary to find an explanation that fits in better with the features of cultural industries.

Trade restrictions (via taxes, tariffs and quotas) in the cultural field were justified by the belief in national cultural sovereignty and the need to coun-ter American imperialism. American cultural products were perceived as a threat to the societies receiving them, blamed for eroding their values and cultural identities. On the other hand, US film companies strenuously defended the free trade regime in an attempt to preserve the integrity of their products. This choice was, of course, the product of a different economic "mentality", but also reflected an awareness that international protection-ism would bring unsustainable costs.[3]

Technology, culture and globalisation have interacted to create a strong level of conflict in cultural industries, especially filmed entertainment, caus-ing international disputes over trade rules, market access and subsidies.

Protectionism in the movie industry has taken the form of an unusual variety of trade instruments (import quotas, taxes, import licenses, tariffs) and cultural policies (subsidies to domestic producers, language require-ments, screen quotas, national schools and festivals). There is a lack of dis-tinction between trade policies and cultural policies in existing works, and this leads to poor understanding about the evolution of the motion picture industry. Trade and cultural policies originate from different lobbies and institutions. Trade and cultural policies are both state activities that can overlap, but it is necessary to make an analytical distinction between them, although they influence each other. The distinction is necessary because the two types of policy respond to different needs and have different impacts on industrial development. Policy makers have worked to promote and regulate the movie industry not only to achieve economic goals but also to achieve broader national purposes, such as defending national cultural sov-ereignty. It is usually supposed that protectionism is a feature of totalitar-ian government, but this is not true. France and Britain adopted restricted measures during the '20 and the '30s, as did Italy and Germany. Even in post-war democratic Italy, the government was influenced by the interests of the different professional categories (producers, distributors and exhibitors) and took a protectionist approach. For example, it is interesting to note that ANICA (the Italian National Association of Movie Industry Profes-sionals) invoked a free market, which should have selected only solid film companies, while at the same time the equivocal presence of short- and mid-term targets (relaunching production with public funds and selecting the most reliable companies) prevented this kind of "hard selection" by market forces. Therefore, adoption of certain regulatory tools favouring protection-ism or a free market is the consequence of interactions between different forces, such as market structure, type of government, and the strength of economic and cultural institutions involved in the film industry.

In order to provide a theoretical framework, the most important academic contributions to this topic are summarized here. The problem of protectionism and free-trade in the creative industries can be framed by referring to two main categories of theories: on the one hand, the "cultural exemption theory" is useful for understanding why films (and other creative and cultural products) can be considered exempt from free trade. On the other hand, industrial dynamics and some theories of international economics help to highlight the relationship between industrial policy choices and industrial life cycle. In general, the cultural exemption theory provides a justification for the adoption of tariffs, quotas, screen quotas and direct subsidies: cultural goods embody externalities that market pricing fails to capture, and homegrown culture is usually associated with positive externalities. By contrast, economic theory claims that goods should circulate in a global market, without distinctions based on national origin, and that protectionism does not seem to provide effective protection for domestic creative industries.[4]

The need for protection in the film industry is based on the assumption[5] that "a film represents more than a mere commodity to be bartered against others". More specific characteristics are used to explain government intervention: films suffer a cultural discount when traded across borders, and they are public goods[6] that may generate external benefits. Since the cinema is a creative industry, a tension arises between its cultural and economic features. Thus, movies are the result of a process involving both material and immaterial features, and it is primarily because of their symbolic content that they are exempt from free trade. Given the specific characteristics of cinema, cultural policies have been investigated by cultural and mass communication researchers and economists. In the first case, the problem of policy-making in the creative industries has been approached to offer answers to urgent matters of culture and to equip agents of cultural policy with new instrument of understanding. On the other hand, economists discuss policy choices by testing the effectiveness of specific instruments, like tariffs, quotas and subsidies, on industry dynamics, and trying to explain whether protectionism is a successful or unsuccessful policy for creative industries.

## The Cultural Exemption Argument

The debate about the public and private features of movies, and more generally about all performing arts, is controversial (Baumol-Bowen 1966, Blaug-King 1976, Scitovsky 1976). At least five rationales are used to justify government intervention in the cultural and creative industries. Firstly, investment in the arts gives current and future generations more cultural options and has a positive impact on improving the quality of life of individuals (Baumol-Bowen 1966). The second rationale is that "fast industrial growth may have altered the preferences of the average consumer that is acquiring leisure faster than the preparation for using it (Scitovsky 1972)".[7] The third argument states that the government must subsidize cultural and creative industries because these industries play a determining role in shaping national culture and identity. The fourth rationale is linked to the positive externalities generated by the development of culture and artistic heritage. The final justification is linked to the "Baumol disease" affecting the performing arts: industrial development has led to a dramatic increase in art production costs, and government patronage is considered necessary. All these arguments have been used to justify cultural exemption,[8] i.e. those policies adopted by a government to correct international distortion caused by free trade in cinema and audiovisual markets.[9] Cultural exemption goes arm in arm with the theory of national cultural sovereignty[10] used to justify reaction against American cultural imperialism.[11] Protectionism is not a problem of highly industrialized nations versus less developed countries or of English-speaking nations versus others. American films encounter different protectionist barriers in most countries. What is usually criticized in this perspective is the difficulty of explaining the meaning of national culture since "the role of film policy in building a collective consciousness about nationhood is itself complex and contentious".[12] This controversial debate has led to a new stream of academic research based on cultural imperialism argument and the assumption that "the presence of a production sector in local culture industries is a necessary and sufficient condition for the cultural expression of a population. Imported material cannot have this kind of authentic relationship with national audiences, and this lead to cultural debilitation".[13] National cultures are usually perceived as vulnerable, especially in countries where market forces are insufficient to protect domestic industries. A further important factor to consider in the explanation of cultural protectionism is that according to the cultural transmission theory, American movies were—and still are—able to affect different national cultures, and do so regardless of tariffs. This effect is peculiar to movies. Explanations of the use of trade barriers and protectionist measures were based on the assumption that movies were embedded with national cultural identities, values, beliefs and languages. On the other hand, the US perceived films as a marketable commodity, and the State Department came under pressure to respond to European protectionist policies between the wars. The tension seemed to end in 1947 when the General Agreement on tariffs and Trade authorized screen quotas, since they were included in Article IV. The debate continued during the 1960s and '70s after the growth of television broadcasting: the relationship between trade and cultural policy was discussed during the UNESCO debate over the New International Information Order.[14]

To sum up, according to exceptionists, each country has the right to conduct its national policies to support domestic cultural industries. They consider the global market as a "false market" dominated by a few American multinationals, and they consider cinema to be an art form and not simply entertainment; however, they do not seek to erect an iron curtain because they recognize their dependence on American goods. On the other hand, free traders consider the movie industry as pure entertainment, an industry like any other. They reject any idea of protectionism because they themselves have no federal policy regarding communication, information and culture.[15] Differences between these views can also be found in the political structures responsible for cultural and creative industries. European countries usually have a Ministry for Arts and Culture, whereas it is the Ministry of Economy and Trade that manages cinema affairs in the USA.

## Industry Dynamics and Policy Choices

History provides many examples of protectionist policies and shows that it is difficult to have "one single story capable of linking development and trade policies".[16] Most countries have varied their degree of openness and protection during their development over time.[17] Classic economic theories are based on the assumption that markets work efficiently, and, although most economists agree that these models are somewhat idealized, "the conventional wisdom is still that markets do a very good job".[18] This view is also applied to international markets, since export and import activities are seen as similar to other economic activities. Thus, the message from conventional economic theory is that "international markets are not very different from domestic markets, so a general policy of letting markets work should be applied to both".[19] Reality, however, can differ from models, and protectionism is a crucial point in the ongoing economic debate. In the last few years, empirical research about international trade in manufactured goods has spurred by examining how globalization impacts on productivity and testing the Heckscher-Ohlin model. Only a few research papers have dealt with international trade in services[20]—and cinema is generally considered to belong to the broad services category.

Economic justifications for the adoption of this kind of policy usually refer to protection of an infant industry, reactions against import dumping, market failure, and non-economic reasons. In the first case, protectionism is adopted to shield infant industries, that is to say, industries with a potential, but still latent, comparative advantage, which has not been exploited. Once protected, the infant industry is able to bridge the gap with its more technologically advanced foreign competitors.[21] The second argument for protectionism is based on tariffs imposed on dumper goods and is usually justified in order to prevent the long-term exploitation of consumers: consumers may temporarily benefit from low prices of foreign products dumped on the market, but in the long term, once the foreign monopoly is established, foreign firms are free to increase prices. Market failure is given as the justification for protectionism in the case of senile industries: "labor markets in advanced industrial countries are too inflexible to cope with imports".[22]

Other versions of the argument concern the "threat posed by rapid surges of imports, broader shifts in comparative advantage or the unfair trade practices of developing countries".[23] Although imports can provide benefits, supporters of senile industry protection argue that these benefits "are outweighed by the extensive costs of adjustment imposed on declining industries, and temporary import protection is considered necessary to ease the cost of adjustment".[24] Non-economic arguments adopted to justify protectionism regard national security, and cultural and sociological considerations. The need to protect national movie production is thus a part of these non-economic arguments. Although the term "cultural protectionism" was first introduced to describe reactions to American cultural imperialism during the 1980s and '90s, European countries have developed different measures to shield their national cultural industries, especially films, since the 1920s.

If these are justifications for protectionism, on the other hand, some economists consider it as economically inefficient, as are deviations from pure market rules. In addition, protectionism is considered as a deprivation of individual freedom, since it prevents personal freedom of choice. There is a vast empirical literature on the issue of free trade and protectionism, and their impact on business productivity performance. Some studies suggest that higher productivity is related to lower tariffs,[25] while others suggest the opposite, and some research states that there is no evidence of a correlation between tariffs and productivity.

In the case of a creative industry, specifically filmed entertainment, the debate over the effectiveness of protectionism is complicated because of the need to define whether economic or not cultural goals are achieved and how they can be measured. As stated before, many countries have adopted a great variety of protectionist measures, such as tariffs, quotas and direct subsidies. Economists usually claim that these tools do not appear to provide effective protection for the domestic movie industry (Marvasti and Canterbury, 2005). Bagella and Becchetti (1999) demonstrated that the net impact of public funding on the box-office performance of Italian movies (1985–1996) was insignificant, mainly because the production companies invested little on immaterial features (directors, actors and so on).

A recent contribution (Jansen 2005) analyses the German movie industry, the determinants of movie performance, and the impact of subsidies (committee and reference subsidies); via an empirical analysis, the author suggests that subsidies cause producers to make movies suited to audience preferences. The author concludes that, even though the subsidy reference system has a positive impact on movie performance at the box office, the government should not subsidize the movie industry. This appears to be an ideological conclusion. More recent contributions (Lee, Kim and Il Kim, 2008) evaluate the direct impact of screen-quotas on the box-office performance of Korean movies, and find a negative correlation.

While there are many empirical studies on factors that can influence the film market (Hoskins, McFayden and Finn, 1997; Litman 1982; Marvasti

2000; Oh 2001; Wildman 1995; Wildman and Siwek 1993), the literature regarding the impact of regulatory factors on the film industry is surprisingly scant. There are more studies about the effect of television program quotas on the broadcasting market than about the film industry. In the case of Italy, this scarcity is justified by the difficulty of gaining access to data, especially historical records; researchers do not yet have access to documents on public funding by the Ministry. In addition, facts and figures must be crosschecked using more than three sources, meaning that there is a real risk of not having enough data to provide a complete picture of the situation. Data may also turn out to be unreliable, because it is very common for public institutions and private companies to provide figures that enhance their image as much as possible.

## The State and the Film Industry Before Fascism: Censure and Taxation

The relationship between the state and the film industry began in the 1910s with repressive interventions mainly prompted by safety issues (the first film reels easily caught fire) and moral concerns. The religious and political authorities viewed the cinema as a danger, with enormous power to seduce all social classes, especially young people, who were more likely to fall under the spell of the "flickering shadows of life which appear on the screen and could be mistaken for reality". The trade and non-trade press of the time was the battlefield for the conflict between the film industry and the theatre; in particular, the authorities were accused of not exercising the same type of control over the cinema as they did over the theatre. Cinema tickets were cheap, making it accessible to young people and the working classes, a public not considered as having a sufficient level of culture and critical maturity to see films judged as indecent, crude and unhealthy. The cinema's potential to corrupt was perceived especially in films containing particularly realistic representations of violence and criminal acts. There were two currents of Catholic thought about the cinema: one had the same moralising approach, while the other recognised the cinema's potential for educational purposes. Catholic groups were founded in Turin, Rome, Naples and Venice to propagate a religious cinema; Turin production company *Unitas*, founded in 1909, specialised in religious subjects and was connected to the cinema magazine "*Lux et Verbo*". In general, these first years of the cinema were a time of actions and reactions concerning the most diverse aspects of the cinema: from evening closing times to fines for the distribution of advertising leaflets.[26]

The campaign against the film industry began in the first years of the century, and culminated in 1912 with an article in the *Giornale d'Italia* by the state prosecutor of the Rome Appeal Court, *Commendatore* Avellone. He denounced the cinema as being akin to usury and illegal gambling dens, appealing for state intervention to prohibit "horrid shows reproducing adulterers, suicides, financial disasters caused by scams, falsehoods and frauds, shameless love affairs and lascivious plots". The first consequence of the stance taken by the so-called "avellonists" was a Directive issued in February 1913, establishing the criteria for *prefetti* (local representatives of national government) to apply when granting cinema licences, in order to stop the cinema from becoming "a school for bad behaviour". Concern about protecting public decorum culminated in the creation of a censorship office on 25 June 1913 (Law no.785, subsequently published in the *Gazzetta Ufficiale* on 14 July 1913), known in the film industry as "Madama Anastasia". The law contained just one article, establishing generic "vigilance over production" and creating a tax to pay for it. The following year saw the publication of regulations specifying the way the law was to be applied. "Vigilance over films intends to prevent public presentation of: a) spectacles which are offensive to morality, to public decency and to private citizens. b) spectacles which are contrary to the national reputation and decorum or to the reputation of the police, or which may upset international relations, c) spectacles which are offensive to the decorum and prestige of the institutions and authorities, police officers and agents. d) violent, repugnant or cruel scenes, and in general, perverse actions or events which may teach or encourage criminal behaviour, disturb or incite wickedness".

In each city, the Ministry of the Interior (*Direzione di Pubblica Sicurezza— Ufficio Centrale di Revisione Cinematografica*) delegated jurisdiction over film "review requests" to the offices of the Prefecture; in order to obtain a screening permit, each production company had to present a document containing technical information about the film, its title, the trademark and length, as well as a detailed description of the subject.

In addition to censorship regulations, there were also taxes: the same law creating the film censorship bureau also imposed a tax of 10 cents on every metre of film to finance censorship procedures.

Just as the state had understood the social impact of the cinema, it had also understood its economic potential, not so much in terms of enhancing the industry, but rather as a source of revenue. On 15 December 1914, a stamp duty was introduced on cinema tickets: 5 cents on tickets costing 10 or 50 cents, and 20 cents on tickets costing 1 lira or more. The state's recognition of the importance of the cinema took the form of censorship and taxation.

## The Cinema in the Early Years of Fascism

Analysis of the relationship between the cinema and fascism is a vast area, the domain of specialist historians. For this reason, only a brief description of the subject is given here, focusing on the economics of the industry and the relevant social and political aspects, while the following chapter will look in more detail at Cines-Pittaluga. In Italy, studies of the fascist era create a division between film and mass media critics and historians, on the one hand, and historians *tout court*, on the other. The most important period for historical research was between 1968 and the early 1980s, when the theoretical paradigms for analysis of the cinema in the Mussolini era were defined: the cinema during the 1930s, the *Istituto Luce*, the work of Luigi Freddi, the relationship between the fascist cinema and neo-realism, the problem of consensus, and journals. In this context, cinema began to be seen as an important tool for investigating the economic and political structures and socio-cultural components of fascist Italy, in line with Mussolini's statements.

The most important of the complex issues to resolve was that of fascist cinema policy during the 1930s. Fascism's attitude towards the cinema was ambivalent, and it took initially little interest in the sector; a great number of laws were passed, but no organisation possessed complete jurisdiction over the film industry. The absence of this type of unified structure denoted the lack of precise policy guidelines. This immediately gives rises to some important questions: Why did the regime intervene to support the film industry after years of virtual passivity? How did it intervene, and what was its objective or what were the opposing objectives? This opens up a wider series of questions: Is a development policy for the cinema always necessary? How can this kind of policy have a positive or negative influence on outcomes for the film industry?

Fascism began to take an active interventionist interest in the cinema only in the 1930s, following the advent of talking films.

The chronological question raised is not simply a theoretical distinction applied in order to more clearly delineate the period analysed, nor does it correspond to just one single evaluation given by cinema historians to this period. The tendency that has taken shape in historiography highlights that fascism's attitude towards the film industry was rather indolent until 1929, and that the transformation process that fascism began in the early 1930s lasted until the end of the Second World War. Even after the fall of the fascist regime, the political attitude to the film industry remained closely connected to the interventionist approach as defined during the twenty-year fascist era.

The fascist model of intervention in the film industry has been defined as schizophrenic.[27] Reconstruction of the debate about cultural and cinema policy has highlighted the coexistence of different projects carried out by people to whom the regime entrusted the task of controlling the cinema. In its later years, the fascist cinema appeared as an increasingly complex model, a continually expanding world of relations and connections. In this context, one area of research, which began in the 1980s, concerns film production companies. However, this has often produced studies lacking a wider perspective of the economic history and social conditions of the period in question.

According to Cannistraro, it is premature to speak of a true *cinema policy* in the 1920s, since the regime did not yet have a clear idea of the relations possible between state and cinema, and was still defining its own political and institutional structure. The first fascist measure regarding the cinema was fiscal, and there was no particular break with the cinema policy of the liberal state. *Taxes on cinemas and other public spectacles* were introduced in November 1923. At the same time, censorship was reinforced as centralised control was given to the Interior Ministry, and changes were made to the film evaluation commission.[28] With regard to this issue, fascism confirmed *in toto* the legislative framework of the preceding period: centralised control was exercised by a ministry (initially the Interior Ministry, then from 1934 the Ministry of Popular Culture, by various titles) and by the binding decision of the first and second level revision commissions. Censorship played an essentially bureaucratic role until 1934, when the creation of the *Direzione Generale per la Cinematografia* expanded its functions (first and foremost it exercised an effective preventive control over screenplays) and increased the system's general rigidity, at least until Luigi Freddi left his post as head of the *Direzione Generale* in March 1939. In the meantime, the original purpose of the revision commissions gradually changed, as they became increasingly incorporated into the fascist framework of governance: in practice, the real power of censorship was exercised less by the commissions than by high-ranking officials, (the Director General of the film industry, the Ministers of Popular Culture, and the *Duce* himself).

Some authors maintain that cinema was not part of a real cultural and economic policy for the cinema, and that fascism did not always have a systematic commitment in this sense.[29] There seems to be a discrepancy between fascism's declared interest in the cinema—recognised as a potential tool for communication and propaganda—and the real effectiveness of legislative measures; there was a cultural policy which did not always fully materialise as an effective economic policy for the film industry.[30]

In order to understand the change in fascism's attitude towards cinema, it must be noted that the number of Italian films produced in the early 1920s was so small that the regime's lack of interest in the industry is unsurprising. Any sign of an underlying policy,[31] even in the early years of fascism, must be associated prevalently with a private venture, the *Società Anonima Stefano Pittaluga*, to be discussed in a later chapter.

Although it was not immediately clear which direction government policy would take in regulating the cinema, industry exponents were interested from the very outset in a government they saw as a *deus ex machina* for improving the situation of Italian cinema. The fascist revolution presented itself as a universal panacea, and Italian film producers imagined that fascism would find the best ways to revive the fortunes of the national cinema.

One of the first problems raised by the study of fascist documentary sources concerns the relation between the definition of a cinema policy and the wider cultural policy of fascism, and consequently also concerns the shift from the cultural level to an economic policy for the industry. In his essay "*La fabbrica del consenso*", Cannistraro claims that the fascist regime used cinema in an attempt to make culture and propaganda converge: "The

regime did not create the cinema in Italy, but recognised its valuable potential for propaganda. After hesitance in the 1920s, fascism began to move
more resolutely towards integrating the film industry into the wider cultural
organisation of the State". The hesitance of the early years can be justified
by the regime's attention to the more important problems involved in consolidating its own structures to achieve the aims of its revolution: "to create
a state and a regime". Cannistraro's book highlighted for the first time the
entire fascist propaganda machine (press, radio, cinema), starting with the
idea that the regime relied more on propaganda than on concrete achievements and popular support.[32]

Cinema, therefore, was a part of the more complex framework that the
regime aimed to construct in order to control the nation's social and cultural
life. For this reason, it is impossible to fully understand the state interventions in favour of the film industry without referring to fascist ideology
in its widest sense. The need to make culture and propaganda converge
and to define a cultural policy led fascism to take over control of the main
instruments of communication—the press, radio and the cinema—in order
to promote a mass culture and the gradual political and social integration of
ordinary citizens. Each area of culture was overshadowed and deeply influenced by the political and moral imperatives of the totalitarian state and the
single party. Cinema, too, would become a sounding board for the values
of the fascist revolution, with its project based "on the rebirth of the Italian
race and the creation of a new state, which would regenerate the nation to
renew the imperial and universal spirit of Roman tradition in the Italians of
the present".[33]

Control of culture and propaganda in an authoritarian state required the
creation of a central control bureaucracy in order to achieve the state's cultural objectives. It has been observed that regimes aspiring to cultural totali-
tarianism regularly attempt to gain control of all propaganda instruments
and to institutionalise these in a branch of governmental bureaucracy. For
Italian cinema, this took place in 1934 with the creation of the *Direzione
Generale per la Cinematografia*. The regime's intervention was necessary
because this new means of communication had such extraordinary power to
influence the masses, their sentiments and their ideas, that no nation could
allow itself not to control politics, morals and economics via the cinema.

There were three reasons why the regime recognised the possibilities
offered by the cinema. Firstly, it was a means of expressing the human
sentiments and ideas; secondly, it had the means "to raise this elementary
original condition to heights of power and strength equalling the greatest
masterpieces ever created, and finally, the cinema was the true and typical
product of the 20th century".[34]

Above all, the cinema could contribute to the fascist revolution that
aimed to create a new man and a new culture: every aspect of life was to
be guided by the great teacher, as Gentile defined the National Fascist Party
(NFP). The objective was nationalisation and an integration of the masses

that would fuse civilian and military society together. The fascist revolution aimed to "consecrate the cult of the nation and regenerate the people in order to create a strong and united community, able to meet the challenge of the modern world, to conquer a new position of leadership, to carry out a cultural mission to revive the spirit and grandeur of Rome in modern times".[35]

> The vastness of the "film industry" becomes the common denominator of contemporary culture, involving the dignity of States and giving rise to impellent needs of prestige and duty.[36]

Most believed that the advent of the fascist state would harmoniously recompose all the many interests within the Italian film industry: the material and spiritual interests, technical and artistic needs, moral duties and spectacular opportunities.

The principal characteristics of the cinema justifying state intervention were its ethical and political function as an "extremely imposing propaganda weapon",[37] which the state aimed to enhance via the *Istituto Luce* and the *Istituto Internazionale di Cinematografia Educativa* (International Institute of Educational Cinema).

The creation of film masterpieces was perceived not only as a success for the nation's industrial capacity, but also—and above all—as demonstrating "the intelligence, the talent, the organisation, and the perfect discipline of the people".

## The Ideal of the Cinema Revival: "Italian Cinematographic Renaissance"

The starting point for the fascist interventions in favour of the cinema was the ideal of reviving Italian cinema, to restore it, as already recalled, to the ancient glory and splendour of the years of silent film, when *Cabiria* had enchanted international audiences.

"Excellency, the Italian film industry is dying miserably, sadly, abandoned and forgotten. In one or two years at most, if no measures are taken, it will be just a memory".

These were Augusto Genina's words to Mussolini in 1925 when he presented the project for the revival of the film industry in Italy. Genina was also speaking on behalf of Gabriele D'Annunzio and Carmine Gallone, and it is interesting to note that one of the very first points in Genina's proposal was protectionist intervention by the government, the only course of action *able to restore the fortunes of the film industry and consent its revival.*

Genina requested "three simple measures: two to help, and the third to defend" Italy's film industry. The first two proposals were that all Italian cinemas be obliged to show one Italian film for every ten foreign films, and that the state relinquish the duty on cinema tickets for Italian films in order to benefit producers.[38]

The defensive measure consisted of increased duty on foreign films. The aim was to ensure that Italian films were protected on the home market in order to cover production costs.

The national market required greater guarantees in order to attract new capital investments in the film industry and to bring back to Italy the skilled artists who had miserably sought fortune abroad. Genina asked the *Duce* for an intervention to miraculously revive Italian cinema; it did not deserve to die because "it speaks the universal language, and arrives everywhere. . . . Precise, and rapid, with a colossal influence on the masses, it leaves deep and lasting impressions on the heart". The archives reveal that Mussolini received Genina, D'Annunzio and Gallone, and that after reading the proposal he declared himself in favour, at least when it came to introducing the quota system for Italian films.[39]

To many, the ideal of a revival appeared an objective that could be achieved only via an intervention by the *Duce*. Mussolini, seen as gifted with superior intelligence, was believed to be the only leader capable of revitalising all the arts and reviving the cinema.

The Cabinet Office (*Presidenza del Consiglio*) received many impressive projects (at least in their intentions): from the establishment of new companies for the production of strictly Italian films, to the foundation of institutes and revival committees. For example, Elena Mazzantini Rosso was a promoter of the National Committee for the revival of the Italian film industry.[40] The committee aimed to establish the *Ente Morale Industrie Cinematografiche* (EMIC—Italian Film Industry Foundation), in order to guarantee and defend the cinema's function of cultural, spiritual and educational propaganda and to free the Italian film industry from its complete subjugation to foreign films.

The most important initiative, a truly novel forerunner of things to come, was the first of a long series of production prizes, although the initial idea did not come from the state. On 22 July 1926, the fascist newspaper "*Il Tevere*" published the announcement of "A grand competition for an Italian film"[41] with a prize of 50,000 lire. Underlying this was obviously the desire to produce a fascist film, not a propaganda film, but a film reflecting the values and culture of the regime. Italian producers naturally hoped that this initiative would become institutional, as it subsequently did. The fact that a party newspaper took this initiative, placing it within the framework of outcomes of the new ideology, could certainly be seen as providing plenty of potential for future requests by exponents of the film industry.

Besides this initiative, in these early years the regime's attitude to the constant decline of the Italian film industry was actually one of inertia in relation to its industrial and economic aspects. One fact is sufficient to illustrate the situation at the time: the annual output of full-length films fell from 150

films in 1920 to just 60 in 1921. It was not the cinema as a form of entertainment that was in decline, but the entire Italian film industry.[42]

During these years, fascism took an essentially ideological interest in the
cinema, in the form of censorship and propaganda. The regime sensed that
the new means of communication was increasingly influential, and saw the
cinema within its wider project of using culture as a propaganda tool and
an effective means of controlling the masses. This was achieved with the creation of the national institute known as LUCE, *L'Unione Cinematografica
Educativa*, (Educational Cinema Union).[43] This began life as the *Sindacato
Istruzione Cinematografica* (Cinema Education Union), promoted by Luciano de Feo as a private initiative for the production and diffusion of educational films. In September 1924, this became a public limited company with
a capital of 2,500,000 lire, guaranteed by various state-controlled bodies.[44]
In 1925, the Institute became a non-profit "moral institution" regulated by
public law, thus completing the formation of fascism's principal film propaganda organisation. LUCE's cinema newsreels dealt directly with the issues
the regime considered most important: it is no coincidence that the first
newsreels focused on the state's policy for rural development and followed
government initiatives very closely. In 1928, Royal decree no. 20125 of 6
September created the *Istituto Internazionale di Cinematografia Educativa*
(International Institute of Educational Cinema)[45] to spread information
about farming methods.

This was a very difficult time for the Italian cinema industry in general.
The shift from silent to sound films involved learning new techniques and
transforming production methods. New professional figures had to be created from zero (sound technicians and engineers); actors and directors had
to adapt to the new production processes, and, film cameras and projection
systems and machinery had to be replaced.

This need for total renovation was the final blow to a film industry
already in deep crisis. 1927 saw the closure of the UCI (Italian Cinema
Union), the consortium of the most important Italian film production companies, which had been formed immediately after World War I in order to
deal with competition from the American movie industry. The UCI collapsed under its huge debts incurred as it attempted to monopolise film
production and control the market. The policy of purchasing every film
made in Italy—including those made non-members of the consortium—
meant the UCI paid out large sums of money to buy even poor-quality
films. At the end of the 1930s, the number of films made in Italy was very
small, so that many directors, technicians and actors had to emigrate and
seek work abroad, mainly in France and Germany.

American films dominated the market. In 1931, Italian films managed to
account for 10% of films distributed in the country, but the remaining 90%
of films shown came exclusively from the USA.

The situation regarding film distribution was very similar. In 1927 MGM,
Fox and Paramount studios opened their own branches in Italy without

having to go through Italian import agents. Warner Bros. granted exclusive distribution rights to Stefano Pittaluga's SASP, while the four smaller American studios (Universal, RKO, United Artists and Columbia) granted distribution rights of their films to Italian companies in which they owned a share, in return for a guaranteed minimum profit and a percentage of the box-office takings. Even regional film distribution was dominated by foreign films. This situation was largely responsible for delaying the development of the Italian industry; the backlog of unused US silent films waiting to be shown delayed the introduction of sound technology into Italian cinemas. At the beginning of 1929, no Italian cinema was capable of showing a sound film, and the shift to sound film eventually took place between 1934 and 1935.

In relation to state intervention (discussed in more depth in the following paragraphs), two contrasting positions are seen. The first position favoured a nationalised film industry at the service of the state as an instrument of propaganda. In contrast, the second position held that it was more useful to aid the growth and development of the private film industry providing escapism and entertainment as an indirect and concealed means of achieving alignment with the dominant ideology.

During the 1920s, the cinema had grown constantly, and in 1927 cinema box-office takings were higher than those of all other types of show for the first time.[46] Cinema continued to attract big audiences because it provided a few minutes of escapism, rapid social elevation and happiness at the price of a cheap ticket. According to Minister Alfieri, cinema: "had discovered the technology of the industry of sentiment and made the public its captive. It has succeeded in creating heroes and heroines that the theatre does not have, popular idols whose tastes and clothes the public imitate".

Although prices had risen from the early years when a cinema ticket cost just 20 cents, the cinema remained economically accessible compared with

*Table 3.1* Italian and Foreign Films Released in Italy, 1930–1939

| Year | American films | Other foreign films | Italian films | Total | % Italian films |
|------|------|------|------|------|------|
| 1930 | 234 | 127 | 12 | 373 | 3% |
| 1931 | 171 | 85 | 13 | 269 | 5% |
| 1932 | 139 | 87 | 26 | 252 | 11% |
| 1933 | 172 | 101 | 26 | 299 | 9% |
| 1934 | 172 | 86 | 30 | 288 | 10% |
| 1935 | 127 | 72 | 40 | 239 | 17% |
| 1936 | 105 | 82 | 32 | 219 | 15% |
| 1937 | 190 | 93 | 31 | 314 | 10% |
| 1938 | 161 | 64 | 45 | 270 | 17% |
| 1939 | 60 | 106 | 50 | 216 | 23% |

Source: author's elaboration from Società Italiana degli Autori ed Editori (SIAE) data.

the theatre. However, faced with a constantly growing demand, the output of Italian films was insufficient; until the mid-1930s Italian films accounted for approximately 10% of all films shown, most of which were produced in the USA. The US studios further consolidated their dominant position when the major studios began to distribute their films directly, without requiring the services of Italian importers. Between 1930 and 1939, US films accounted for an average of about half the films shown. After World War I, Italian and European audiences began to prefer American films and the word "cinema" became synonymous with Hollywood productions.

Moreover, the US government strongly supported the movie industry, and served as a critical intelligence source for it. The MPPDA (Motion Picture Producers and Distributors of America), Hollywood's trade association, was founded in 1922 and was known as the "Little State Department". Movies were considered the most efficient means for spreading the "American way of life" around the world. General Will H. Hays was appointed as its President and the Hollywood international trade strategy was informed by Hays's belief that trade no longer "followed the flag" but instead followed films. According to Hays, "a really good motion picture, no matter by whom it might have been made, is bound to have proper distribution and exhibition".[47]

Last, but not least, the average budgets of American movies heavily increased from $20,000 in 1914, to $60,000 in 1920. Outlays in creative inputs, such as actors, directors, the acquisition of literary works increased, and movies became branded products: film companies started to use stars to promote their movies and invested from 2% to 10% of the total budget in advertising, with fan magazines, newspaper and poster campaigns. Film producers soon became aware of the positive correlation between production costs, marketing investments, the creation of the star system, and box office returns. According to American observers, "people who are satisfied with the predominance of our pictures are the exhibitors and the great mass of people who attend motion picture performances. Audience likes our pictures because they are better than any other pictures they can see".[48]

Between 1930 and 1939, US films accounted for an average of about half the films shown. After the First World War, Italian and European audiences had begun to prefer American films and the word "cinema" became synonymous with Hollywood productions. In this context, fascism planned and created a new economic policy around the cinema.

## The State Builds a Framework: Aids, Rewards and Controls

> It is the duty of the state to go into the matter, that is to make known phase by phase its own qualitative need, first of all because also the aesthetic education of the people is part of their ethical education, and secondly because the legitimacy of intervention by the state in these matters of the cinema as well as deriving from general rights, also derives from the specific right of the state to participate in the production with its own capital.[49]

The collapse of Europe after the war led to a shift in public policies for the movie industry. Before the 1920s, European governments intervened in the regulation of the industry mainly through ticket levies and censorship. Movies were considered immoral entertainment, something very far from the "high culture" represented by literature and theatre. At the end of the First World War, with the rise of nationalism, the movie industry became part of the political agenda, and movies were used as powerful instruments of propaganda, as in the case of fascist Italy, and, later on, Nazi Germany.

The intervention of European governments followed a twofold path: first of all, financial incentives were given to national producers, and screen-time quotas were introduced to guarantee the projection of national movies. Second, the number of imported American movies was reduced with the introduction of contingents: the first country to adopt such measure was Germany with the *Kontingent Law* (1925).

After five years of *laissez-faire* during which Italian producers had demonstrated their own ineptitude compared with the competition from foreign films, especially those from the USA, state intervention would become increasingly influential, especially in the late 1920s.

"The American began their market incursion modestly, without fanfare, unloading in Italy a great quantity of well-made, easily enjoyed films for which they negotiated exclusive agencies to all of Italy at prices from one thousands to thirty thousand dollars. Naturally, exhibitors and distributors convinced that it was an exceptional bargain (and it was) rushed to make contacts and sign deals. The terms were excellent, the films very good. Their novelty, the attractiveness of subjects, the skill of their direction, the new and interesting faces of the actors very quickly created in Italy a wave of sympathy and fascination from American films".[50]

The relationship with the American film industry was an ambiguous one. The very rapid consolidation of American economic power in the Italian economy after WWI made a direct opposition nearly impossible. If, on the one hand, movie producers asked for a strong national industry, on the other, distributors and exhibitors made profits thanks to American movies.

Professional journals started a heated campaign asking the government to do something concrete for the Italian cinematographic renaissance. The debate over the best solutions to be adopted was heated and revealed different perspectives. Time and modalities of public intervention in the movie industry were linked to the evolution of fascism itself.

Effective governance of the Italian cinema industry required unambiguous policies, or at least policies sharing common objectives. However, with hindsight, it can be seen that there was no such clear definition of shared intentions, to the point that conflicting objectives led to real power struggles.

Although figures like Luigi Freddi spoke in favour of a policy of self-sufficiency, resistance by the Italian producers and big US studios led to other approaches, subsequently structured as government interventions and often supported by very important political figures, who appeared as the supreme architects of the Italian cinema revival.

Fascist cinema policy was certainly wide-ranging. Laws protected national film production and provided incentives by "encouraging the creation of long-term programmes and steering production companies towards huge films of high artistic quality".[51] New bodies and bureaucratic structures came into being: the *Direzione Generale per la Cinematografia* (General Film Board), and the *Ente National delle Industrie Cinematografiche* (National Film Organisation), Cinecitta` and the *Centro Sperimentale di Cinematografia* (Experimental Film Centre). The theoretical debate was revived on the pages of "*Bianco e Nero*", the monthly journal of the *Centro*. Interest increased in gathering data about the film industry: the number of companies in the three branches of the value chain, the annual number of films produced, the quantity of films imported and exported, the list of technicians and artists, consumer statistics. The quantitative aspect of cinema was generally communicated to the public in yearbooks (*almanacchi*), a sign that the sector was alive and working uninterruptedly.[52] It is important also to consider the wider economic context of those years in the wake of the upheaval caused when the New York Stock Market crashed in October 1929.

The economic crisis began to have a tragic effect in summer 1930, as hundreds of thousands of jobs were lost in both industry and in agriculture. The government's economic policy initially headed in two directions: wage reductions and price control. As this process went ahead, the idea developed that economic forces should no longer be left to operate freely or be regulated by the market, thus paving the way for state intervention.

Italy's problem was starkly evident from the start: the country's financial and industrial systems needed support in order to reorganise. On the one hand, this led to a process of business mergers and concentrations, and, on the other hand, there was a growing need for government intervention. This type of intervention was not intended to replace private initiative, as Mussolini himself clearly stated in 1932 when interviewed by German journalist Emil Ludwig: "We call this economic policy *State intervention*, as defined in the *Carta del Lavoro*: if something does not work, then the State intervenes". From a purely theoretical point of view, this auxiliary nature of state intervention is not substantially different from what Keynes delineated in his most important work. Roosevelt's *New Deal* in the United States attempted to change the relationship between public and private interests, giving the state the role of both integrating and correcting the mechanism of capitalism. Fascist officials constantly stressed that extraordinary nature of state intervention, although it seems certain that the "crisis of the system and not in the system", as Mussolini put it, would require much wider-ranging state involvement. This is the context surrounding the legislative intervention plan for the film industry.

"At the time of the greatest failures, when capital fled and technical possibilities dissolved", [53] the regime established a complex legislative and institutional framework; between 1934 and 1939 this helped to create the conditions necessary for revival of the Italian film industry. The first fascist cinema law was the so-called Belluzzo Law (no. 1121 of 16 June 1927), named after the Minister of the National Economy who signed it. It introduced obligatory showing of Italian films: first-run cinemas had to show Italian films for 27 days. However, the measure proved ineffective because there were just not enough Italian films to cover the number of days required by the law. In addition, the law considered only first-run cinemas (estimated at a hundred across the entire country) and did not include the 92 days (from 1 July to 30 September) of the summer season. This meant that a cinema could actually comply with the law by screening only six to seven Italian films per year if each film stayed on the programme for a maximum of seven days. In a period when cinema-going in Italy was growing fast and the national film industry was practically inexistent, the law requiring the screening of Italian films could appear a firm guarantee that even a mediocre film would be distributed across the whole country.

> Everything is lacking: directorial criteria, directors, technicians and actors. There is no doubt that the benefits of providing cinemas with all the Italian films the *quota system* allows to be shown suggest making low-budget films, and there is no doubt that it is difficult for a low-budget film to be an excellent film.[54]

Cinema owners criticised the law and mostly ignored it.[55] However, the fact remains that the Belluzzo Law established certain basic criteria, such as the Italian origin of films and distinct categories of cinema.

In 1930, a delegation consisting of Giuseppe Bottai, Leandro Arpinati, Stefano Pittaluga, Giuseppe Barattolo, Gustavo Lombardo and Nicola de Pirro presented Mussolini with a list of criticisms of the Belluzzo Law. The response to their objections arrived with Law no. 918 of 18 June 1931, signed by Minister Bottai; this defined the criteria necessary for a new film to qualify as Italian, but most importantly, it introduced direct financial aid for films with particular artistic status. This was the first intervention giving an incentive to the Italian film industry, and corresponded to a formula that all Italian film entrepreneurs had more or less wished for, despite the vagueness of the term "sufficient artistic status".

This law marked a fundamental turning point in the relationship between state and cinema, establishing that a grant equivalent to 10% of gross takings: this was actually tantamount to reimbursing half the 20% tax on cinema tickets. The premium was awarded by the Ministry of Corporations, which had a special commission to evaluate the artistic quality of films. However, the law was so imprecise in this respect that all films made in 1930–1931 received funding, and state aid went to all without distinction. In addition, since funding was linked to takings, the biggest-earning films received most funding, in line with Bottai's vision of the cinema. The report accompanying the law when it was presented to the Chamber of Deputies emphasised that the precise intention was "to help the entire film industry without distinction, and therefore to give greater rewards to those who best interpreted public taste".[56] This intention returned *in toto* with the 1938 Alfieri Law, and also appeared in the legislation of post-war democratic Italy.

The 1931 Law had opened up the way for public aid to the film industry. Although this was an absolute novelty for the sector, it is worth remembering that a consequence of the post-1929 Depression was that subsidies and nationalisations were now the norm. This interest in the film industry was not due only to the sector's economic problems; the idea was taking shape that the cinema was not just a form of escapism, but could also play an important social and political role, as in Soviet Russia and Nazi Germany. The Russian cinema was seen as a model for the quality of its films, while the German cinema was a model of organisation; this had been Hitler's priority from the outset.

The film production situation in this period was quite unusual, as the Italian market was completely dominated by just one production company from 1927 to 1932; SASP (*Società Anonima Stefano Pittaluga*) accounted for approximately 90% of Italian output during these years. In 1930 Pittaluga (based at Cines studios) produced 83% of all Italian films; in 1931 this percentage rose to 92%, and once again in 1932 SASP produced 43% of all Italian films. Stefano Pittaluga became the symbol of the Italian cinema revival, entrusted with the task of reanimating the dying industry. The Genoese entrepreneur was greeted as a hero: "an Italian industrialist, Stefano Pittaluga, strong, courageous, and immune to difficulties—with the first 100% talking film, *La canzone dell'amore (The Song of Love)*, has raised the cinema to heights I had not believed possible". Public opinion became convinced that SASP would lead Italian cinema to equal, if not actually overtake, the US film industry.[57] It was also believed that Pittaluga would give Italian films plenty of space on his own cinema circuit.

SASP was also the only example of a vertically integrated organisation modelled on the US studios. The production monopoly occurred almost automatically, since Pittaluga's was the only company that had invested in conversion to sound technology, reorganising the old Cines studios in Via Vejo and installing RCA's Photophone system. This was enabled by funding from the COMIT. The history of SASP can be considered as representing the main organisational, artistic, financial and economic shortcomings of the Italian film industry, and will be discussed in a separate chapter, based on the documents in the Archive of the *Banca Commerciale Italiana*. It is a story in which adoption or importation of the American model was not sufficient to revive Italian film production; this meant that changes to the Italian cinema industry would need to involve its industrial-organisational and artistic aspects, as well as its cinema style and language.

Together with Stefano Pittaluga, who died prematurely in 1931, other producers began to emerge: Gustavo Lombardo, founder of Titanus in

1928; Giuseppe Amato whose popular-regional cinema featured comic actors speaking in dialect; editor Angelo Rizzoli, and Carlo Roncoroni.

Alongside these few solid business ventures, the first laws seemed to leave unresolved the eternal problem of Italian cinema: the excessive number of cinema projects launched by speculators.

> It is painfully surprising to observe the growing numbers of companies and tiny companies that make a film . . . and then perish[58]

The Italian market appeared, therefore, to be full of producers whose main interest was to serve the obligation to show Italian films. They were prepared to invest only small amounts of capital, and their conviction that the public appreciated "a funny little story and the grimaces of an old actor or actress" led to the creation of companies making what the critics judged to be poor-quality films.

Between 1930 and 1944, a total of 255 production companies were formed (producing a total of 945 films), of which 52% were short-lived speculative ventures that made only one film (14% of all films produced in this period). This type of short-lived production company boomed between 1934 and 1938; they were 39% of production companies in 1934, peaked at 42% in 1936 and then dropped to 29% in 1938. The film industry seemed to suffer from a structural weakness it would have been difficult to overcome even with state intervention. Between 1931 and 1945, 78% of production companies made fewer than five films. For example, in the 1935–1936 season, the 40 films in circulation were edited by 27 production companies; five of these produced two films, two produced three films, and only one produced four films. The remaining films were made by short-lived production companies.

It was hoped that the state would intervene to create the conditions needed for an entrepreneurial approach to production and for continuity, for the vertical integration of production companies (since without distribution a production company could never be considered as truly industrial), and for improvements in technology. Regulation and reorganisation of the production system contributed to making the cinema a powerful ethical and political tool for use by the state. The regime was aware that the industry consisted of just a few groups of producers who had *serious organisations, a sound economic situation, good technical skills, and almost always the support of excellent rental organisations.*

In this production context, the first ideas about protectionism and commercial control began to circulate, eventually culminating in the ENIC monopoly.

The first measures to support Italian production (obligatory screening quotas introduced in 1927) seemed like a bland imposition. Therefore, Law no. 1414 of 1933 perfected the system of obligatory screening and introduced dubbing vouchers (for every Italian-made film, the producer received three dubbing vouchers which gave exemption from the tax on imported foreign films). Articles 1 and 2 stated that "in the Kingdom's cinemas, it is forbidden to show non-Italian sound films over 1000 metres long which have been adapted into Italian (dubbing and post-synchronisation) abroad".

Article 5 established a tax of 25,000 lire on every foreign film dubbed into Italian; a type of copyright for the Italian language held by the state. Producers of Italian films were exempt from this tax at a rate of three dubbed films for each Italian film produced. This meant that Italian producers were guaranteed earnings of around 8% of the average cost of making a film.

The system of dubbing vouchers remained unchanged during the following decade, with some adjustments to the number of vouchers and their face value.

The new law was not yet fully satisfactory because it neglected an extremely important aspect, i.e. effective compliance with law regarding the number of days when it was mandatory to show Italian films. A cinema owner could actually show an Italian film for one day and foreign films for months. Moreover, the small number of Italian films compared with the vast number of foreign films made it impossible to apply the law in this sense. For example, in 1938 there were 30 Italian films versus 258 foreign-made films, i.e. one Italian film for every 8.6 foreign imports. This situation would have continued to make the law ineffective if the ENIC monopoly had not come into effect, changing the rules of play. Quaglietti's data on films shown in the city of Rome in 1934 confirm that the law was ignored.[59] The law then reiterated the policy of incentives introduced in 1931, rewarding films with outstanding artistic and technical qualities. When the laws passed in 1931 and 1933 are compared, it becomes evident that there was a desire to change the criteria for the rewards; the objective was to move away from a blanket subsidy for all films and to encourage quality productions, removing the automatic subsidies assigned by a commission in which politicians played a determining role.[60] Thus, support for the cinema became closely linked to control of political power.

However, this measure did not have particularly important effects, since the number of films receiving subsidies remained quite constant: 25 films in the 1933–1934 season, 18 films in 1934–1935, 21 films in 1936–1937, and 18 in 1937–1938[61]. A subsequent law passed in July 1934 increased the number of obligatory screenings for Italian films from the number required by the previous 1927 law. The ratio of foreign films to Italian films had been 10:1 but now became 3:1, and the legal obligation was also extended to second-run cinemas in cities with over 50,000 inhabitants.[62] As Quaglietti has shown, compliance with the law meant that at least 54 Italian films should have been produced, rather than the 30 actually made.[63] Thus, a law was passed which tended towards protectionism at the same time as it encouraged national film production.

The fascist transformation of the cinema culminated in 1934, with the creation of the following bodies: the *Corporazione dello Spettacolo* (the

Show Business Corporation) by Royal decree on 23 June, the *Federazione Nazionale Fascista degli Industriali dello Spettacolo* (National Fascist Federation of Show Business Industrialists) by Royal decree on 16 August, and the *Sottosegretariato per la Stampa e la Propaganda* (Under-Secretariat for Press and Propaganda) by Royal decree on 6 September 1934), the future *Minculpop*. The changes made by RD 18 September 1934, no.1565 made an addition to the three original *Direzioni Generali* (Directorate-Generals): the Italian press, foreign press, and propaganda. The new *Direzione Generale per la Cinematografia* (Directorate-General for the Film Industry) was headed by a Galeazzo Ciano's close friend Luigi Freddi, a journalist at "*Il Popolo d'Italia*", director of the NFP propaganda office, and secretary of the *fasci all'estero* (fascists abroad). Freddi, and the political struggle during which he was at the centre of Italian cinema, are fundamental in cinema historiography, not only because of the importance of his post, but also because he himself wrote two volumes detailing the events in which he was involved. Although allowance must be made for an inevitable bias, Freddi's work is an essential source that must be taken into account.

The *Direzione* was set up to take care of administration, censorship and funding for the cinema. It was intended to be "the central organ propelling and perfecting that formidable complex of activities which is growing up around the cinema as each day goes by".[64] It had four divisions: general affairs; supervision of production; cultural issues and cinema press; censorship, awards and commerce. Almost all the division directors had backgrounds in artistic and cultural sectors.

Examination of the archive documents reveals a vast output of interventions in favour of the film industry: fascism fully understood that its importance was both economic and cultural, and that its structures required intervention, aware of the importance of films in influencing the psychology of the masses and the formation of a collective identity. Fascist cinema policy was not without contradictions or internal conflicts; these reflected the two opposing visions of the cinema. Freddi aimed for a more nationalised and totalitarian cinema, eternally committed to expressing the fascist idea of man and life. According to Freddi, every aspect of the cinema had to be controlled, from the economic aspect of private production to control of the artistic sphere via preventive censorship of subjects and screenplays. Freddi was convinced that abandonment of the project of a state cinema would constitute betrayal of the spirit of fascism.

In contrast, Alfieri (who eventually triumphed) held that state intervention should be limited to providing industrial structures and other instruments such as access to funding and legislation, in order to protect and supervise the private film industry without excessive interference in its artistic and creative aspects, i.e. film content. In a letter to Freddi, Alfieri recalls that "the *Direzione Generale per la Cinematografia* must provide clear and rigid ethical and political directives, must exercise necessary control over the effective consistency and seriousness of ventures, but must not in any way take the place of producers during the making of the film. . . . The *Direzione* has the immensely important task of stimulating, enriching, and assisting all the activity of the cinema industry, but at the level of command and not of implementation"[65].

The importance of the cinema in the formation of national feeling and popular cultural aspirations led to interventions aimed at resolving the financial, industrial, technical and artistic problems responsible for the industry's great weakness and low production levels.

> He recognised that without raising this artistic part to levels which can interest, excite and convince the public, the other part would not take root and become once again, as in the era of the pre-war film industry, a very powerful source of economic development for the Nation and a very powerful means for spreading ideas.[66]

The regime began to promote a systematic investigation of the film industry, producing studies and analytical documents in order to understand the system's most intrinsic mechanisms, with a view to defining the most suitable lines of legislative intervention. It was necessary to provide the film industry with a solid industrial structure directed at producing quality films for export to foreign markets, because film was a product with great export potential. This made it necessary to remove sporadic ventures, to create a profound industrial consciousness, to strengthen the technical and artistic base and train cinema criticism.

From Freddi's point of view, the Italian film industry in 1934 had not changed its old ways, and improvisation was still the main driving force behind business ventures: "The Italian film industry has always been at least five years behind the industry of other countries. In every way and from every point of view: industrial organisation, technical equipment, production principles and capacity, artistic criteria, direction methods and orientations, performer quality, subject matter, and distribution means.[67]

The reference models were the American film industry and its mighty Hollywood machine, with its system of tax breaks and free private initiative (a model where the state did not intervene directly but created opportunities), and the state cinema in Russia, with its control over funding and even more importantly over film content. Here was a level of control which fascism would never achieve.

The idea advanced by Freddi was precisely that of every other entrepreneur who saw the integration of the three branches of the film industry (production, distribution and cinemas) as the solution to the problems of Italian cinema. This meant complete achievement of what Pittaluga had not lived to see. The American model's economic and industrial structure was admired, as were its technical and aesthetic results, and Freddi's production model was a kind of state-owned MGM. His formula was very straightforward: strong control over private production, preventive censorship of subjects and screenplays, and the Hays Code as an example to imitate more for its political and social aspects rather than for its moral stance. Although Freddi declared that "the economic and the artistic functions of the film industry cannot be separated from its ethical functions",[68] there was no attempt to subjugate the cinema to any fascist ideology. Freddi was definite in his opposition to direct propaganda in films, and even viewed the *Luce* newsreels with disfavour. He preferred to use social demagogy, or the assertion of an abstract heroic moral code: historical myths celebrated in relation to the present. The ideal cinema for Freddi was that of the USA, i.e. a refined show with "an ethical content, artistic quality, technical competence".[69]

At the level of industrial production, the regime attempted to a structural reorganisation to reduce the number of production companies and encouraged the creation of consortiums or corporations. The aim was to create vertically structured groups, a condition still shown to be necessary in the late 1930s in order to "make companies active, since production is not at present a largely and rapidly remunerative undertaking". By integrating the three stages of the film industry, it was hoped that distribution and cinemas would be able to cover the production sector's budget deficits.

Once he had obtained his prestigious post, Freddi immediately began a process of achieving centralised control: Law no. 1566 of 20 September 1934 placed all measures connected with vigilance and encouragement of the national film industry under the control of the Under-Secretariat for Press and Propaganda, which was given special vigilance and appeal commissions. The composition of the commissions reiterated the dual state functions of incentive and censorship. The decisions of control commissions had to respect what were prevalently reasons of state and the party's wishes, but when a decision concerned aesthetics or was vaguely related to economics or strategy, film industry exponents were also involved.

The *Direzione* became operational on the 24th of September, when a new law gave it control of censorship, which had been a function of the Ministry of the Interior, and of financial aid to film production, which had been a function of the Ministry of Corporations.

A similar organisation had already been in operation for over a year in Germany. On the 14th of March 1933 Joseph Goebbels was appointed Minister for Education and Propaganda, stating that "the sole objective of propaganda is to win over the masses. Every means of achieving this aim is good, every means which impedes this is bad".[70] The immediacy of cinema images made it the good means *par excellence*. All German cinema studios, distribution organisations, the most important cinema projection circuits and, above all, the most important production companies (UFA, Tobis, Bavaria) were placed under the direct control of the Reich in order to represent National Socialist ideology. The Nazi regime created the *Filmkreditbank* in order to finance the film industry, which was in a state of crisis. The bank was created as a limited company: the capital was provided by UFA and the principal German banks,[71] and was a real model for Italy's

*Sezione di credito cinematografico* (film industry credit agency) established in 1935 as a part of the *Banca Nazionale del Lavoro*.

The foundation of S.A.C.C. was inspired by the German Filmkreditbank, even though the functioning was different, since in Germany the bank did not directly fund but acted as an intermediary between production companies and credit institutions.

The Sezione would give the film industry access to credit via direct loans. The financial system was certainly one of the factors enabling the complex structure of the film industry to function. During the 1930s, fascism took an interest in observing the situation in the USA, Germany, Austria and France, where the banks had an important role in financing the film industry.

It was therefore seen as vital for the production of big budget films and masterpieces to gain the trust of the credit system:

> Money is needed, but it is above all the attitude of high finance and the banks, which has to change. They need to know that the cinema industry exists, they need to trust it, respect it and take an interest, and the sad preconception that it involves only adventurers and failed entrepreneurs has to end.[72]

The aim of Sacc was "to support the growth of national movie production through funding at special conditions to companies active in the production, distribution and exhibition branches. The Section can also: give credit to companies for buying, editing and distributing foreign movies; advance revenues on foreign distribution of national movies; advance prizes given by the Ministry to production companies".[73] The section had an independent patrimony, separated by the Bank. The Ministry of Finance, in agreement with Ministero per la Stampa e la Propaganda, made vigilance on its activity.

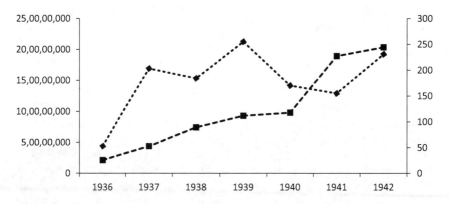

*Graph 3.1* Number of Loans and Total Amount of Funding by S.A.C.C., 1936–1942.

Source: author's elaboration from historical archive of Banca Nazionale del Lavoro.

The Section was administrated by: a Board of Directors, an Executive Committee and a Director. The president and the general director of the Bank were respectively the president and the director of S.A.C.C.

The Board of Directors was made of nine members: a representative from the Ministry of Finance; one from the Ministry of Popular Culture (Ministero della Cultura Popolare); the president, the general director and two representatives of Banca Nazionale del Lavoro (they have to be part of the Board of Directors of the Bank); a representative of Federazione Nazionale Fascista Industriali dello Spettacolo and two representatives of those institutions that took part in the endowment fund of S.A.C.C.

The S.A.C.C. board of directors was responsible for funding requests, guarantees, stiffening endorsement and bail bonds. It also decided for competencies given to Executive committee and the Section's director. The executive committee was made up of the president and the director of S.A.C.C. and five members of the Board.

Production companies have to respect very strict rules to get access to funding and loans requests have to be equipped with: 1) a copy of the statute; 2) a list of company managers; 3) a copy of balance sheets; 4) reports on company activities, technical equipments and capabilities. For funding requests of new movies, companies had to hand in these documents too: 1) official approval by the *Ministero per la Stampa e Propaganda* and license from the *Federazione Nazionale Fascista degli Industriali dello Spettacolo*; 2) a copy of the story; 3) a copy of the final screenplay; 4) an artistic plan; 5) a working plan; 6) an estimated budget; 7) a detailed financial plan; 8) a copy of all contracts both for producing and distribution.

The total amount of the loan could cover at least 60% of movie production costs, after having deducted the public fund the company could obtain from the *Ministero della Stampa e Propaganda*. Generally speaking, a loan could not last more than 24 months. Allotments could start after the beneficiary demonstrated to spend the difference between the estimated budget and the granted loan.

It is quite clear from the mechanism depicted above that the government had the overall control on the funding process, and a production company could not get access to credit without having obtained previous approval from the *Ministero per la Stampa e la Propaganda*.

Although the fascist bureaucratic structure was modelled on that of Germany, and Mussolini defined cinema as "the strongest weapon", unlike Germany, Italy did not have a state film industry, nor were strictly political films produced.

While the top levels of government were attempting to centralise every industrial and market activity, the small and very small film companies began to show their discontent. They saw Freddi's policy merely as an obstacle to their habit of making easy money from speculation. Even the fascist political class demonstrated a certain distaste for the policy of the Direzione generale. State control over the cinema was interesting only up to a point, and after an initial stage of reorganisation, everyone would have preferred to maintain the *status quo*. In this context, Freddi's approach became increasingly troublesome, and, in parallel with his controls, other state measures began to encourage private enterprise; it was placed under suitable control, but no one wanted to see it disappear. This is the perspective from which to consider the financial benefits contained in Law no.1143 of 13 June 1935, according to which the Secretariat could advance up to a third of the estimated production costs for each film.

Fascism continued to build a legislative framework for the cinema with Decree no.861 of 29 April 1937, which modified the Law of 5 February 1934. In particular, it extended the screening ban to foreign films between 500 and 1,000 metres long, raised the dubbing tax, and increased the number of dubbing vouchers to four. In addition, it introduced further taxes on dubbed films that earned over a certain amount at the box office.

This was also the time of the first big conflicts between Freddi's line of action and that of Parliament Member Dino Alfieri, called in to replace Galeazzo Ciano at the Ministry of Popular Culture.

Freddi supported state intervention in production to achieve balance in the anarchy of an industry with production companies that closed down, while others were involved in non-stop production, an industry that did not always take the trouble to make films able to satisfy public demands. It could be said that Italian films were still not very competitive, despite the activity of the *Direzione generale*, but this would not be a completely objective assessment. At the very time when Freddi's policy could have had a decisive effect, Italian producers found that Alfieri was more inclined to maintain their old privileges. Although Freddi's approach remained that of a coordinating intervention, a new law was passed on 16 June 1938, known as the Alfieri Law. One of its most important points was the introduction of a premium for producers' corporations: the basic mechanism was 12% of gross taking, up to a maximum of 25% if takings in the three years after release equalled six million lire. This law marked the definitive victory of private interests. The new law undoubtedly benefitted the industry because it increased the number of films produced, led to greater industrial concentration in the film industry, and loosened censorship controls.

The Alfieri Law unleashed a flood of film production, but, despite the laws, Italian films were still unable to make any impact on the American competition, which continued to take the lion's share at the box office. Producers requested even more drastic measures, and in the climate of nationalism marking Mussolinian autarchy, on 4 September 1938 (Royal decree no.1389) came the "Monopoly for the purchase, importation and distribution of foreign films", known as ENIC. The four biggest American studios had no intention of distributing their films under the ENIC aegis and abandoned the market, leaving it wide open to Italian producers. The protectionist measures of the new law forced distributors and cinema owners to distribute and show Italian films. The Italian habit of cinema-going proved stronger than attachment to a certain product; despite the drop in the number of American films, ticket sales continued to rise and the box-office takings of Italian films reached 50% of the total in 1942. Italian production increased from the 33 films made in 1937 to 96 in 1942.

The revival of the national industry saw constantly rising audience numbers. Box-office takings rose from 439 million lire in 1936 to 525 million in 1937, and up to 586 million in 1938. At the same time, there was also a noticeable increase in the number of days on which films were shown, and in ticket sales. The cinema had now spread across the entire country, with 2,720 private cinemas alongside 1,428 run by the *Opera Nazionale Dopolavoro* (National Recreational Club), and by religious and other bodies.[74]

Fascist state intervention also attempted to move towards the theoretical debate surrounding the cinema, towards definition of a critical cinema theory, another integral part of the process of re-creation and requalification of the film industry. Once again, artistic and industrial interests were closely interwoven. Capital and legislation were not enough to revive Italian cinema from its stagnant inferiority. It also needed renewal from within to enhance the cinema's expressive potential. In order to achieve this, the artistic side of the industry required work in the form of training for actors, directors, production managers and screenwriters. The *Centro Sperimentale di Cinematografia* (Experimental Film Centre) was founded in 1935 as a school for the new creative talents of the Italian film industry; the *Centro* would provide rational training for technicians and artists, with a unified approach to ensure that the process of film creation was effective. Mussolini defined the *Centro* as the vital precondition for achieving the supremacy of the Italian film industry.[75]

The *Centro* offered 100 pupils a two-year training course in the following subjects: acting, artistic creation (direction, screenplay writing, editing), sound engineering, cinematography, stage management, costumes, special effects and production. The regime's aim was also to allow the centre to produce films, although limited to just two films a year, in order to have effective control over production costs and *to guide the artistic and economic aspects of Italian film production, in accordance with the international tasks that will be assigned to Italy.*[76] The *Centro* was undoubtedly an important training school and constituted a fertile environment for those who would later be the principal exponents of neorealism.

Theoretical production was entrusted to a new journal, "*Bianco e Nero*", directed by Luigi Chiarini, presented as a monthly publication of the *Centro Sperimentale di Cinematografia*. In his introduction to the first edition of January 1937, Luigi Freddi wrote that its primary aim was not *to use the film industry for publicity or editorial purposes, as do many journals and newspapers, but to be useful to the cinema.* There was criticism of years of empty debate regarding cinema theory and criticism, too often left to aesthetes, who had summarised the problem by declaring that the Italian film industry did not exist, without realising that a finished film was the result of combining artistic, technical and industrial factors in an extremely complex process. *Bianco e Nero* intended to create a new cinema aesthetic, based on substance (on what Walter Benjamin defined as the specificity of cinema) and not only on form. The cinema was a mechanical medium with its own aesthetic content and form of expression. According to the magazine, the aesthetic backwardness of Italian cinema was due to too much theorising about the technical and technological components. This was further accentuated because producers were unable to invest in innovation, and since they were averse to risk and anxious for almost guaranteed box-office success, they produced the same old films with the same well-worn stylistic features and narrative forms, and used the same old actors, who would supposedly draw the public into the cinemas: "So the films are always the same, with the same foolish events. The producers have no courage and this is why they cannot make the Italian film industry work".[77]

Fascism also tackled the problem of artistic recognition for the film industry. The Venice International Film Festival was founded in 1932 as part of the National Institute for Educational Cinema, and became a legally autonomous body in 1936: "The 'Biennial International Art Exhibition', an autonomous board established according to Royal decree no.33 of 13 January 1930 to manage the figurative art show, is permanently authorised to promote and manage a yearly International Film Festival in Venice, in addition to the activities for which it was founded".[78] The purpose of the Festival (Art. 2) was to "be the supreme expression of the year's best films from every country", to recognise and to reward the films that aspired to be genuine expressions of art.

The regime had attempted to resolve the industrial problem of Italian cinema with a set of measures (the quota system, awards, dubbing vouchers, loans), but the number of business ventures remained low, at least in relation to the needs of the home market. There were few companies that existed "exclusively, continuously for film production, with a clear and precise programme and solid discipline"[79] and that could be a reference point for independent producers, giving them "support and integration for their own work".[80]

Financial, economic, organisational and aesthetic factors were among the many different explanations offered for the difficulties of Italian cinema in regaining an important international position. Analytical study of the *Societa` Anonima Stefano Pittaluga* shows the extreme complexity of film industry management and organisation, and this will be discussed in the next chapter. Regarding film industry organisation, cinema journals always attributed the disappointing achievements of Italian cinema to the lack of collaboration between the different stages of the production system; in particular, the film distributors were accused of acting immorally because of their straightjacket contracts with producers and excessive percentages imposed on cinema managers.

Relations between the production and distribution sectors conditioned the chances of returns on the capital invested. Production companies did not always possess a vertically integrated organisational structure allowing them to distribute their own films on a circuit of cinemas they owned. In most cases, the production company used a distributor who dealt with "Italian films from various companies and the foreign films they owned". The distributors were responsible for launching, promoting and scheduling films; it therefore appears understandable that they had more of an interest in the films they owned, which ensured them greater financial returns. Although this limited exploitation of the home and international markets, the distributors claimed they were distributing the films the public preferred: foreign films that were considered artistically superior to Italian-made films. Their advantage in the distribution of American films was also economic. A Hollywood film managed to recoup a large percentage of its production costs on the circuit of first-run cinemas in the USA. This made it possible to sell the film abroad at a lower price than Italian producers could offer, so that Italian producers were forced to make low-budget films in order to survive the competition.

Many forces conditioned the dynamics of the Italian film industry; economic, political and artistic factors were closely interconnected, and each had a different impact on the sector.

The production companies were positioned between the state, with its attempts to provide incentives and exercise control, and the unavoidable forces of market competition. The national market was always seen as being too small for a film production company to flourish, making it necessary to go abroad, where the pressure of competition had increased. This move required consolidation of the production organisations, which needed to concentrate on more long-term business projects, and it also required improvements in terms of style and expression in order for Italian films to adapt to the tastes of an international audience.

The search for an "Italian way" in the cinema would require training in management and professional, technical and artistic skills because of its complex nature as a cultural industry, meaning that it was important to find a balance between art and the dictates of industry and of the market.

## Notes

1 Carlo Roncoroni during the parliamentary discussion on 8 May 1936, in Atti Parlamentari, Legislatura XXIX, Prima sessione, Discussioni.
2 Among the most important works, see: Bakker, Gerben 2008, *Entertainment Industrialised—The Emergence of the International Film Industry*, Cambridge, UK: Cambridge University Press; Bakker, Gerben 2005, "The Decline and Fall of the European Film Industry: Sunk Costs, Market Size, and Market Structure, 1890–1927", *Economic History Review*, 58 (2): 310–351; Bakker, Gerben 2004, "Stars and Stories: How Films Became Branded Products", in Sedgwick, John, Pokorny, Michael, (eds.), *An Economic History of Film. Routledge*,

London: Routledge, pp. 48–85; Higson, Andrew, Maltby, Richard 1999, *"Film Europe" and "Film America": Cinema, Commerce and Cultural Exchange 1920–1939*, Exeter: University of Exeter Press; Segrave, Kerry 1997, *American Films Abroad: Hollywood's Domination of the World's Movie Screens from the 1890's to the Present*, Jefferson, NC: McFarland; Jarvie, Jan 1992, *Hollywood's Overseas Campaign: The North Atlantic Movie Trade, 1920–1950*, Cambridge: Cambridge University Press; Balio, Tino (ed.) 1985, *The American Film Industry*, Madison: University of Wisconsin Press; Thompson, Kristin 1985, *Exporting Entertainment: America in the World Film market 1907–1934*, London: British Film Institute; Guback, Thomas 1969, *The International Film Industry: Western Europe and America since 1945*, Bloomington: Indiana University Press.

3 "The Government believes sincerely that the interests of the motion-picture industry are best promoted by the freest possible interchange of films, based solely on the quality of the product". American diplomats complained about the fact that European legislative barriers, more than any other form of artificial restrictions, depended on "the arbitrary will of the administration", *Trade Barriers to Exports of U.S. Filmed Entertainment*, Motion Picture Association of America, 2010.

4 See Bagella, Michele, Becchetti, Leonardo 1999, "The Determinants of Motion Picture Box Office Performance: Evidence from Movies Produced in Italy", *Journal of Cultural Economics*, 23: 237–256; Marvasti, Akbar, Canterbery, Ray 2005, "Cultural and Other Barriers to Motion Pictures Trade", *Economic Inquiry*, 43 (1): 39–54.

5 *Tendencies to Monopoly in the Cinematograph Film Industry*, Report of a committee appointed by the British Cinematograph Films Council, published by the Board of Trade, July 1944.

6 "All motion pictures have the characteristic of non-rivalness because their consumption by one moviegoer does not affect their availability to others. Filmmaking, along with television and radio programming, is a quasi-public good export by virtue of the strength of its non-rival economic characteristic", Flibbert, Andrew 2007, *Commerce in Culture: State and Markets in the World Film Trade*, New York: Palgrave, pp. 36–37. The other property is that it is impossible or too costly to exclude any person from consuming a good that has been produced.

7 Bagella and Becchetti, cit.

8 Jack Lang, the French Minister of Culture in the '80s, was the first to use the term "cultural exemption" during the Intergovernmental Conference on Cultural Policies for Development, held in Mexico in 1982.

9 McAnany, Emilie, Wilkinson, Kenton (eds.) 1996, *Mass Media and Free Trade: Nafta and the Cultural Industries*, Austin: University of Texas Press, pp. 3–4.

10 For the debate on the problematic nature of the term "national culture" and on cultural sovereignty, see Collins, Richard 1990, *Television: Policy and Culture*, London: Unwin; Raquel Salinas, Leena Paldan 1979, "Culture in the Process of Dependent Development: Theoretical Perspectives", in Nordenstreng, Kaarle, Schiller, Herbert (eds.), *National Sovereignty and International Communication*, Norwood, NJ: Ablex Publishing, pp. 82–98; Crane, Diana, Kawashima Nobuko, Kawasaki Ken'ichi (eds) 2002, *Global Culture: Media, Arts, Policy, and Globalization*, New York: Routledge; Mulcahy, Kevin Winter 2002, "Cultural Imperialism and Cultural Sovereignty: U.S.-Canadian Cultural Relations", *The Journal of Arts Management, Law, and Society*, 31 (4): 265–278; Frederick, Howard 1992, *Global Communications & International Relations*, Belmont, CA: Wadsworth Publishing Company; Downing, John, Wartella, Ellen,

Mcquail, Denis (eds.) 2004, *The Sage Handbook of Media Studies*, London/
Thousand Oaks, CA/New Dehli: Sage.

11 The opposition between European countries and the US is well summarised by this claim of Mitterand during the Uruguay Round of the GATT: "Who could be blind today to the threat of a world gradually invaded by Anglo-Saxon culture, under the cover of economic liberalism?" quoted in Bremmer, Charles 20 October 1993, "Mitterand Musters Troop to Defend the Culture Cocoon", *The Australian*, p. 9.

12 Hill, John 1999, *British Cinema in the 1980s*, Oxford: Oxford Unversity Press.

13 Moran, Albert (ed.) 1996, *Film Policy: International, National and Regional Perspective*, London/New York: Routledge.

14 See UNESCO 1982, *Cultural Industries: A Challenge for the Future of Culture*, Paris: Unesco.

15 Strong criticism to cultural exemption was expressed by Jack Valenti, president of the Motion Picture Association of America, according to whom: "cultural exemption is an elitist and backward looking approach; protectionism is a contravention of freedom of expression and consumption; State implication in culture does not foster talent and harms art; the "cultural exemption" favours the development of an artists-in-the-unemployment-line mentality; it constitutes a block on competition and a perversion of the market; refusal to reduce costs menaces living standard improvement for the entire planet; protectionism's inefficiency leads to wastage of government funds". See Frau-Megis, Divina 2002,"Cultural Exemption", National Policies and Globalization: Imperatives in Democratisation and Promotion of Contemporary Culture", *Quaderns del CAC* (Catalan Audiovisual Council), 14: 1–16.

16 Albornoz, Facundo, Vanin, Paolo 2010, "Trade Protection and Industrial Structure", *The B.E Journal of Economic Analysis and Policy*, 10 (1), Article 57, pp. 1–29.

17 Chang, Ha-Joon 2002, *Kicking Away the Ladder? Policies and Institutions for Economic Development in Historical Perspective*, London: Anthem Press.

18 Krugman, Paul 1986, *Strategic Trade Policy and the New International Economics*, Cambridge, MA: The MIT Press, pp. 10–11.

19 Ibid.

20 See Freund, Caroline, Weinhold, Diana October 2002, "The Internet and International Trade in Services", *American Economic Review*, 92 (2): 236–240; Amiti, Mary, Wei, Shang-Jin 2005, "Fear of Service Outsourcing: Is It Justified?", *Economic Policy*, 20 (42): 308–347; Marvasti, Akbar, Canterbery, Ray 2005, "Cultural and Other Barriers to Motion Pictures Trade", *Economic Inquiry*, 43 (1): 39–54.

21 See Saggi, Kamal, Pack, Howard 2006, "Is There a Case for Industrial Policy? A Critical Survey", *World Bank Research Observer*, 21 (2): 267–297.

22 For a general discussion on economic justifications to protectionism, see Carbaugh, Robert 2009, *International Economics*, Mason, OH: South-Western Cengage Learning.

23 Ibid.

24 Ibid.

25 On the positive effect of low trade barriers on productivity see Paudel, Krishna, Debasis, Mitra 1998, "Trade Liberalization, Market Discipline and Productivity Growth: New Evidence from India", *Journal of Development Economics*, 56 (2), 447–462; Pavcnik, Nina 2002, "Trade Liberalization, Exit, and Productivity Improvements: Evidence from Chilean Plants", *Review of Economic Studies*, 69: 245–276; Amiti, Mari, Konings, Joep 2005, "Trade Liberalization, Intermediate Inputs, and Productivity: Evidence from Indonesia", *IMF Working Papers*,

5/146. On the positive relationship between tariff protection and productivity see Konings, Joep, Vandenbussche, Hylke 2004, "Antidumping Protection and Productivity Growth of Domestic Firms", *Journal of International Economics*, 65: 151–165. On the absence of relationship see Trefler, Daniel 2004, "The Long and Short of the Canada-U.S. Free Trade Agreement", *American Economic Review*, 94: 870–895.

26  See Bernardini, Aldo 1996, *Il cinema muto italiano*, vol. II, Rome: Nuova ERI/ Centro Sperimentale di Cinematografia, p. 210.

27  Zagarrio, Vito 2006, "Schizofrenie del modello fascista", in Caldiron, Orio, *Storia del cinema italiano 1934–1939*, Rome: Edizioni Bianco e Nero, pp. 37–61.

28  Law 24 June 1929 no.1103, Modifiche alle vigenti disposizioni relative alla vigilanza governativa sulle pellicole cinematografiche.

29  See Cannistraro, Paul 1974, *La fabbrica del consenso. Fascismo e mass-media*, Rome-Bari: Laterza; Veneruso, Danilo 1981, *L'Italia fascista. Storia d'Italia dal Risorgimento alla Repubblica. IV Volume*, Bologna: Il Mulino. Zagarrio, Vito 2004, *Cinema e fascismo. Film, modelli, immaginari*, Venice: Marsilio; Ben-Ghiat, Ruth 2000, *La cultura fascista*, Bologna: Il Mulino.

30  ACS, PCM 1928, Fascicolo 3.1.7, Protocollo 4426. Nello Signorelli in a letter to the Duce dated 19 September1928.

31  Brunetta, Gian Piero 1975, *Cinema italiano fra le due guerre. Fascismo e politica cinematografica*, Milan: Mursia.

32  See Cannistraro, *cit.*

33  Gentile, Emilio, 1993, *Il culto del Littorio*, Rome-Bari: Laterza.

34  ACS, PCM 1934–1936, Fascicolo 3.2.2, protocollo 1397, "Luigi Freddi— Questione relativa all'attuazione di un suo progetto nell'interesse della cinematografia italiana".

35  Gentile, cit.

36  ACS, PCM 1934–1936, Fascicolo 3.2.2, protocollo 1397.

37  *Camerata* Maggi during the parliamentary discussions on 13 May 1937, in Atti Parlamentari, Discussioni dal 3 maggio 1937 al 31 dicembre 1937, Prima Sessione, Discussioni, Tornata del 13 Maggio 1937.

38  There were different opinions about reducing the duties on cinema tickets. On the one hand, they were seen as being too little to bring about what turned out to be a vast change. On the other hand, based on a report by the Ministry of Corporations, this would have brought more members of the public into cinemas—due to the drop in ticket prices—and would also have improved the earnings from each single film, usually distributed in different proportions between producers and cinema owners. All in all, a reduction would not have meant large losses in State revenue, but Minister Bottai held that the measure was not very opportune at that particular time because the revival should be constructed not only via the straightforward reduction of a certain group of duties or taxes, but above all via *greater consolidation and increase in national economic output.*

39  "In reply to the letter from the Cabinet Office, I have the pleasure of informing you that, with the intention of promoting the production of Italian films, this Ministry has already prepared a design for a Law Decree which embraces the concept of a quota system, contained in the document presented by the representatives of the industrialists and of the fascist cinema Corporations. At present it is not possible to do the same with regard to the State cutting the tax on cinema tickets for Italian films". This communiqué was sent by the Ministry of the National Economy to the Cabinet Office on 16 August 1925, ACS, PCM 1925, 3.8 protocollo 1086.

40  ACS, PCM 1925, Fascicolo 3.8, protocollo 1086, *Comitato per la rinascita della cinematografia in Italia. Richiesta di appoggio del Governo.*

41 Il Tevere, 22 July 1926.

42 Paradisi, Umberto 15 settembre 1921, "La voce delle cifre nel grido della crisi cinematografica", in *Il giornale d'Italia*, quoted in Redi, Riccardo, Camerini, Claudio (eds.) 1958, *Cinecittà I: industria e mercato nel cinema italiano tra le due guerre*, Venice: Marsilio, pp. 29–33.

43 Regio decreto-legge 6 settembre 1924 n. 2025, Fondazione in Roma di un Istituto Internazionale per la cinematografia educativa.

44 Commissariato Generale per l'Emigrazione, Cassa Nazionale per le Assicurazioni Sociali, Istituto Nazionale delle Assicurazioni, Cassa Nazionale Assicurazione Infortuni sul Lavoro.

45 ACS, Fondo PCM 1931–34, fasc. 5.1, prot. 6893.

46 SIAE, *Lo spettacolo in Italia*.

47 Will Hays speech at the Inland Press Association Convention, 26 May 1925, quoted in Higson and Maltby (cit.), p. 188.

48 Col. Edward G. Lowry, "Certain Factors and Considerations Affecting the European Market", internal MPPDA memo, 25 October 1928, quoted in Higson and Maltby (cit.), p. 36.

49 Alessandro Pavolini, 3 June 1941.

50 Chiti, Roberto, Quargnolo, Mario 1957, "La malinconica storia dell'UCI", *Bianco e Nero*, 7: 21–35.

51 ASBI, US., n 18, fasc.4.

52 V. Mussolini in the introduction to *Almanacco del cinema italiano*, Rome: Società Anonima Editrice Cinema, 1939-XVII.

53 The phrase is on the first page of the bi-monthly publication *Cinema* of 25 April 1937, no. 20.

54 ASI-BCI, Carte di Raffaele Mattioli, Corrispondenza A-Z (CM), cart.127, fasc. "GIORDANA Tullio", N. 5/455. Journalist Tullio Giordana founded the liberal-democratic journal "L'Epoca" in 1917.

55 Bassoli, Carlo 1927, "Contingentamento", *L'Eco del Cinema*, 41, quoted in Quaglietti, Lorenzo 1975, "Il cinema degli anni trenta in Italia: primi elementi per una analisi politico-strutturale", Various Authors, *Materiali sul cinema italiano 1929/1943*, Quaderno informativo della Mostra del Nuovo Cinema, 63, Venice: Marsilio, pp. 294–295.

56 Brunetta, 1975, p. 41.

57 Mussolini was credited with the following statement about the role of SASP after the first sound film: "Continue like this and the Americans will be afraid of Italian films".

58 La Cinematografia. Giornale d'arte e di battaglia, 15–30 maggio 1929. The quote is from the article entitled *La nostra battaglia: Cinemania*.

59 Quaglietti, 1975, p. 290.

60 The commission consisted of representatives from the Corporazione dello Spettacolo, the Ministry of Corporations, the Ministry of Finance, the Minister of the Interior, the Federazione nazionale degli industriali dello spettacolo, and two experts nominated by the Corporazione dello spettacolo, in Ciliberti, Ferruccio 1942, *Legislazione italiana per la cinematografia*, Siena: Edizioni Ex Combattenti.

61 Freddi, Luigi 1949, *Il cinema*, Rome: L'arnia, p.129.

62 RDL 20 July 1934, no.1301

63 Quaglietti, 1975, *cit.*

64 *Camerata* Castellini during the discussion of the budget of the Ministry of the Press and Propaganda from 1 July 1936 to 30 June 1937, in Atti Parlamentari, Discussioni dal 4 maggio 1936 al 18 marzo 1937, Prima sessione, Tornata del 7 maggio 1936.

65  ACS, PCM 1934–1936, 3.2.2 protocollo 1397, *Lettera di Dino Alfieri a Luigi Freddi, dated 15 May 1937*.
66  *Camerata* Maraini. ATTI PARLAMENTARI, Legislatura XXIX Discussioni dal 4 Maggio 1936 al 18 Marzo 1937, Prima Sessione—Discussioni—Tornata Del 7 Maggio 1936, *Discussione del disegno di legge: Stato di previsione della spesa del Ministero della stampa e propaganda per l'esercizio finanziario dal 1 luglio 1936 al 30 giugno 1937*.
67  ACS, PCM 1934–1936, Fascicolo 3.2.2, protocollo 1397.
68  Freddi, Luigi 1936, "Rapporto sulla cinematografia italiana", in *Lo Schermo*, II, vol. 1, January, p. 11.
69  Ibid.
70  Goebbels as reported in the introduction by L. Lochner to Goebbels, Joseph, 1948, *Diari intimi*, Milan: Mondadori.
71  Petley, Julian 1979, *German Cinema 1933–45*, London: BFI, p. 53.
72  "As long as the banks prefer to install pastry shops and make Christmas cakes, obstinately refusing to take an interest in this extremely important sector of the economy and national prestige, Italy will never be able to get the respectful attention of the production and commercial sphere of the cinema", Argo 18 November 1934, "Cinematografia", *Il cinema e le banche*, p. 2.
73  Official Statute of S.A.C.C., art. 2.
74  L'industria cinematografica italiana negli ultimi dieci anni, in *Almanacco del cinema italiano*, pp. 24–25.
75  ACS, Fondo Minculpop, busta 68 "Rapporti sulla situazione industria cinematografica 1931–1945", 2ff sul Centro Sperimentale di Cinematografia.
76  Ibid.
77  Editorial in the first edition of Bianco e Nero.
78  R.D.L 13 febbraio 1936, n.891, ACS, Fondo PCM 1934–36, fasc. 14.1, protocollo 4677.
79  Roncoroni, Carlo 15 maggio 1936, "Cinematografia", *Il discorso Roncoroni alla Camera. Compiti e Realta` del cinema in Italia*, p. 1.
80  Ibid.

## Bibliography

ALBORNOZ, Facundo, VANIN, Paolo 2010, "Trade Protection and Industrial Structure", *The B.E Journal of Economic Analysis and Policy*, 10 (1): Article 57, 1–29

AMITI, Mari, KONINGS, Joep 2005, "Trade Liberalization, Intermediate Inputs, and Productivity: Evidence from Indonesia", *IMF Working Papers* 5/146

AMITI, Mari, WEI, Shang-Jin 2005, "Fear of Service Outsourcing: Is It Justified?", *Economic Policy* 20 (42) (Oct): 308–347

BAGELLA, Michele, BECCHETTI, Leonardo 1999, "The Determinants of Motion Picture Box Office Performance: Evidence from Movies Produced in Italy", *Journal of Cultural Economics*, 23: 237–256

BAKKER, Gerben 2008, *Entertainment Industrialised—The Emergence of the International Film Industry*, Cambridge, UK: Cambridge University Press

_____. 2005, "The Decline and Fall of the European Film Industry: Sunk Costs, Market Size, and Market Structure, 1890–1927", *Economic History Review*, 58 (2): 310–351

_____. 2004, "Stars and Stories: How Films Became Branded Products", in SEDGWICK, John, POKORNY, Michael (eds.), 2004, *An Economic History of Film*, London: Routledge, pp. 461–502

BALIO, Tino (ed.) 1985, *The American Film Industry*, Madison: University of Wisconsin Press

BAUMOL, William, BOWEN, William 1966, *Performing Arts, The Economic Dilemma: a study of problems common to theater, opera, music, and dance*, New York: Twentieth Century Fund

BEN-GHIAT, Ruth 2000, *La cultura fascista*, Bologna: Il Mulino

BLAUG, Mark, KING, Karen 1976, "Does the arts council know what it is doing?" in Blaug, Mark (ed.), *The economics of the arts*, London: Martin Robertson, pp. 101–125

BRUNETTA, Gian Piero 1975, *Cinema italiano fra le due guerre. Fascismo e politica cinematografica*, Milan: Mursia

CANNISTRARO, Paul 1974, *La fabbrica del consenso. Fascismo e mass-media*, Rome-Bari: Laterza

CARBAUGH, Robert 2009, *International Economics*, Mason, OH: South-Western Cengage Learning

CHANG, Ha-Joon 2002, *Kicking Away the Ladder? Policies and Institutions for Economic Development in Historical Perspective*, London: Anthem Press

CILIBERTI, Ferruccio 1942, *Legislazione italiana per la cinematografia*, Siena: Edizioni Ex Combattenti

COLLINS, Richard 1990, *Television: Policy and Culture*, London: Unwin

CRANE, Diana, KAWASHIMA Nobuko, KAWASAKI Ken'ichi (eds.) 2002, *Global Culture: Media, Arts, Policy, and Globalization*, New York: Routledge

DOWNING, John, WARTELLA, Ellen, MCQUAIL, Denis (eds.) 2004, *The Sage Handbook of Media Studies*, London, Thousand Oaks, CA, New Dehli: Sage

FREDERICK, Howard 1992, *Global Communications & International Relations*, Belmont, CA: Wadsworth Publishing Company

FLIBBERT, Andrew 2007, *Commerce in Culture: State and Markets in the World Film Trade*, New York: Palgrave

FRAU-MEGIS, Divina 2002, "Cultural Exemption", *National Policies and Globalization: Imperatives in Democratisation and Promotion of Contemporary Culture* Quaderns del CAC (Catalan Audiovisual Council), 14: 1–16

FREDDI, Luigi 1949, *Il Cinema*, Rome: L'arnia

FREDERICK, Howard 1992, *Global Communications & International Relations*, Belmont, CA: Wadsworth Publishing Company

FREUND, Caroline, WEINHOLD, Diana 2002, "The Internet and International Trade in Services", *American Economic Review*, 92 (2): 236–240

GENTILE, Emilio 1993, *Il culto del Littorio*, Rome-Bari: Laterza

GOEBBELS, Joseph 1948, *Diari intimi*, Milan: Mondadori

GUBACK, Thomas 1969, *The International Film Industry: Western Europe and America since 1945*, Bloomington: Indiana University Press

HIGSON, Andrew, MALTBY, Richard 1999, 'Film Europe' and 'Film America': Cinema, Commerce and Cultural Exchange 1920–1939, Exeter: University of Exeter Press

HILL, John 1999, *British Cinema in the 1980s*, Oxford: Oxford Unversity Press

JANSEN, Christian 2005, "The Performance of German Motion Pictures: Profits and Subsidies", *Journal of Cultural Economics*, 29: 191–212

JARVIE, Jan 1992, *Hollywood's Overseas Campaign: The North Atlantic Movie Trade, 1920–1950*, Cambridge: Cambridge University Press

KONINGS, Joep, VANDENBUSSCHE, Hylke 2004, "Antidumping Protection and Productivity Growth of Domestic Firms", *Journal of International Economics*, 65: 151–165

KRUGMAN, Paul 1986, *Strategic Trade Policy and the New International Economics*, Cambridge, MA: The MIT Press

LEE, Kim, KIM, Il 2008, "The Effect of the Korean Screen Quota System on Box Office Performance", *Journal of World Trade*, 42 (2): 335–346

LITMAN, Barry 1982, "Decision Making in the Film Industry: The Influence of the TV Market", *Journal of Communications*, 32 (3): 33–52

MARVASTI, Akbar 2000, "Motion Pictures Industry: Economics of Scale and Trade", *International Journal of the Economics of Business*, 7 (1): 99–114

MARVASTI, Akbar, CANTERBERY, Ray 2005, "Cultural and Other Barriers to Motion Pictures Trade", *Economic Inquiry*, 43 (1): 39–54

MCANANY, Emilie, WILKINSON, Kenton (eds.) 1996, *Mass Media and Free Trade: Nafta and the Cultural Industries*, Austin: University of Texas Press

MORAN, Albert (ed.) 1996, *Film Policy: International, National and Regional Perspective*, London, New York: Routledge

MOTION PICTURE ASSOCIATION OF AMERICA 2010, *Trade Barriers to Exports of U.S. Filmed Entertainment*, online publication

MULCAHY, Kevin 2002, "Cultural Imperialism and Cultural Sovereignty: U.S.-Canadian Cultural Relations", *The Journal of Arts Management, Law, and Society*, 31 (4) (Winter): 265–278

NORDENSTRENG, Kaarle, SCHILLER, Herbert (eds.) 1979, *National Sovereignty and International Communication*, Norwood, NJ: Ablex Publishing

OH, Jeongho 2001, "Internation trade in films and the self sufficiency ratio", *Journal of Media Economics*, 14 (1): 31–44

PAUDEL, Krishna, DEBASIS, Mitra 1998, "Trade Liberalization, Market Discipline and Productivity Growth: New Evidence from India", *Journal of Development Economics*, 56 (2): 447–462

PAVCNIK, Nina 2002, "Trade Liberalization, Exit, and Productivity Improvements: Evidence from Chilean Plants", *Review of Economic Studies*, 69: 245–276

PETLEY, Julian 1979, *German Cinema 1933–45*, London: BFI

QUAGLIETTI, Lorenzo 1975, "Il cinema degli anni trenta in Italia: primi elementi per una analisi politico-strutturale", Various Authors, *Materiali sul cinema italiano 1929/1943*, Quaderno informativo della mostra del nuovo cinema, 63, Pesaro

REDI, Riccardo, CAMERINI, Claudio (eds.) 1958, *Cinecittà I: industria e mercato nel cinema italiano tra le due guerre*, Quaderni della mostra internazionale del Nuovo Cinema di Pesaro, Padova: Marsilio

SAGGI, Kamal, PACK, Howard 2006, "Is There a Case for Industrial Policy? A Critical Survey", *World Bank Research Observer* 21 (2): 267–297

SCITOVSKY, Tibor 1976, *The joyless economy: an inquiry into human satisfaction and consumer dissatisfaction*, Oxford: Oxford University Press

_____. 1972, "What is wrong with the arts is what's wrong with society", *American Ecnomics Review*, 62 (2): 62–69

SEDGWICK, John, POKORNY, Michael, (eds.) 2004, *An Economic History of Film. Routledge*, London: Routledge

SEGRAVE, Kerry 1997, *American Films Abroad: Hollywood's Domination of the World's Movie Screens from the 1890's to the Present*, Jefferson, NC: McFarland

SIAE 1937, *Lo spettacolo in Italia*, Rome: Società Italiana degli Autori e degli Editori

THOMPSON, Kristin 1985, *Exporting Entertainment: America in the World Film market 1907–1934*, London: British Film Institute

TREFLER, Daniel 2004, "The Long and Short of the Canada-U.S. Free Trade Agreement", *American Economic Review*, 94: 870–895

UNESCO 1982, *Cultural Industries: A Challenge for the Future of Culture*, Paris: Unesco

VENERUSO, Danilo 1981, *L'Italia fascista. Storia d'Italia dal Risorgimento alla Repubblica. IV Volume*, Bologna: Il Mulino

WILDMAN, Steven 1995, "Trade Liberalization and Policy for Media Industries: A Theoretical Examination of Media Flows", *Canadian Journal of Communication*, 20 (3): 367–388

WILDMAN, Steven S., SIWEK, Stephen E. 1993, "The economics of trade in recorded media products in a multilingual world: Implications for national media policies", in Noam, Eli M., Millonzi, Joel C. (eds.), *The international marked in film and television programs*, Norwood, NJ: Ablex, pp. 13–40

ZAGARRIO, Vito 2006, "Schizofrenie del modello fascista", in Caldiron, Orio, *Storia del cinema italiano 1934–1939*, Rome: Edizioni Bianco e Nero

_____. 2004, *Cinema e fascismo. Film, modelli, immaginari*, Venice: Marsilio

# 4   "We Can Be Like Hollywood"

An Italian film industry really exists and works.
It has three production plants, twelve movie cameras.
three sound systems . . .
and more than five hundred artistic and technical workers.
God bless Stefano Pittaluga.[1]

## A New Technological Breakthrough: The Advent of Sound Film

At the end of the decade, the state-of-the-art of European movie industries was much more complicated than ever because of both the external and the internal forces at play. The Great Depression and the subsequent political upheavals have shaken European economies. Individual nations drew back from international co-operation and erected barriers in attempts to protect their own economies. National industries tried to raise exports and lower imports.

Sound film arrived after the structural consolidation of the entire film production chain (production, distribution, exhibition), when cinema had begun working towards cultural legitimation by developing a critical and aesthetic discussion. The aim was to provide cinema with the solid theoretical foundations it needed to overcome its long-standing inferiority complex in relation to the traditional arts, especially theatre, music, dance and literature.

*Don Juan*, the first talking picture, was shown to public acclaim on 15 August 1926 at the Warner Theatre in New York. This sparked a new patents war between production companies, eager to convert to the new technology and defend their market positions.

In the first difficult years of the film industry, technology had always been fundamentally important for progress. From the outset, the technical aspect of the cinema had attracted attention: the public was captivated by the incredible new techniques. After the initial stage, there was a lack of technological innovation during the first decade of the 1900s, and attention was concentrated on narrative innovations: cinema no longer represented just itself but began to tell stories. The introduction of longer films provided more possibilities for telling a story on the screen, allowing a more complete narrative "beyond" that of a simple image.

Films with sound and colour were from the outset seen as a way to increase the public's perception of reality, since real life was in sound and colour. No film show had ever been completely silent (the very first film shows were accompanied by a pianist or organist), but the first great innovation was sound and picture synchronization.

The consequences of this second technological leap (the first was the passage from short to long movies) forward affected the entire production chain, especially production and exhibition. The introduction of sound film required huge investments to convert film studios and install the new and sophisticated technology. Incandescent lighting replaced noisier arc-lighting, cine cameras had to be silent, and there was a need to create new professional figures (sound technicians). From the creative point of view, the integration of sound and images transformed the development of screenplays, and many actors had to adapt their artistic skills to a new form of acting; some discovered that their voices were not "phonogenic".

On the European markets, talking film created two problems. The first was that it required investing heavily in new recording and projection systems, and the second concerned linguistic barriers; the production system now had to deal with the expense of adapting films to different national markets, which generated forms of nationalism aimed at defending the domestic film industry. This marked the beginning of the national film industries.

European audiences greeted American films with catcalls, and Great Britain and France actually banned them, because the public disliked the strong accents of the US actors. This opened a great window of opportunity for European film industries to develop their output, which had not always been adequately exploited thus far.

Before subtitles and dubbing were introduced, producers had to find strategies to overcome the problem of distributing their films on the international circuit, but these were expensive and not always satisfactory. There were the so-called multiple versions; the same story was shot in different languages in the same studio, changing actors and sometimes film director.[2] Sound film built barriers between nations in a much more effective way than any customs duty.[3]

During the 1929 Paris Conference of Cinema Exhibitors (and the subsequent 1930 Brussels meeting), sound had become the major issue since it was an obstacle to exports and to the very existence of national movie industries. Multiple-language productions were discussed as possible solutions to overcome language and cultural barriers. Multiple-language films shared the same plot but were shot with actors able to speak the appropriate language for a specific foreign market. This strategy was progressively abandoned after a few years when dubbing was technically improved and became cheaper. The language issue, however, was not completely overcome and the sense of national and cultural identity became even stronger, as the French case demonstrates: "the audience of the popular houses only want to hear films speaking French and they are quite right too. The vast cinema-going public of Paris, the provinces and the colonies, will not tolerate having its eardrums assaulted by the sounds of an incomprehensible language". Sound showed that audiences preferred movies from their own country, and Europe cultural diversity was a delicate matter. In 1932, Erich Pommer declared: "The international talking film is an accomplished fact. It was thought that the internationality of silence could not be adequately replaced by the national limitation of language. The spoken word appeared to have become an insurmountable barrier. It was considered that the end of the international film had arrived and at the same time this is the end of film as the incomparable medium of culture and propaganda that it had been".[4]

The increased production costs due to the new technology and the uncertainty of success on single markets made it even more strategically important to occupy the international markets with a widespread distribution network. The challenges of international competition led many European countries to define commercial and cultural policies for the cinema, in order to defend both market shares and their national culture and identity. During the 1930s, the events most closely involving the film industry were therefore very much interconnected with political and social events.

Adaptation to the new technology was a slow process in Italy, and for several years silent and sound films continued to coexist alongside each other because the capital needed to invest in technological conversion was not always available.[5] Besides this, there was a stock of silent films still waiting to be shown, and this delayed the introduction of sound technology in the cinemas. At the start of 1929, not one single cinema had the technology to show sound films, and in 1930 only 4% had converted. At the end of 1929, only 18% of cinemas in Europe were able to project sound films; the first to convert were the first-run cinemas in cities, followed by the smaller cinemas. In Europe, Great Britain converted most rapidly to the new sound technology (22% of cinemas in 1929; 63% by the end of 1930). Germany was slower, and it was only in 1932 that 60% of German cinemas were ready to project talkies. The percentages rose in the following years: 15% in 1931, 32% in 1932, and 43% in 1933. Between 1934 and 1935, all cinemas converted to sound technology. This created the same economic problems everywhere, since it involved spending large amounts of money on making the films and on installing the new technology in the studios and cinemas.

In Italy, the first production company to release a completely talking film was SASP, *Società Anonima Stefano Pittaluga*, which seemed to have understood "the rebirth of national possibilities with sound, and the artistic advantages of sound for the cinema".[6]

The documents used for reconstructing the economic magnitude of the Italian film industry are the same for analysing the silent film era. The greater quantity of official statistics makes it easier to do research on the number of companies in the three branches of the movie value chain, the number of films produced each year, the quantity of films imported and exported, lists of technical and artistic staff, consumption statistics. The public received information about the quantitative aspects of the film industry from the *almanacchi* (albums), which became an indication of the sector's liveliness and endless output, and also of beneficial state intervention in favour of reviving the cinema, since cinema was perceived as a powerful social instrument, equalled only by the press. Although the statistical data of the time is more systematic, some gaps and doubts remain; abundant information about certain companies often accompanies a lack of sources for other companies, especially the smaller ones.

In order to give an idea of the Italian film industry at the introduction of sound film, a total of 12 films were made in 1930–1931, including one silent film. In the following season, the number rose to 13, from 1932–1933 it rose to 25, and in 1934–1935 the number was 30. This was too small a number to be the base for a revival of the Italian film industry. In addition, these were seen as poor-quality films, produced with the sole aim of making money.

The industry structure was not greatly different from the previous period, at least in the number of companies and the number of so-called meteoric companies.

Between 1930 and 1945, a total of 255 production companies formed (which made a total of 945 films); 52% were short-lived companies speculative ventures that produced just one film (Graph 4.1, below), accounting for 14% of total output.

The short-lived companies registered the highest percentages of the total number in the years between 1934 and 1938, when they accounted for 39% and 29% of the market respectively (with a peak of 42% in 1936).

It is plausible that the measures favouring the film industry contained in Law no.1143 (13 June 1935) encouraged the formation of these production companies, whose principal aim was to gain access to state funding.

Another factor to consider when explaining the constant presence of meteoric companies during this period is the so-called "*contingentamento*", the quota system limiting the number of foreign films imported and obliging

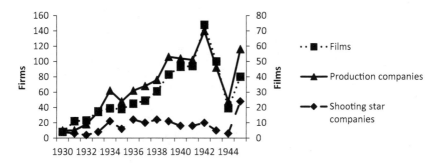

*Graph 4.1* Italian Cinema Production Companies, 1930–1945.

Source: author's elaboration on Bernardini.

exhibitors to dedicate a certain share of the programme to Italian films (cf. Law no.1121/16 June 1927).

Another aspect similar to the silent film era that was analysed in the previous chapters is capital investment in the sector. Taking the companies whose share capital is documented, it emerges that 62% were formed with a capital of 500,000 lire, and that 16% had a share capital equal to 1 million lire. Apart from Pittaluga, (whose capital amounted to 100 million lire) and some projects promoted by the government, like LUCE (L'Unione Cinematografica Educativa), the average amount of share capital was 800,000 lire. In general, the greater its share capital, the longer the company survived and the more films it produced. Phoebus Film was formed in 1938 with a capital of 10,000 lire, and made just one film; Itala Film was founded in 1937 with a capital of 300,000 lire, and was active on the Italian market until 1955, producing 22 films; Scalera was formed in 1938 with a share capital of 1 million lire, and produced a total of 68 films until 1951. However, a share capital of hundreds of thousands of lire was not always synonymous with productivity, confirming that the container alone was not enough without content. Companies with a share capital of 500,000 lire generally had greater production capacity. The total amount of capital invested in the industry was considered insufficient to revive production, especially since films were now more expensive to make. In order to compete with the other film industries, small investments of four or five hundred thousand lire were no longer seen as possible. Big productions needed budgets of over a million lire, and could require as much as 8 million, as in the case of *Scipione l'Africano*. Yet, despite these declarations of intent, industry experts declared that company survival depended on spending no more than 700,000 lire for each film produced. Although there was an apparently widespread belief that a big budget was synonymous with quality and box office success, economic and market constraints imposed limits on production costs.

The technological innovation of talking films certainly revolutionised the production process, but it must be remembered that Italian cinema was already in recession before sound film was patented: after the disastrous collapse of the Unione Cinematografica Italian, only one single company was still active at the end of the 1920s. The greatest problem lay in production capacity and consequently in the possibility of exploiting economies of scale that would ensure production on a larger scale. However, Italian companies were unable to release more than two or three films a season. The exception was SASP, which was the only big company and could produce 15 films a year, but only until 1934. The situation was similar in other European countries (Germany, France and England), which found themselves in the same situation of inferiority to the United States during the 1920s. Hollywood's competitive advantage lay in large-scale production, enabled by its quintessential production model: the consolidated Studio System. The American market during the sound era was dominated by the five majors (a.k.a. the "Big Five), i.e. Metro-Goldwyn-Mayer (MGM), Warner Bros, Paramount, 20th Century Fox, and Radio-Keith-Orpheum (RKO); all except RKO have survived to this day. Each major had its own buildings housing film studios and all the post-production processes. It had a stable pool of technical and artistic staff under contract, and had its own precise artistic policy for genre and style. The market strength of these big studios depended on controlling distribution channels in the USA and abroad and the first-run cinema circuits. In the 1930s, competition with American cinema was a daily topic in ministry offices and in advertising; Hollywood was the industrial, technical and commercial model *par excellence*. Everyone appeared eager to learn the American lesson, and scapegoats were blamed for the mistakes of the past. Producers were the first to come under attack, accused mostly of being incapable of technical and artistic innovation, since their primary objective was to make money for themselves. In similar situations, for example the French film industry, no tendency can be seen towards vertical integration of production companies as a result of sound film: large distributors like Gaumont were now only marginally involved in production, and their profits mostly depended on the success of American films. According to the trade press, the French market was full of short-lived companies, and although France had produced films "with first-grade artistic and technical qualities, worthy of universal admiration", it still did not have the organisation needed to resolve the cinema's industrial problem: "the so-called film industrialists are merely people without any idea of capitalism or organisation, who go into production unprepared, forming a company often with just the legally minimum capital destined to the first advertisement proclaiming production of a *superfilm*. Short-lived companies spring up, multiply and collapse without leaving a trace, except for their creditors. Their intentions are not very serious, their unilateral vision of the industry sees only speculation, their means are insufficient and their energy is dispersed. The problem: the lack of Government intervention. The possibilities of development for the film industry are industrial, spiritual and healthy government protection".[7]

This lack of integration between production and distribution prevented producers from expanding their activities on a larger scale and did not help to reduce the fragmentation of the European markets, even more divided now that sound film had reduced the export potential of films.

## To the Rescue: "One Day A Great Company Was Founded"[8]

> The Italian film industry once led the way in artistic production, but was defeated by the Americans, French and Germans, and disappeared from the market. However, a great company was founded; Pittaluga Films began to produce excellent films and what is more important, they were very commercial.[9]

The history of Società Anonima Stefano Pittaluga (SASP) covers a period of about 20 years from its foundation in 1919 to 1936 when it went into liquidation.

The history of SASP presents impressively interwoven political, economic and cultural interests among the entrepreneur, the state, the bank. On the one hand, fascism elected Pittaluga as the "national champion", the saviour of the Italian film industry. COMIT, which means the bank, was left with the task of managing this heavy and difficult burden and the many problems involving the creation of *ad hoc* financial tools for evaluating a new art like the cinema. Cines was seen as the means whereby Italian output and quality would be improved; it was surely destined to become a breeding ground for talent.

What is certain is that Pittaluga and his company's activity aroused contrasting feelings within the film industry: detractors criticised him for his ambiguous behaviour and choices that were apparently directed more at distributing American films than at increasing Italian film production. Supporters, on the other hand, claimed that SASP strategies completely reflected not only with the interests of the company itself but also, and especially, national interests. The creation of a chain of cinemas should not be interpreted as an attempt to obtain a monopoly, but rather as the farsighted creation of organisational structures able to withstand the American competition.

SASP is an interesting case and provides many elements for analysis and reflection: its role in reviving the fortunes of the Italian film industry, the challenge of technological innovation (the advent of sound film), the failed "transplant" of the studio system model, the problem of funding and investment evaluation, its organisational complexities, its artistic and stylistic/ expressive deficits. The history of Pittaluga is certainly an interesting business history, but also illustrates the interaction of economic and cultural factors, political and artistic factors, with the creation of production studios capable of competing on the international markets. The process of identifying links and interpretation will not be linear, not least because the documents about Cines-Pittaluga have been dispersed.

Stefano Pittaluga began working in 1919 as a distributor and then moved into production, firstly with the purchase of FERT (1922) and Rodolfi Film (1923) and then with Cines in 1926, one of the longest-lived Italian production companies. The purchase of Cines was one of the most significant events, because from then on the history of Pittaluga's company became part of the political/ cultural context and the wider history of the Italian cinema. For about a decade, SASP coincided with the entire film industry, since it was one of the very few companies to stay active at a time of great difficulty for the Italian film sector. All that remained were a few dozen production companies, producing the same number of films per year.

Before World War I, Italy had occupied a position of international importance, covering 20% of the German market, while American films covered 25% and French films 30%.[10]

The war ended a period of growing production, and the attempt to combat the Hollywood invasion with UCI (a consortium of producers, distributors and exhibitors) had failed miserably after only four years. Many Italian actors, technicians and directors emigrated abroad, especially to Germany, in search of better working conditions.

Cines-Pittaluga was therefore a driving force for the Italian film industry, "a unique example of a studio with production facilities, stable management, and intervention and development plans". [11] This was where industrial reorganisation came together with the ideological needs for the creation of an Italian style of cinema. The studios in Via Vejo symbolically expressed the fascist intention to use the cinema as a means of transforming the Italian people, and the films made there show the difficulties involved in creating an authentic national cinema. They demonstrate the search for a balance between the commercial demands of the box office and political dictates, a combination of "the desire to entertain as well as to persuade". [12] According to Brunetta, Pittaluga was the only entrepreneur able to understand the problems of the Italian film industry, with a modern and international approach to business strategy. [13] Another cinema historian, Lorenzo Quaglietti, was less positive in his judgement; he considered Pittaluga to be excessively idealised, overlooking the fact that "his business initiative corresponded to Government lines". [14] The same variety of opinions is found among Pittaluga's contemporary admirers and detractors.

Pittaluga began working in the film industry as a small rental agent for Liguria within the family business company "Pittaluga e Tassoni". The first foreign films were distributed in 1912, and came from Denmark (4), Germany (13), Italy (21) and the USA (2). After World War I he moved to Turin and founded Società Anonima Stefano Pittaluga. Some commentators believed that Pittaluga stood apart from the other companies in the film sector because it was the first "serious and honest" company in Italy, unlike all the other ventures inspired by speculation that continued to spring up.

The company gradually succeeded in creating a chain of cinemas throughout the country: Veneto, Friuli, Piemonte, Liguria, Lombardy, Emilia Romagna, Tuscany, Lazio, Sicily and Campania. Società Anonima Stefano Pittaluga was officially formed on 19 March 1919 with a share capital of 2,000,000 lire, divided between Stefano Pittaluga (800 shares), and Vittorio Sacerdote, Levi Ottavio, Artom Vittorio, Ferrero Giovanni, Chiarella Achille, Levi Cesare, Molineri Luigi, Marco Carlo, Luca Attilio (each with 120 shares). The aim of the company was to buy, sell and rent cinema films", while cinema purchase, sale and rental was entrusted to the Società Anonima Immobiliare Toscana, formed in1921 "with a share capital of one million has Pittaluga as its Managing Director". Anonima Immobiliare, which will return below as the Società Anonima Immobiliare Cinematografica Italian (SAICI), absorbed the FERT studios and Itala film complex, which became the SASP management headquarters. [15]

At the end of the 1920s, Pittaluga's empire included around 200 cinemas (under direct management or rented) and supplies films to more than 1,500 cinemas throughout the country. [16]

This created plenty of bad feeling in the industry; cinema owners accused the company of exercising a total monopoly and protested that SASP managed to grab the best European and American films. The cinema magazines warned about the danger of a monopoly. [17] On the contrary, some saw

Pittaluga's strategy as essential for dealing with the American competition. "Pittaluga understood that his time had come: the time in which the first brave man to forge ahead would be an easy winner. His desire for victory was perfectly human. Who should he have allowed to take the prize? His Italian rivals? Even worse: his foreign competitors?".[18]

After consolidating rental and cinema management, Pittaluga concentrated on film production. First, he reopened the studios belonging to FERT and Rodolfi Film of Turin, and then bought the Cines studios, which meant that the company could begin making sound films, since the studios had been fitted with sound technology.[19]

Pittaluga also consolidated other sectors connected with the film industry: the chemical industry and printing/publishing. His dominant approach was directed towards vertical integration of all the sectors connected with film production and use. It was therefore strategic for the company to develop and print the film copies needed for the cinema chain, and also to print every kind of paper material: tickets, posters, *bordereaux*, magazines, books, musical scores, circulars, *leaflets* (veline) and writing paper. It became especially necessary to consolidate all these sectors after Pittaluga bought up the *Unione cinematografica italiana* in 1926.

The choice of backward vertical integration was probably due to the far-sightedness that his contemporaries recognised in Pittaluga. Until then, SASP had dealt with the sectors of the film production chain in closest contact with the public. A cinema owner knew his audience's tastes and used this to make up his programme of films: backward vertical integration meant that Pittaluga would be able to produce films that could then be distributed in the cinemas on his own widespread chain. Pittaluga "knew well how a film worked on the emotions of an Italian crowd, because he knew how the crowd worked, what made it tick".[20]

Pittaluga appeared to have very clear ideas about the kind of cinema the public loved and appreciated most:

> The real cinema, that fills seats, that makes the crowd sob and saves box office takings does not consist of exceptional films or films based on everyday life. The audience want to get away from reality, they want to escape, dream and feel like millionaires.[21]

SASP did not follow a particularly creative line with its productions; it always attempted to make films that would be commercially successful, and, in some cases, it tended to propose films that had been successful abroad in order to minimise the risks of distribution. Pittaluga himself stated the need to follow this direction in his 1923 Report: "We intend to make artistic productions, but principally to do commercial work".[22] This rather ambiguous statement suggests the promise of improved quality in Italian cinema with a stylistic renewal, but above all it suggests the company's real interest: a sure commercial work able to ensure box office takings. Pittaluga favoured comedies, musicals, operas, and melodramas, deriving plots from literature and theatre. It was not unusual for him to intervene in the choice of actors and screenplay, making changes where he felt the film would be made more attractive to the public.

Unlike other Italian producers, SASP would never have to compete on a market where there was a total lack of cooperation between production, distribution and exhibition. The films it made would be shown in the company's own cinemas.

Returning to the reasons for Pittaluga's vertical integration, it must be recalled that the 1920s were the years when the vertically integrated Hollywood "Studios" were at the height of their success. The European cinema saw the US giants and their organisation as a model that they should imitate in order to attempt a reaction to the invasion of American films.[23] Not only did the Hollywood studios have perfectly coordinated production, distribution and exhibition operations, but they also attributed value to intangible assets and provided job security for their technical and artistic staff working under contract.

Besides the impetus that may have come from the competitive dynamics of the national and international markets, Pittaluga's choice was very probably influenced by political pressures, and by the importance given at the time to the issue of reviving the film industry. SASP's relations with fascism are still unclear, mainly due to the lack of documents; as is often the case for Italian cinema, these materials have been lost or are no longer available. However, political considerations certainly had an important role, if Pittaluga was officially given the task of saving Italian cinema and if Law no. 918 (18 June 1931) created awards for Italian films.[24] This law seemed tailor-made for SASP, as it was really the only active production company in Italy at the time.

## "L'Ollivud Semo Noi"[25] (We Can Be Like Hollywood)

SASP showed the first signs of interest in film production in the year it was founded; one of the first shareholders was *Cavaliere* Giovanni Ferrero, a large landowner, who purchased 120 shares at 1,000 lire each (a large sum out of a starting capital of 2,000,000 lire), and the following year *Ing.* Guglielmo Olivetti bought a package of 10 shares. He was given the job of creating the new studios for FERT, a production company founded in 1919 by Enrico Fiori; FERT was—as already mentioned—bought up by SASP, which in October 1923 then began to produce its own films.

The Fert-Pittaluga story is not always clear, and even after it was bought by Pittaluga, Fert produced films under its own label and under the Fert-Pittaluga label. In 1924, Fert released 10 films and one film under the joint label, in 1926 Bernardini finds one FERT film and one Fert-Pittaluga film, and also in the following year. According to Bernardini, Fert alone also produced one film in 1930.

In 1924 Pittaluga announced and distributed the following titles: *Dall'Italia all'Equatore*, *Saetta impara a vivere* and *La taverna d'America*, together with a film that was a milestone for the company's activity: *Maciste ed il nipote d'America*. In 1926, various films were presented to the public: *Beatrice Cenci*, *Il transatlantico*, *Il gigante delle Dolomiti*, *I martiri d'Italia*, *L'ultimo Lord* and *Maciste nella gabbia dei leoni*, announced as the "season's biggest hit".

Despite all the praise, and despite the advertising campaigns in "Films Pittaluga" (the company magazine), the number of films produced in that period was quite small. In addition, the titles were always the same and were offered again to the public over several seasons. The company's strongest product was the Maciste series: *Maciste all'inferno* (1926, by Guido Brignone), *Maciste contro lo sceicco* (1926, by Mario Camerini), and *Maciste nella gabbia dei leoni* (1926, by Guido Brignone). The production company clung to the myth of Maciste as a lifeline at a time when the entire film industry was in a deep crisis. Pittaluga was convinced that the Italian film industry could be revived only gradually, starting with commercial films that did not involve too much in the way of artistic experiments, since the principal objective was to re-launch the industry. Pittaluga believed that film production should be directed towards making big films with greater sales potential: "exceptional films, made with the right technical and artistic skill have all the potential for sale on any market".

> The film industry can only be revived gradually, with a new style of production that meets all the essential artistic requirements, that acquires universal appeal in its story-lines and the way it is made. In other words, it must satisfy the tastes of all audiences, and use really accomplished artists each time who can captivate not only our cinema audiences, but the entire world.[26]

According to Pittaluga's advisors, the main reason behind the collapse of Italian cinema was the difficulty of exporting films that were very Italian and not sufficiently international. Besides this, the war years had seen an increase in production companies in the large cities, leading to overproduction. The problem was further aggravated because the films were generally unable to find an outlet abroad. When they did succeed, it was clear that "they were poor quality goods, so that the few Italian films that managed to cross the frontiers gave foreign audiences the impression that "the Italian film industry had not kept up with the times and with the changes in audience tastes".[27]

This was the national situation, but on the pages of its own magazine (Films Pittaluga), SASP had assured its readers of a direct and constant commitment to restore Italian cinema to its former glory; proof came when the FERT studios were re-opened and film production was restarted. Pittaluga had never made a secret of his approach to reviving the industry, based on the conviction that international cooperation was important and necessary for maintaining friendly and useful relations with the foreign countries producing films.

Pittaluga did not consider a total boycott of foreign films to be necessary, because even if "Italian films were at the peak of quantity or quality, we would still need foreign films, if only to ensure product variety and to keep us abreast of technical and artistic advances". The best way to fight the Italian and European crisis was to establish "a programme of agreements to increase the earning potential of the film. The European crisis is serious, and the different European countries, taken separately, are weaker than America, but this could change completely if the principal film-producing countries were to form an artistic, technical and financial partnership for making films".[28] SASP had always boasted of its international cooperation, and its magazine celebrated the distribution of Italian films, but especially of international films.

Pittaluga was one of the promoters of the so-called *Film Europe*, an attempt to contrast Hollywood avalanche during the '20s.

The first practical step for the establishment of Film Europe was a contract of mutual distribution agreement signed during summer of 1924 between the German *Ufa* and *Etablissements Aubert*, one of the biggest French distributors: they exchanged distribution rights for France and Belgium with those for Germany and Central Europe.

The mutual agreement was different from the typical distribution contract[29] since it was based upon the willingness to open markets for a two-way exchange. Eric Pommer, head of *Ufa* and the main supporter of this pact, was considered as a potential leader in a pan-European industry: "I think that European producers must at least think of establishing a certain cooperation among themselves. It is imperative to establish a system of regular trade which will enable the producers to amortize their films rapidly."[30] On the French part, the contract was seen as something important for future plans, as Louis Aubert pointed out: "European cinema will, alongside preservation and highlighting of the respective national identities, together form a uniform whole which can counter the superior competition of America. We are not opposed to America, but we also want our place in the sun, as we deserve."[31]

In 1928, Pittaluga signed a co-production agreement with *Terra Film*, an important production company. Ludwig Klizsch, the director of *Ufa*, commented: "A European film cartel is actually established now. The German-Italian agreement was only an incidental step in a whole series of general European agreements. A number of leading film enterprises in important European film countries has joined to form a solid front against America in order to be able to negotiate on terms of equality with the greatest film factory in the world."[32] This was part of a larger project designed at European level to establish a "planned film economy". Big movies would have been financed according to a formula based upon the distribution potential of each country: 22% for Britain, 18% for Germany, 16% for France, 10% for Italy, 12% for Scandinavia, 12% for Austria, and the remaining 10% falling to the country of origin.[33]

Pittaluga also understood that the Italian movie sector might have remained small, local and declining without competition from foreign films. Such competition would have spurred creativity and allowed Italian films to compete in the international arena.

At this point, it is possible to begin seeing the problems that company decisions created for the Italian market. Since SASP was one of the few—if not the only—production company with a similar structure to the vertically integrated studios, it was seen as the vehicle for reviving the Italian film industry. However, it also had the interests of a private company, with the apparent aim of producing films as long as this activity should prove sustainable. Pittaluga would never give up his interests in distribution at a time when cinemas were flourishing thanks to foreign films, and film production could not ensure immediate profits. "All film markets are organised, or are getting organised, in a system of cinema chains, firstly because producers have the right to know more or less how many film runs they can count on, and then because it is impossible in Italy to establish any unified and orderly internal organisation, whereas we see the Americans reaching out towards the cinemas, not only those in their own country".[34]

According to Pittaluga's critics, his cinema chain was used not so much to ensure a guaranteed commercial outlet for Italian films, but for the "loved and hated" American films.[35]

From the entrepreneurial point of view, the principal evils of the Italian film industry were fiscal pressure, taxes, and the customs duties on imported films. So it is no surprise that Pittaluga made sure he became President of the *Federazione nazionale industriali, commercianti film ed esercenti cinema,* (National Federation of Industrialists, Film Exhibitors and Cinema Operators), or that it was Pittaluga who brought to Government attention the Federazione's requests as they emerged from three congresses held between 1923 and 1926. The requests hinged on the following points: no protectionism or special film quota law could miraculously revive the Italian film industry; it was necessary to create a commercial organisation abroad and to involve foreign capital in producing Italian films; production standards needed improvements to align with the artistic and technical standards of international films; cinema owners' needs should be considered; producers should have the same access to credit from the banks as other industries. Pittaluga considered the cinema an international industry in need of continuous and constant exchanges and inputs. Foreign films were fundamentally important for Italian cinema, not just for the cinemas to survive, but above all to improve the standard of Italian films and make them more competitive.

Pittaluga was received by the Minister of Finance, Volpi di Misurata, and insisted on the proposal. Volpi's exact answer is not known, but it must have been negative because there was no reduction in fiscal pressure. Given the lack of Government support, Pittaluga stressed that the current situation did not allow any planning of large-scale film production.[36] Pittaluga also added that it would be counterproductive to compete with the US film industry at a time when Italian cinema was in crisis. SASP managed to obtain exclusive distribution rights for many films from the major American studios. The pages of "Films Pittaluga" were full of American cinema idols, and the public grew fond of Hollywood stars: Buster Keaton, Douglas Fairbanks, Rodolfo Valentino, Pola Negri, Charlie Chaplin and many more. The message was very clear: for the time being, given the stagnation of the Italian film industry, survival was impossible without American films. During the 1929–1930 season, Pittaluga's catalogue contained around 140 titles; only six were Italian (produced by Cines), a very small number for launching a revival of the Italian film industry. The other titles came from the following countries: Great Britain (16 films from British International Pictures), United States (89 films of which 50 from Warner Bros-First National, 25 from Universal and 14 from P.D.C), other European countries including France and Germany (a total of 29).

> Pittaluga needs to understand, once and for all, that making two or three films does not resolve anything at all, and does not give anyone the authority to talk of a revival.[37]

Although Pittaluga was described as a sensible businessman, able to defend the national prestige of Italian cinema, it was also possible to view him as an industrialist attracted by mere profit rather than by the ideals of reviving the film industry.

Clearly, Società Pittaluga also profited from distributing foreign films— which was not always to the liking of the regime. In 1928, the firm had exclusive distribution rights to 50 films from Universal Studios, 30 from First National and Warner Brothers, 25 from Producers Distributing Corporation, as well as 47 German, 17 French, and four English films. *Uncle's Tom Cabin* (Universal), *The Desired Woman* (Warner Bros.), *La passion de Jeanne d'Arc* (Société Génèral de Films), and *Das Mädchen Der Straße* (Nero Film, Germany) were some of the titles he imported that were successful in the Italian market. While Pittaluga was pressured by the government to produce films, he knew that the distribution of foreign films were indispensable to the profitability of his company.[38] In order to encourage the public acceptance of foreign-language films, Pittaluga even created a dubbing facility at Società Pittaluga plants and he equipped cinemas with the necessary sound technology.[39]

Clearly, Pittaluga wanted to defend his commercial interests. However, he was under pressure from the regime to be the saviour of Italian film.[40] The bank, BCI, would have preferred to judge Pittaluga's results on the basis of efficiency and the ability to generate income and repay investors.

Nevertheless, it was clear to bank management that significant losses had to be sustained for political reasons.[41]

## UCI-Pittaluga and the New Cines-Pittaluga

Pittaluga's debut in film production is linked to the story of the *Unione Cinematografica Italiana* (UCI), a consortium of producers formed in 1919 with financial backing from the Banca Commerciale Italiana and the Banca Italiana di Sconto (BIS). The consortium aimed to "unify defensive action against foreign competition, around a powerful technical and financial group. The company promoters intended it to have a monopoly in Italy to ensure the wider conquest of international markets and to compete with the other powerful world organisations formed by collaboration between gigantic financial bodies, especially in Germany and America".[42]

During the COMIT Board meeting on 20 December 1922, the UCI already appeared to be in a state of difficulty needing urgent and radical reorganisation. On 31 December 1924 it was decided to go into liquidation. In September 1926, Banca Commerciale Italiana entrusted Rag. Angelo Piperno, an accountant, with the task of writing a report on the UCI's financial situation, in order to proceed towards the merger of "*Unione Cinematografica Italiana* and *Società Anonima Stefano Pittaluga*".[43] The main reasons for the UCI's failure were the collapse of the BIS and weaknesses in its own accounting, administration and finances; UCI closed down in September 1926.[44]

In a letter to the Managing Director, Angelo Piperno—given the job of evaluating the assets of the moribund UCI—stressed the need to continue negotiations with the SASP:[45] "I also want to talk in person to illustrate what I consider to be very favourable reasons for a possible fusion with the *Società Anonima Pittaluga*. I have advocated this and I have worked to re-open the negotiations; these are now in process, and I am participating actively as instructed by Ing. Garbagni". According to Piperno, Pittaluga appeared to have all the qualities considered essential in a production manager: "organisational ability, culture, especially regarding history, literature and art, indisputable technical competence and irreproachable honesty".[46]

According to Piperno, Pittaluga seemed the only entrepreneur capable of resolving a problem that was both economic and also political: "I confess that I don't feel able to examine the possibility and the advantage of industrial recovery of production *by the UCI* (our italics) . . . however, it is certain that, for reasons of evident economic necessity, and for a lofty question of prestige and political advantage, restarting production is advisable and can be profitable".[47] The documents in the Banca Commerciale Italiana archives do not totally clarify the motives for the UCI-Pittaluga merger. Perhaps the most plausible explanation can be found in the last few lines of Piperno's report, where he talks about economic necessities (for the bank) and also about prestige and political advantage, since the UCI had signed a contract with the Istituto LUCE for an "industrial partnership to produce some historical or moral narrative films". For this reason, it seemed at least advisable to re-start production, despite "the 60 million lire of bank credit which makes it impossible for the company to be financially flexible, and which unequivocally threatens its balance sheet".[48]

*Films Pittaluga* celebrated the potential of the UCI, predicting that SASP would become one of the most important film organisations in Italy and Europe. A broad programme was announced for every branch of activity. Film exhibition and cinemas would be consolidated to ensure better use of the films and to increase audience figures, production would improve in artistic quality, and the company would apply solid management criteria.

The new Cines-Pittaluga studios were officially opened in May 1930 in the presence of Minister Bottai with a ceremony officially recognising Pittaluga's role in reviving the film industry.

During the ceremony, Pittaluga said that the movie industry was a difficult and risky one and was now dependent on help from the government. The Minister of Corporations Giuseppe Bottai replied: "Mr. Pittaluga, the film industry concerns the art, the economics and the politics of a nation. . . . We have prepared a set of benefits and laws to economically and financially help Italian movie production".[49]

Pittaluga announced production of six new films: *Cesare Augusto* "the glorification of Imperial Rome"; a *national narrative film* "the creation of fascist Italy"; *Le catacombe* "a re-evocation of Christian Rome"; *an Italian opera* "a musical film with Italian performers, orchestras and conductors"; *Figlia di re* "a modern Rome with Ancient Egypt", and a *commedia Italiana* (probably *La canzone dell'amore*) "a dialogue film with actors from the theatre and cinema". The programme actually changed several times, and the most interesting episode involves *Resurrectio* by Alessandro Blasetti, presented as the first Italian sound film; it suddenly disappeared from advertisements and was replaced by Gennaro Righelli's *La Canzone dell'Amore*. Pittaluga seems to have thought the time was not yet ripe to release an innovative psychological drama that may not have been a box-office success.

The site of the "second Cines" studios was in Via Vejo 51, the south of Rome. The recording studios were those of the first Cines founded in 1905 by Alberini and Santoni, which had been converted to sound film technology with RCA Photophone recording equipment. The new Cines-Pittaluga complex had three recording studios: two for sound film and one for silent film. Each studio had offices for technical and artistic services, dressing rooms for the actors, the bit part players and the extras. Then there were the painters, decorators, plasterers, the generator room, the machinery for the mechanical and electrical workshops, for the carpentry and the scenery store. Not to mention the synchronisation and sound projection room, a lab for developing negatives, and a restaurant that could seat 200.[50]

Once the studio buildings were finished, it was a case of completing the plan to revitalise the Italian film industry by defining a production policy.

Pittaluga's first concern was to recruit technical and artistic staff recalled from abroad. These included dressmakers, carpenters, prop managers and upholsterers, makeup artists, electricians, stagehands, mechanics and labourers. There was an editing office, a "short film" office, a "story office" and a "press" office. The personnel working on the set included: the stage manager, a set secretary, a production inspector, an editing secretary and an assistant stage manager.

Cines' artistic policy was to encourage young talents, and it sought to collaborate with Alessandro Blasetti, Aldo Vergano and Mario Serandrei from "Cinematografo" magazine (founded as "Lo Schermo"), which just a few years previously had accused it of suffocating the revival of Italian cinema. Aldo Vergano was put in charge of the Script Office, while the actors engaged included some already famous names like Ettore Petrolini, Armando Falconi, Lia Franca, Dria Pola and Isa Pola, Elio Steiner and Giorgio Bianchi, always great favourites with audiences.

However, commercial concerns always accompanied the need for artistic innovation, which explains why Cines employees recall arguments between Pittaluga and the artistic director. According to his collaborators, Pittaluga "as an industrialist, with the idea of the easiest deal, insisted on one artistic genre for all categories", and it was not unusual for him to intervene "in the choice of a storyline and details of the screenplay, scenes, editing, and especially in the choice of actors and the style of the production".[51]

Under Pittaluga's direction, the new Cines produced about ten sound films, including *Resurrectio* by Alessandro Blasetti, *La Canzone dell'Amore* by Gennaro Righelli, *Nerone* by Alessandro Blasetti, *Napoli che canta* by Mario Almirante, *Corte d'Assise* by Guido Brignone, *Medico per forza* by Carlo Campogalliani, *Terra Madre* by Alessandro Blasetti, *Rubacuori* by Guido Brignone, and *Vele ammainate* by Anton Giulio Bragaglia.

When distribution and production are compared (Table 4.1), it can be seen that SASP distributed on average 38% of the US films on the Italian market. The number of films it produced was actually very small, especially considering the potential of the Italian market and the technical equipment in the new Cines studios.

*Table 4.1* Distribution and Production Activities by SASP

| Years | American films | Distributed by SASP | Films produced by SASP |
|-------|----------------|---------------------|------------------------|
| 1930 | 234 | 98 | 4 |
| 1931 | 171 | 50 | 14 |
| 1932 | 139 | 86 | 10 |
| 1933 | 172 | 54 | 13 |
| 1934 | 172 | 52 | 2 |

Source: author's elaboration on SASP archival materials.

In the slow conversion to sound film, SASP should have considered the possibility of expanding its own export markets by attempting to produce films for an international audience and abandoning the romantic genre that found little favour with foreign audiences. Such a complex organisation could have offered "contents" more in line with public tastes, whereas it actually appears to have created a sort of discrepancy between the organisation—whose production capacity was under-used—and the films produced. Eric Hobsbawm writes that "Tastes and fashions, notably in popular entertainment, can be 'created' only within very narrow limits; they have to be discovered before being exploited and shaped".[52] Many variables affect the film market. A production company builds up its competitive advantages through control of the production chain and access to financial resources, using popular actors and actresses, and creating "stories" to entertain audiences, giving them the chance to dream. Hobsbawn claims that public tastes can be "created", i.e. influenced, but before this can be done, it is necessary to discover what they are, and then use this information to create suitable production and communication strategies. The criticisms levelled at Cines-Pittaluga in the cinema magazines were due to this lack of perception regarding cinema audience tastes. Stylistic and expressive innovation should not necessarily have produced artistically superior films that were difficult to sell, but the enhancement of artistic elements should have led to a greater awareness of the language of the cinema and of its potential. Commercial demands cannot always be reconciled with the cinema's need for artistic experimentation and development. In this context, it can be stressed that its artistic decisions were as important for Cines-Pittaluga to function as were its management, administration and organisation, at a time when the international competition focused on the quality of all the aspects making the cinema a means of expression: technical standards, acting, expression, editing, direction and photography.[53]

Few Cines-Pittaluga films produced in 1930–1931 earned more than they cost to be produced. The export area for Società Pittaluga's films included Europe, Latin America, the United States, Canada, and Australia. In most cases, the distribution contract was based on a minimum guarantee, in which the distributor pays a fixed amount to the producer for the marketing of the movie. It was non-refundable in case the movie failed to cover the minimum guaranteed amount. In the United States, Pittaluga films were licensed in a 50:50 net deal, in which all distribution costs were deducted off the top and then the net split on a 50:50 basis between the distributor and the producer, the American distributor also being paid a guaranteed minimum of $4,000. While the films were distributed across a wide geographical area, their foreign revenues were not high: apart from just a few films, like *La Canzone dell'amore* (1930), *Terra Madre* and *L'Uomo dell'artiglio* (both made in 1931).

*Terra Madre* was coproduced in Germany, with the company Atlas-film, and had clear propagandistic aims. "The subsequent return home (to the countryside) by the aristocratic hero signals not only a disillusion with and a rejection of the urban and its alien values, but also the reaffirmation/celebration of all those authentic rural values (religion, family, hierarchy, community, harmony), informing what is presented as an immutable cultural identity on which in turn the nation and nationalism depends."[54]

The movie was at best a moderate success in Germany and box office results were quite good in the United States and France. According to some cinema historians, Blasetti, the director of *Terra Madre*, was especially influenced by American and Soviet cinema, and recoded their conventions to meet Mussolini's desire for a "truly national film".[55] Both in Italy and abroad, Blasetti was respected as one of the most innovative film-makers. He was convinced of the importance of realism as the basis for a national film aesthetic. *Terra Madre* is an example of realism used for political ends.[56] The film was a precursor to the postwar neorealist films that finally brought Italian cinema acclaim.

## The End of Società Pittaluga

The effort to keep Società Pittaluga profitable, and to keep it a source of foreign film distribution, came to a sudden end in 1931. In that year, Stefano Pittaluga died prematurely of cancer. With Pittaluga gone, the company lacked clear leadership and direction.

Ludovico Toeplitz, son of the chief executive of BCI, was appointed General Director of Società Pittaluga in order to protect the interests of the bank. Emilio Cecchi, intellectual and writer, was appointed director of production (from 1932 to 1933) by a joint decision of the board of directors of the bank and the company. The choice of Cecchi was political. At a time when Mussolini was attempting to enroll the support of intellectuals, Cecchi was a leading figure in Italy and his interest in the cinema made him one of the few who could mediate between the worlds of politics, film, and culture. Furthermore, Cecchi had visited the United States in 1931 and had learned about Hollywood production methods.

Cecchi's efforts to modernize Italian cinema were generally approved by contemporary intellectuals, but BCI, which had hoped to solve Società Pittaluga's economic difficulties, viewed him as a failure.[57] Out of a total of 18 films made, only one, *Non sono gelosa*, a commercial comedy about a jealous wife, was able to cover production costs (the meager profit was $6,400), but the returns could not cover the losses of other films, such as *Acciaio* (released in 1933), a high-concept collaboration between Pirandello and German director Walter Ruttmann that flopped at the box office because it lacked both technically and stylistically.[58] The film cost over $84,000 and earned only $33,000 both in Italy and abroad.[59] In 1933, both Toeplitz and Cecchi resigned from the company. The firm's balance sheet recorded heavy losses in all sectors of activity. In July 1933, the bank wrote to Pedrazzini,

"Owing to objective and market difficulties, this bank can no longer finance the losses incurred by the company."[60]

In 1931, despite the rather poor economic results, Dr. Adamoli—in charge of controlling management—held that there was not enough information for a definitive judgement about Cines Pittaluga's prospects. According to Adamoli, the company was just starting up, and the situation was made even more difficult by the general crisis of the cinema and by the cost of investing in sound film technology, which increased general expenses and therefore production costs. At the end of 1932, two years after embarking on film production, Adamoli had changed his mind. He now saw the prospects for improving results as "not very positive and discouraging",[61] since there was a persistent deficit between expenses and returns as evident from the Graph below.

From 1930 to 1934, the revenue for all movies produced by the company was over 32 million lire domestically (about $2.6 million) and over 9 million abroad ($758,573). Some movies were great successes abroad, like *La canzone dell'Amore* and *Terra Madre*, but most flopped.

According to Adamoli, besides making suitable corrections to the general accounting system and improvements in management to contain general and collective expenses, the most important intervention concerned production processes, specifically coordination between the Script Office, and the company's production and marketing departments. The marketing office should have had information about audience tastes and should have known which types of film were most popular.

Thus it was a case of constantly updating the linguistic-expressive aspects of production to "produce films which the public like"[62] to avoid having to improvise a screenplay, perhaps inspired by a successful film of the past. If we go through archival materials, it's interesting to notice that immaterial assets represented a small percentage of the overall budget: in most cases the script and the screenplay scarcely get 3%, a much lower figure than the 10% figure cited by professional journals like *Kines, La Vita Cinematografica, La Cinematografia,*

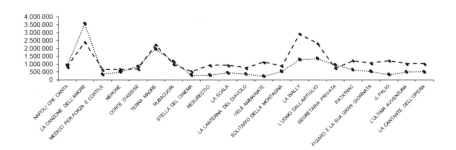

*Graph 4.2* Pittaluga Movies: Costs and Earnings.

Source: author's elaboration on archival materials, ASI-BCI, SOF, 309.

and *La Rivista Cinematografica*. If an Italian film cost on average $40,000 in the 1930s, then $4,000 would have been the ideal development and script-writing budget—a long way from the $150 spent on the screenplays of the Pittaluga films *Nerone, Vele ammainate*, and *La Lanterna del Diavolo*.[63] The Italian average production costs were about one-eighth of American, a quarter of French, and a third of British movies.[64] In Pittaluga's film budgets, the lion's share is usually made by organizational and management costs, with 30 to 40% of the budget. According to contemporary commentators, for a good movie, the company should have invested at least 10% in the screenplay.

At the time Stefano Pittaluga died, the Cines-Pittaluga label still dominated film production: in 1930, it accounted for 84% of films produced in Italy, 92.3% the following year and 43.3% in 1932. In 1933, there was a large drop, both in absolute terms and also in comparison with the other companies, with Cines accounting for 20% of all films produced.

This situation was also due to the production incentives ushered in by law in 1931; this initially favoured the big Cines productions, but over time provided an incentive to the small businessmen whose interest in the cinema was mostly to do with speculation. Between Stefano Pittaluga's early death and the creation of the *Direzione Generale per la Cinematografia* (1934), the small and medium production companies dominated the industry. These were the so-called *Independents*, i.e. companies without sound stages and formed with a share capital of 500,000 lire, which mostly concentrated on popular types of film. Although the Independents were essential for avoiding the dispersal of productive energy, it was impossible to imagine that they would ever be able to resolve the problems faced by the Italian film industry.

The opinion of cinema critics and experts was as follows:

> The Independents haven't saved the film industry. And everyone knows this is not because they don't want to. An independent is obliged to produce in much worse conditions than those who have, or manage, a factory or organisation. An Independent has to work on a film that is

*Table 4.2* Approximate Percentage Expenditure of Two Pittaluga Films

| La canzone dell'amore | | Napoli che canta | |
|---|---|---|---|
| *Macro costs* | *Percentage* | *Macro costs* | *Percentage* |
| Screenplay, copyright | 2,17 | Screenplay, copyright | 0,8 |
| Director | 5 | Director | 5,39 |
| Architects and set designers | 0,2 | Architects and set designers | 2,05 |
| Set design | 8 | Actors | 17 |
| Actors | | Actors | |
| Collective costs | 43,56 | Collective costs | 43,30 |

Source: author's elaboration on ASI-BCI, SOF, cart. 236.

guaranteed to be successful or at least break even. This of course means that these films are not original, and are often devoid of art.[65]

Italian film production was now dominated by a large number of small production companies that made no more than four films per season. Instead of a strategy based on economies of scale and on consolidating production, the preferred course of action was to create a new company to obtain access to state aid more profitably.

In 1934, SASP company management came close to abandoning direct production, preferring to hire facilities and make films in partnership with independent Italian film-makers (who came and went in the space of a few years). According to the bank supervisors, the partnership formula was a failure because Società Pittaluga would be burdened financially.[66] Furthermore, the production quality was low, the storylines located between the "comic and the sentimental," and thus difficult to be exported successfully.[67] The newspapers and magazines at the time spoke of the imminent collapse of the company, blaming the incompetence of the directors and excessive bureaucracy.[68]

Equally important, however, was the change that was occurring in the government's film policy. Mussolini ended up adopting a mixed policy by simultaneously developing state-controlled administrative bodies and pursuing incentives to private enterprises.[69] This policy was the result of an internal debate between those like Luigi Freddi, general director of Direzione Generale per la Cinematografia, who advocated a state-controlled movie industry, and those like Dino Alfieri, Subsecretary of the Press and Propaganda Ministry, later minister of Popular Culture, who believed that the government should only provide some legislative tools, such as credit facility or state ads, leaving producers free to decide the content of features.[70] Thus, the regime did not have a coherent plan for its relations with the film industry until the mid-1930s.

When Società Anonima Stefano Pittaluga went into liquidation, the film industry—at least the production sector—was fragmented; during the central years, there was no dominant operator, and market shares were divided among a great many production companies. In 1935, for example, there was the following structure (Table 4.3):

*Table 4.3* Production Companies and Market Shares, 1935

| No. production companies | Movies | Market share |
| --- | --- | --- |
| 15 | 1 | 39,47 |
| 5 | 2 | 26,32 |
| 3 | 3 | 23,68 |
| 1 | 4 | 10,53 |

Source: author's elaboration on Bernardini.

In the following years (1936, 1937, 1938, 1939), the structure is also similar to that in Table 4.3, with about 20 companies producing one single film each, and a few companies (1–9) producing from 2 to 9 films.

Given this data, Freddi's approach of advocating a more concentrated industry under state guidance was defeated. Italian film companies were attracted by production bonuses, and made as many film as they could without much concern for quality:

> Instead of 40 films made by 40 different companies, [there should be] 40 films made by 10 companies that work all year, with a well-defined industrial programme, with their own directors, actors and technicians, according to a unified plan, with an organised policy for selecting scripts.[71]

Until the mid-1930s, Italian films accounted for about 10% of the total films in circulation, most of which came from the USA. From 1930 to 1939, American films covered on average over half the Italian market and accounted for as much as 80% of total box-office earnings.

Although nationalism dictated defence of Italian cinema, the closure of the market had important economic repercussions; the dearth of films affected the cinemas, whose takings contributed to the producer's earnings and were an important source of state revenue (20–23% of gross takings went in tax).

The main problem of the sound era was that production capacity was considerably less than the demands of a constantly growing market. The cinema continued to attract crowds of spectators because it gave them a brief escape from reality, a dream of easy social elevation and happiness at a small price.

When the *Sezione Autonoma di Credito Cinematografico* (SACC) was created, investment in the industry boomed from 18 million lire in 1934–1935 to 71 million in 1936–1937. Although this seems to show a growing industry, when the capital really invested is scrutinised more closely, it turns out that it was 10 million lire: "We must take into account 6 million in advance credit and 18 million in loans granted by SACC, 4 million in state awards to producers, and another 6 million in dubbing vouchers. It must also be considered that out of thirty films, at least ten have had the rental fees in advance".[72] It is not surprising that these details are from *Film*, a magazine close to the fascist regime. This kind of criticism supported the state as it turned towards Alfieri, who had recognised the problems inherent in previous legislation and had a new approach to the film industry.

In 1935, the government decided to take over BCI's industrial shares, including those of Società Pittaluga, through the Istituto per la Ricostruzione Industriale (IRI). The same year, the Cines-Pittaluga facilities were destroyed by a suspicious fire.[73] Luigi Freddi, head of the Direzione Generale per la Cinematografia, supported the rebuilding of a movie production centre and in 1937, Cinecittà, the "Hollywood on the Tiber" was inaugurated. Thus, by the late 1930s, the government had taken over the film industry.

## Conclusions Part I and II

Italy played a leading role in the heroic and chaotic era of cinema pioneers that ended with World War I. It is difficult, but not impossible, to identify what prevented the Italian and European cinemas from developing according to their production potential, and what favoured the growth and success of the American cinema. These conditions still persist in part today, due to a cultural delay limiting understanding of the cultural, economic and technical process generated by the creative industry, particularly when it comes to the characteristics of an audio-visual production.

The situation then resembled the present situation in some ways. Not all films that were made reached the cinemas: for example, only 222 out of 410 films made in 1920 were screened. According to contemporary observers, the cinemas made excessive profits and producers were able to cover only one-fifth, or at most one-quarter, of production costs. This was why it was important to export films abroad, but the foreign market was becoming increasingly inaccessible.

Here is what Paradisi, journalist, film director, actor and producer wrote in *"Il Giornale d'Italia"* on 13 September 1931. "If the production monopoly has brought our film industry these disastrous results, the cinema monopoly will bring complete ruin. Why? For the simple reason that foreign films have a domestic market of their own, so that they come onto the Italian market at such low prices that any cinema owner would be happy because he can earn double or triple the amount he earns with Italian films".

A few days later, in the same newspaper, Paradisi recalled that 222 Italian films were shown in 1920 against 130 foreign films: 67 American, 44 German, 24 French and seven from other countries. "This year the lords of the Italian monopoly have bought 187 American films, 270 German films, and 24 French films, meaning that 481 foreign films were brought into Italy, obviously to be launched on cinema screens".

If this was the state of the art in the early 1920s, once fascism had understood the importance of the cinema as an instrument of propaganda, it attempted to provide the industry with a more industrial organisation. The story of Società Anonima Stefano Pittaluga shows how the film industry became a target of the government's interest and interference. Mussolini perceived the usefulness of various communications industries—radio and print as well as film—to his rule. Mussolini tried to use the film industry to shape national identity. Subsidies for domestic producers, import licenses, screen-time quotas, state-financed productions, state-sponsored awards, and censorship were all tools to promote the development of the movie industry. Fascist policy was a mix of restrictive (screen quotas, import tariffs, censorship) and supportive measures (bank and credit loans, production subsidies) designed to prevent a total takeover of the local market by foreign movies. This direct intervention was perceived as a necessity for the survival of the national film industry.

Freddi worked to lay the industrial and ideological foundations of a sort of state-controlled Metro Goldwyn Mayer, attempting to integrate the various organisational and technical branches of the industry. Despite state intervention, American films continued to account for 80% of total box-office takings in Italy until 1938. Only when the protectionist Alfieri Law was introduced was it possible to reduce the share of American films to 22% in 1942, and increase the market share of Italian films to 50%. Takings rose, as did film and cinema numbers, and enough technical, professional and artistic managers were trained that, despite the endless series of unresolved problems, the essential foundations were laid for the film industry and producers would be able to start up again after the end of World War II.

Despite the measures imposed by Mussolini's regime, American films continued to dominate Italian theatres. Nevertheless, the groundwork was set for the Italian film industry to come into its own after World War II. The neorealist style, the beginnings of which could be seen in some of Pittaluga's films, such as *Terra Madre*, enabled Italy to gain international success. From 1949 to 1953, the Italian movie industry jumped from fourth to second place in international ranking, while box office returns rose 120% and income from exports grew 300 percent. The neorealist movement, which was inspired by directors' honest responses to the turmoil and poverty of Italy's postwar condition, represents the democratic renewal of Italian society after fascism and World War II.

## Notes

1 Giannini, Guglielmo 9 July 1927, "La funzione dell'Anonima Pittaluga", *Kines*, 24, quoted in Redi, Riccardo, Camerini, Claudio (eds.) 1958, *Cinecittà I: industria e mercato nel cinema italiano tra le due guerre*, Venice: Marsilio, pp. 97–107.
2 The first Italian talking picture, *La canzone dell'amore*, produced by SASP in 1930 was filmed at the same time in three versions: Italian, French and German.
3 Gromo, Mario 2 December 1932, "Per il film italiano. Rinascerà a Torino un'industria cinematografica?", *La Stampa*.
4 Pommer, Erich "The International Talking Film", quoted in Garncarz, Joseph 1999, "Made in Germany: Multiple-Language Versions and the Eraly German Sound Cinema", in Higson, Andrew and Maltby, Richard, *Film Europe and Film America: Cinema, Commerce and Cultural Exchange, 1920–1939*, Exeter: University of Exeter Press, p. 253.
5 The process was immediate in the US, and in 1929 half of cinemas had sound technology. The last silent film *Il bacio* by producer Jacques Feyder was also made in 1929, cf. Alonge, Giaime, Carluccio, Giulia 2006 *Il cinema americano classico*, Rome-Bari: Laterza, p. 17.
6 Stefano Pittaluga "understood that there was now an exceptional opportunity to attempt a revival of Italian film production. Pittaluga sensed this and acted first, giving the example of re-launching the film industry in this country, which was once a world leader. Nor did he do all of this just in order to speculate. A side to my friend's character that would surprise quite a few people is that as a producer Pittaluga was spurred on by an idealism ready to make sacrifices and to resist

hardships for a long time."Bragaglia, Anton Giulio 31 January 1953, "Stefano Pittaluga", *Cinema*, no. 102.

7 "La crisi cinematografica in Europa", *Cinema*, 25 January 1937.

8 This comment is attributed to Pittaluga, in AMC, Fondo 201/2—Comunicati ufficio stampa 1927, *Comunicato* no. 5, 2 May 1927.

9 This brief statement (no. 5 del 2 May 1927) is taken from a Portugese publication, the Magazine Bertrand, Lisboa, in AMC, Fondo Pittaluga 201/2—Comunicati Ufficio Stampa 1927.

10 Ben-Ghiat, Ruth 2001, *Fascist Modernities: Italy, 1922–1945*, Berkeley: University of California Press.

11 Farassino, Alberto 1982, "Quei dieci anni di cinema italiano", in Various Authors, *Anni Trenta. Arte e cultura in Italia*, Milan: Mazzotta, p. 388.

12 Ghiat, Ben 2001.

13 Brunetta, Gian Piero 1993, *Storia del cinema italiano*, vol. I, Rome: Editori Riuniti, pp. 266–267.

14 Quaglietti, Lorenzo 1980, *Storia economico-politica del cinema italiano 1945–1980*, Rome: Editori Riuniti.

15 Bragaglia, "Stefano Pittaluga".

16 *Films Pittaluga 15*, (15 June—14 July 1924).

17 In 1920, "Cine-fono" magazine spoke with alarm about the danger posed by Pittaluga.

18 Giannini, Giuseppe 9 July 1927, "La funzione dell'Anonima Pittaluga", *Kines*, 24, quoted in Redi, Riccardo, Camerini, Claudio (eds.) 1958, *Cinecittà I: industria e mercato nel cinema italiano tra le due guerre*, Venice: Marsilio, pp. 97–107.

19 Pittaluga was the only company with enough capital to carry out conversion.

20 Bragaglia, "Stefano Pittaluga".

21 Toeplitz, Ludovico 1964, *Ciak a chi tocca*, Milan: Edizioni Milano Nuova, p. 94.

22 AMC, Pittaluga, Fondo 1923, *Atti-Corrispondenza-Inventari, 1920–1934: Relazioni e bilanci della SASP*.

23 "No comparisons therefore to make with foreign production . . . without mentioning the chances of organisation. Where there are ten or more people involved in creating a screenplay from a synopsis, each with his own ideas and experience, all on fixed contracts for this very purpose, in our country, the sums we have stated above allow us only to entrust the screenplay to one person, or two at the most, and they will only have a little experience because they do this work from time to time and are badly paid. In America, the artistic director is one part of a vast mechanism. But here he has to do everything, from the screenplay of the story almost up to working the clapperboard", A. Petrucci, *Difesa del film italiano*. The article is not dated and there is no publication title; it comes from the archives of the Museo del Cinema di Torino, Fondo Pittaluga 204/1 "Rassegna stampa di alcuni film 1931–1934".

24 See Chapter XX.

25 The words are those of Mario Gromo, referring with a touch of irony to the inauguration of the Cines studios in his article *Risorgerà a Torino un'industria cinematografica? Gli uomini e i mezzi*, in "La Stampa", 3 December 1932.

26 Films Pittaluga, no. 1–2, 15 January/15 February 1926, p. 2.

27 AMC, Pittaluga, Fondo 1921–22, *Atti-Corrispondenza-Inventari, 1920–1934: Relazioni e bilanci della SASP*.

28 AMC, Fondo 201/2—Press releases 1927, *Comunicato* no.9, 10 June 1927.

29 In a typical distribution contract, one firm was appointed as the official foreign distribution agent of another.

30 C. de Danilowicz 4 July 1924, "Chez Eric Pommer", *Cinémagazine*, 4 (27): 11, quoted in Thompson, Kristin 1999, "The Rise and Fall of Film Europe", in Higson and Maltby. Higson, Andrew, Maltby, Richard 1999, "Film Europe"

and "Film America": Cinema, Commerce and Cultural Exchange 1920–1939, Exeter: University of Exeter Press, 56–81.

31  "Interview mit Louis Aubert", *Film Kurier*, 24 May 1924, quoted in Saunders, Thomas 1999, "Germany and Film Europe", in Higson and Maltby, p. 162.

32  *New York Times*, 22 June 1928, p. 5, quoted in Thompson, Kristin 1999, "The Rise and Fall of Film Europe", in Andrew Higson and Richard Maltby, pp. 62–63. Higson, Andrew, Maltby, Richard 1999, "Film Europe" and "Film America": Cinema, Commerce and Cultural Exchange 1920–1939, Exeter: University of Exeter Press, 56–81.

33  This project has started to be designed in 1926, during the International Cinema Conference in Paris. The Motion Picture Producers and Distributors of America (MPPDA) did its best to boycott the conference, which was much criticised in the trade press: "some twenty nations will gather in Paris to discuss the future of motion pictures. Some eighty papers will be read in many different languages. That's interesting in view of the fact that there is but one international language—motion picture. Perhaps some constructive, practical thoughts will come from the Paris gathering, but whatever the outcome, it's a good safe bet that American producers will continue on their merry way of giving the public of America and the world what it wants". In "Unidentified American trade paper", quoted in *The Bioscope*, 22 July 1926, p. 21, quoted in Higson, Andrew 1999, "Cultural Policy and Industrial Practice: Film Europe and the International Congresses of the 1920s", in Higson and Maltby, p. 122.

34  Ibid.

35  Bassoli, Carlo February 1926, "Sa la Banca Commerciale Italiana?", *L'eco del cinema*, 27, quoted in Redi, Riccardo, Camerini, Claudio (eds.) 1958, *Cinecittà I: industria e mercato nel cinema italiano tra le due guerre*, Venice: Marsilio, pp. 84–86.

36  "Il Torchio", 5 agosto 1927.

37  Lega, Giuseppe 1 January 1927, "Una proposta concreta", *Il Torchio*, 1.

38  See, "I cinematografi in Italia," *La rivista del cinematografo*, 7–8 July 1930; "Cinematografia italiana nello stato presente," *Quadrante* 6 (1933); SIAE 1934, *Lo Spettacolo in Italia, 1924–1933*, Rome: SIAE; Atti Parlamentari, Legislatura 29, Discussioni dal 3 Maggio 1937 al 31 Dicembre 1937, Prima Sessione—Discussioni—Tornata Del 13 Maggio 1937.

39  "Società Anonima Stefano Pittaluga, 1932–1934," 27 July 1932, Fund, SOF, Folder 309, file 1, ASI-BCI.

40  "Note del prof. Adamoli sulla situazione patrimoniale ed economica del Gruppo Pittaluga nell'anno 1932," SOF, Folder 309, file 1, sf., ASI-BCI.

41  Ibid.

42  Soro, Francesco 1935, *Splendori e miserie del cinema italiano*, Milan: Consalvo, p. 187. The production companies belonging to UCI were: *Itala Film, the Cines Group made up of Celio Film, Palatino Film, Imprese Cinematografiche Italiane, the Barattolo Group, consisting of Caesar Film, Bertini Film, the Mecheri Group consisting of Tiber Film, Film d'Arte, and INCIT*. There were also other smaller companies.

43  This was the title given to the affair and contained in the Notes accompanying the accounts and Repertorio Affari vari, ASI-BCI, UF, r, vol. 10, f. 2878–2881.

44  ASI- BCI, Fondo ST, cart. 47, fasc. 4, sf. 3, "Relazione del Rag. A. Piperno per il Grande Ufficiale Sig. Giuseppe Toeplitz—September 1926

45  ASI-BCI, ST, cart. 47, fasc.4, sf.3.

46  ASI-BCI, ST, cart. 47, fasc.4, sf.3.

47  ASI-BCI, SOF, cart. 236, fasc. 1, "Società Anonima Stefano Pittaluga 1929–1931".

48  ASI-BCI, ST, cart. 47, fasc.4, sf.3.

49 For quote see Riccardo Redi, *La Cines, storia di una casa di produzione* (Bologna, 2009).

50 ASI-BCI, SOF, cart. 310, fasc.3.

51 "He once invited me to make a film entitled *Mare/Sea* which then was secretly called *Vele ammainate*. Aldo Vergano wrote a synopsis and he changed it according to the principle of the seduced and persecuted young maiden saved by the avenging hero. Ruffians and exotic people, sailing ships and storms were in agitation when the story was set in this way. I did my best to avoid banality, but it was impossible", in Bragaglia, "Stefano Pittaluga".

52 Hobsbawn, Eric 1983, *Mass-Producing Tradition: Europe, 1870–1914*, in Hobsbawn, Eric, Ranger, Terence *The Invention of Tradition*, Cambridge: Cambridge University Press, p. 307.

53 Antonello Gerbi, *Teorie sul cinema*, ASI-BCI, P-Gerbi, cart. 5, fasc. 2.

54 Quoted in Brass, Tom 2001, "Reel Images of the Land (Beyond the Forest): Film and the Agrarian Myth", *Journal of Peasant Studies*, 28: 1–56.

55 On this topic, see Ben-Ghiat, 2001 and Landy, Marcia 1986, *Fascism in Italy*, Princeton, NJ: Princeton University Press.

56 Bertellini, Giorgio 2004, *The Cinema of Italy*, London: Wallflower Press.

57 See *Il Cinema italiano*, 20 Apr. 1932; Meccoli, Domenico 15–29 November 1941, "Intervista ad Alessandro Blasetti," *Il Tempo*, Anno V, n. 46; "Promemoria al Capo del Governo, febbraio 1934," SOF, Folder 309, file 3, sf, ASI-BCI.

58 On the history of the movie see Camerini, Claudio 1990, *Acciaio, un film degli anni Trenta. Pagine inedite di una storia italiana*, Turin: Nuova Eri.

59 Only one movie, *Non sono gelosa* (1933, directed by Carlo Ludovico Bragaglia) made a profit. The movie was a classic Italian comedy about love and jealousy.

60 "Lettera del 28 luglio 1933 da Segreteria Affari Finanziari a Solza (president of SASP)," SOF, Folder 309, sf, ASI-BCI.

61 ASI- BCI; SOF, cart. 309, sf. "Note del prof. Adamoli sulla situazione patrimoniale ed economica del gruppo Pittaluga nell'anno 1932".

62 ASI-BCI, SOF, cart. 236, fasc. 1, sf "Relazione del dott. Adamoli sulla visita contabile effettuata negli stabilimenti della Cines nel dicembre 1932".

63 *Nerone* was a parody of ancient imperial Rome; the movie was successful at the box office but not with critics. *Vele ammainate* and *La Lanterna del diavolo* were classical popular drama; these movies had a tepid welcome at the box office but a warmer one with critics.

64 Bakker, *Entertainment Industrialised*, 272–273. See also Sedgwick, John, Pokorny, Michael 2005, "The Film Business in the U.S. and Britain during the 1930s", *Economic History Review* 58: 79–112.

65 The article "Indipendenti, registi, attori, esportazione; ovvero: esame di coscienza" was published on *Cinegiornale*, no. 7, 15 November 1934, for celebrating the birth of *Direzione Generale per la Cinematografia*.

66 SOF, Folder 310, file 3, ASI-BCI. Description of Cines production plants and analysis of economic results of Società Anonima Stefano Pittaluga.

67 Ibid.

68 Giuseppe Sampieri, Vittorio 3 May 1933, "Corriere Romano", *Cinema Illustrazione*, Anno VIII, 36: 2

69 Gili, Jean 1981, *Stato fascista e cinematografia: Repressione e promozione*, Rome: Bulzoni, pp. 120–121.

70 Savio, Francesco 1975, *Ma l'amore no: Realismo, formalismo, propaganda e telefoni bianchi nel cinema italiano di regime (1930–1943)*, Milan: Sonzogno; Redi, Riccardo 2009, *La Cines, storia di una casa di produzione*, Bologna: Persiani Editore; Redi, Riccardo 1979, *Cinema italiano sotto il fascismo*, Venice: Marsilio; Argentieri, Mino 1991, *Risate di regime*, Venice: Marsilio.

71   Bonfiglio, Fabrizio 1–15 November 1936, "Case di produzione a vero e proprio carattere industriale", *Cinegiornale*, Vol.10, quoted in Miccichè, Lino et al. 2006 (eds.), Storia del cinema italiano: 1934, Rome-Venice: Bianco e Nero/Marsilio, p. 678.
72   Sampieri, Giovanni 12 March 1938, "Produzione, noleggio, esercizio", *Film*, Anno 1, n.7, quoted in Brunetta, Gian Piero 2009, *Il cinema italiano di regime. Da "La canzone dell'amore" a "Ossessione"*, Rome-Bari:Laterza.
73   Freddi, Luigi 1949, *Il cinema*, Rome: Arnia, p. 181.

## Bibliography

ALONGE, Giaime, CARLUCCIO, Giulia 2006 *Il cinema americano classico*, Rome-Bari: Laterza, 2006

ARGENTIERI, Mino 1991, *Risate di regime*, Venice: Marsilio
_____. 1974, *La censura nel cinema italiano*, Rome: Editori Riuniti

BAKKER, Gerben 2008, *Entertainment Industrialised*, Cambridge: Cambridge University Press

BEN-GHIAT, Ruth 2001, *Fascist Modernities: Italy, 1922–1945*, Berkeley: University of California Press

BERTELLINI, Giorgio 2004, *The Cinema of Italy*, London: Wallflower Press

BRUNETTA, Gian Piero 2009, *Il cinema italiano di regime: Da "La Canzone dell'amore" a "Ossessione"*, Rome-Bari: Laterza
_____. 1993, *Storia del cinema italiano*, vol. I, Rome: editori Riuniti

CARABBA, Claudio 1974, *Il cinema del ventennio nero*, Florence: Vallecchi

DE GRAZIA, Victoria 1981, *The Culture of Consent: Mass Organization of Leisure in Fascist Italy*, Cambridge: Cambridge University Press

FARASSINO, Alberto 1982, "Quei dieci anni di cinema italiano", in Various Authors, *Anni Trenta. Arte e cultura in Italia*, Milan: Mazzotta, pp. 381–402

FORGACS, David 1990, *Italian Culture in the Industrial Era, 1880–1980: Cultural Industries, Politics and the Public*, Manchester: Manchester University Press

GERBALDO, Paolo 1990, *La Fert: un esempio di casa di produzione cinematografica nella Torino degli anni Venti*, degree thesis, University of Turin

GIANETTO, Claudia, 1998, "Stefano Pittaluga, trait d'union entre muet et parlant", in TOFFETTI, Silvia (ed.), *Un'altra Italia. Pour une historie du cinéma italien*, Paris-Milano: Cinémathèque Française—Mazzotta

GILI, Jean 1981, *Stato fascista e cinematografia: Repressione e promozione*, Rome: Bulzoni

GOMERY, Douglas 1980, "Economic Struggle and Hollywood Imperialism: Europe Converts to Sound", *Yale French Studies* 60: 80–93

HAROLD, James, TANNER Jakob (eds.) 2002, *Enterprise in the Period of Fascism in Europe*, Aldershot: Ashgate

HIGSON, Andrew, MALTBY, Richard 1999, *Film Europe and Film America: Cinema, Commerce and Cultural Exchange, 1920–1939*, Exeter: University of Exeter Press

HOBSBAWN, Eric, RANGER, TERENCE 1983, *The Invention of Tradition*, Cambridge: Cambridge University Press

LUPO, Salvatore 2005, *Il fascismo: La politica di un regime totalitario*, Rome: Donzelli

MOORE, Barrington 1996, *Social Origins of Dictatorship and Democracy: Lord and Peasant in the Making of the Modern World*, Boston, MA: Beacon Press

Nicoli, Marina, 2011, "Entrepreneurs and the State in the Italian Film Industry, 1919–1935", *Business History Review 85* (Winter): 775–798

Paolella, Roberto 1966, *Storia del cinema sonoro (1926–1939)*, Naples: Giannini

Poulantzas, Nicos 1974, *Fascism and Dictatorship: The Third International and the Problem of Fascism*, London: New Left Book

Quargnolo, Mario 1986, *La parola ripudiata*, Udine: La Cineteca del Friuli

Redi, Riccardo 2009, *La Cines, storia di una casa di produzione*, Bologna: Persiani Editore

_____. 1979, *Cinema italiano sotto il fascismo*, Venice: Marsilio

Ricci, Steven 2008, *Cinema and Fascism: Italian Film and Society, 1922–1943*, Berkeley: University of California Press

Rueschemeyer, Dietrich et al. 1992, *Capitalist Development and Democracy*, Chicago: University of Chicago Press

Sanguineti, Tatti 1998, *L'anonimo Pittaluga. Tracce, carte e miti*, Ancona: Transeuropa

Savio, Francesco 1975, *Ma l'amore no: Realismo, formalismo, propaganda e telefoni bianchi nel cinema italiano di regime (1930–1943)*, Milan: Sonzogno, 1975

Sedgwick, John, Pokorny, Michael 2005, "The Film Business in the U.S. and Britain during the 1930s", *Economic History Review 58*: 79–112

Soro, Francesco 1935, *Splendori e miserie del cinema italiano*, Milan: Consalvo

Tannenbaum, Edward 1972, *The Fascist Experience: Italian Society and Culture, 1922–1945*, New York: Basic Books

Toeplitz, Ludovico 1964, *Ciak a chi tocca*, Milan: Edizioni Milano Nuova

Tosi, Virgilio 1997, *Breve storia tecnologica del cinema*, Rome: Bulzoni

# Part III

# Building the Cinematic Miracle

## Cinema under Democracy

# 5  Multiple Actors and the Rebirth of an Industry

European film-makers are not that different from those in America.
Some want to make popular mainstream films;
others are more attracted to quirky independent fare.
What separates the two film industries is that one is run as a business, the other as a charity.[1]

## Beginning from Scratch

"For twenty years the State was the worst of all the producers. But in the present situation I still have hopes in the State, because it has the power to do exactly the opposite of what the previous State did".[2] At the end of the Second World War, Italian cinema appeared to be on its deathbed. Like the rest of Italian society, the cinema lived through the transition from a dictatorship to a democratic regime, and this meant that its role had to be re-defined and negotiated with government. Once again, the relationship between state and cinema was more of a continuation than a break with the past. The path charted out by fascist legislation would not be dismantled, and the Italian film industry would find itself dependent on the "visible hand" of the government.

The American motion picture industry appeared to be anxious to re-conquer the position lost in this market during the war. The US feared that "a new legislation should be enacted in Italy, which would restrict the right freely to import and distribute foreign films in this important market".[3] In fact, after the 1948 Paramount decree (it separated studio's production and distribution branches from exhibition), European markets became much more important for American movie revenues

The situation in the early 1940s was dramatic. There was a German occupation, Italy was divided into two zones, some cinema machinery had been moved north to the Republic of Salò's Cinevillaggio in Venice, and Cinecittà, the most important film production centre, had been devastated and turned into a refugee camp. Nevertheless, after Rome liberation, Italy felt a strong need to define its position within the new European political order.

The international success of some national movies—*Roma città aperta*, *Paisà*, *Il bandito*, *Aquila Nera*—showed that there was a real will to achieve artistic and economic recovery. This is well explained by Gilles Deleuze: "Italian cinema had at its disposal a cinematographic institution which had escaped fascism relatively successfully, on the other hand it could point to a resistance and a popular life underlying oppression, although one without illusion. To grasp these, all that was necessary was a new type of story capable of including the elliptical and the unorganized, as if the cinema had to begin again from zero by questioning afresh all accepted American traditions. The Italians were therefore able to have an intuitive consciousness of a new image as it was being created".[4]

The success of Italian films and their gradual conquest of international markets were destined to become one of the most emblematically significant manifestations of an economic miracle within a mixed economy regime, partly given over to free enterprise and partly subsidized by the state. Of all the European cinemas emerging from the war, whether victors or losers, it was the Italian film industry that made the greatest efforts to move up from a position of inferiority and managed to achieve qualitative and quantitative results that none of the economically more developed countries were able to equal; neither Britain, nor France, nor Germany were able to build up a cinema industry able to compete with Hollywood.

Italy and the Italians emerged from World War II knowing that they had to rebuild a country that wanted to forget the war and the fascist era. The political and social situation was uncertain, and so was national identity. In *Accadde al commissariato* by Giorgio Simonelli (a film released in 1954), a farce sums up the confusion felt in the early 1940s: "We are hanging from a balloon string, and the balloon is called uncertainty". Rediscovering freedom, after 20 long years of government led by Mussolini, was a dual process: together with a natural enthusiasm for the end of the war, there was also a feeling of material and spiritual fragility, mostly due to the rapidity of the transition from dictatorship to democracy.

Italian cinema seemed to have melted away. Nevertheless, film-makers continued to meet among the ruins of occupied Rome to talk about the future, intending to reorganise and revive the cinema once the war ended. Aware of the enormous difficulties to come, they predicted a hard-fought battle with the old arch-enemy: Hollywood.

The American majors had mounted another attack via the Psychological Warfare Branch, the military propaganda office, which was followed by the Allied Italian Film Board, the office dealing with the cinema in Italy. The Americans had every intention of regaining the market position their movie industry had lost with the introduction of the ENIC monopoly. They called for its abolition, together with all the fascist laws supporting the Italian film industry. The Film Board would not accept verbal agreements to this effect, but demanded new laws aimed at opening up a free market for films in Italy.

This American resolve to sweep away fascist laws was clearly stated by US Admiral Ellery Stone during a meeting to discuss the future of Italian cinema. He illustrated the plans: "The so-called Italian cinema was invented by the fascists. So it has to be suppressed. The instruments which created this invention must be suppressed too. All of them, including the Cinecittà. There has never been a film industry in Italy. There have never been film industrialists. Who are these industrialists? Speculators and adventurers, yes, that's what they are. Anyway, Italy is an agricultural country, so what would she need a film industry for?"[5]

Stone's words reflected the American government's gratitude towards Hollywood for its help during the war years, a favour the government was now ready to return by helping Hollywood conquer the European markets. President Truman's strategy of exporting the American dream as part of the fight against communism also involved the cinema, called on to spread a "fair and complete picture of American life and the aims of US government policy".[6]

Military organisations like the PWB and Film Board prepared for the arrival of film companies in Italy when the ENIC Monopoly was formally abolished on 5 October 1945.

Without state funding, the studios at Cinecittà and Pisorno closed, and with its technical and artistic management staff scattered, the Italian film industry attempted to emerge from beneath the ruins. The decade from 1945 to 1955 is its most interesting and dramatic period.

Italian cinema had to face a real invasion. No longer shackled by quotas and dubbing taxes, US films flooded into Italian cinemas: 188 in 1946, 287 in 1947, 344 in 1948, and 369 in 1949. The total was five times the number of Italian films made in the same period. These figures become even more dramatic, not only because new American films arrived in Italy, but also because there were films made during the war that were not distributed in Italy until the conflict ended. To make sure they had direct control of demand, the Hollywood majors returned to Italy in late 1945. First Paramount, then Metro Goldwyn Mayer, 20th Century Fox, Warner Bros, RKO and Universal re-opened their Rome branches, while others preferred to give exclusive rights to Italian distributors, like Columbia Pictures working with *Ceiad* or United Artists with *Artisti Associati*.

Graph 5.1 shows the number of Italian and foreign films released in Italian cinemas from 1945 to 1965. It is quite evident that the market was totally dominated by Hollywood productions in the first four years. In 1946, about 600 American films were released, and from then until 1949 an average of 570 Hollywood films circulated in Italy. The number of Italian cinemas was growing, and going to the cinema accounted for about 2/3 of total spending on entertainment. Public attendance was increasing constantly: from 411 million in 1946 to 697 in 1951 and 768 million in 1953. Cinemas began to be built in small towns that had never had a cinema before this

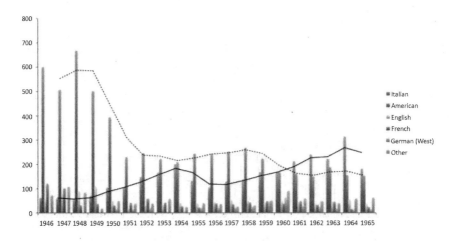

*Graph 5.1* National and Foreign Movies Released in Italy, 1945–1965.
Source: author's elaboration from ANICA official reports.

time: from 1950 to 1952 the number of provinces with no cinema fell from 3,700 to 2,400[7].

Industry professionals thought that, after a few years, the Italian film industry would be able to work in a free market, with no financial support from the state. However, reality soon revealed the difficulty of ending a relationship whose nature and spirit had been defined during the fascist era.

The American conquest had help from many quarters. Italian audiences rediscovered the fascination of Hollywood movies after years of fascist *autarchy*. Cinema owners needed continual supplies of films to meet demand from the rising numbers of cinemas. Distributors made plenty of easy money importing old films from the USA. The Church considered US films to be less morally, ideologically and politically threatening, and *Democrazia Cristiana* used American escapist cinema to create anti-Communist consensus.

On the other side of the barricade, there were opposition forces committed to defending *neorealism* and spreading the Soviet cinema. Film industry workers opposed the US invasion, while producers were initially unsure what to do, but then decided on communication with the enemy.

## From Ruins to Reconstruction

On 10 July 1944, the Italian film producers formed the *Associazione Nazionale Industrie Cinematografiche e Affini* (ANICA), together with distributors and the developing and printing branches. The association is still active today.

The first President was Alfredo Proia, succeeded in 1949 by Eitel Monaco (head of the *Direzione generale per la cinematografia* at the Ministry of Popular Culture 1941–1944), formerly Secretary General, who remained in office until the 1970s. Monaco was suspected of continuing the fascist approach, and he symbolises ANICA's ambivalent policy in the immediate post-war period: laissez-faire professions of hostility to any kind of protectionism were accompanied with actions and demands aimed at defending Italian cinema from the US invasion.

ANICA followed in the steps of the *Federazione Nazionale fascista industriali dello spettacolo* (FNFIS), which had included and represented the interests of producers, distributors and cinema owners. This element of continuity is important, because it was during the fascist era that film industrialists started becoming aware of their own identity.

Under Eitel Monaco's management, steps were taken to consolidate production, train technical and artistic managers, separate industrial from political affairs, and regulate the entire industrial system. At its peak, ANICA directly represented 90% of the Italian film industry. It aimed to create a shared identity for an industry that had never felt this identity. ANICA represented the interests of Italian cinema in Italy and abroad and had its delegates in Italian organisations and committees, and in international organisations.[8] For example, in 1959, ANICA promoted the formation of the *Bureau International du Cinéma*, which brought together the international federations of producers, distributors, technical industries, and cinema owners in order to discuss the problems of the European film industry.

During the fascist era, the cinema industrialists had created an economic/industrial policy that gave them the benefits of an independent private organisation, but with state funding. This para-corporative strategy, adapted to the new context, would allow ANICA members to identify shared policies and to accept the necessary compromises, despite their differing views about industrial culture. This is particularly important, since the post-war government had always considered the film industry as a marginal economic sector, and it was not included in economic reconstruction plans or in the aid programmes that preceded the Marshall Plan.

The producers were aware that they would have to show that the industry actually existed if they wanted it included in government plans. Their decision to form an association made it easier to communicate with the political forces, especially with the United States, now in charge of Italy.

ANICA's primary objective was to acquire legitimacy for the Italian film industry as an industry. The first post-war reports proudly mention the industry's exceptional rate of growth. These reports also show that the association grasped the full scale of the problems besetting the industry; the economic figures were always placed in the international context. The reports did not just register the industry's existence or accumulate facts and figures, but also attempted to identify tendencies and suggest the most appropriate strategies. Emotionally charged and almost uncritical, they made it possible to paint positive scenarios even at the blackest of times. Eitel Monaco, the heart and soul of the association, was conscious that he was managing a complex situation and well aware of the need to identify and solve the problems involving both the domestic market and Italian films on the foreign market. He knew he had to balance artistic and economic interests, that he was obliged to accept compromises with the government in order to obtain adequate support, and that the cinema owners must be persuaded that faith in Italian cinema would be repaid at the box office.

The producers asked directly for state aid in order to combat the influx of American films. On the contrary, the cinema owners formed the *Associazione Generale dello Spettacolo* (AGIS) and opposed any limits on film imports because American films gave high box-office returns.

In an attempt to reconcile the interests of the various categories, in early 1945 a *Commissione temporanea per la cinematografia* (Temporary Cinema Commission) was set up in order to seek an agreement between producers, cinema owners, government and entertainment industry workers. Soon afterwards came an organisation that would have an important role in all events concerning the Italian film industry: the *Sottosegretariato di Stato per la stampa, lo Spettacolo ed il Turismo*, attached to the *Presidenza del Consiglio* (Cabinet Office).

Protected by the US military administration, the American majors opposed any attempt to impose mandatory screenings or import quotas. Legislative Decree no. 678 (5 October 1945) revoked the ENIC Monopoly. Article 1 proclaimed that "film production is an activity free of control", but there was no elimination of censorship. Article 11 actually states that everything was abrogated, apart from "laws regarding public security and regulations for governmental vigilance over cinema films which regulate film censorship". As in the past, the executive acquired a powerful means of control. The decree apparently satisfied all parties, and actually helped film production; in the two years it was in force, the number of Italian films rose from 25 in 1945 to 67 in 1947.

This first attempt at legislation concerning the film industry left behind a mass of contradictions, and marked the start of the Italian cinema's total subordination to government control. Initially, it seemed an essential mean of giving the Italian cinema a chance to recover, an impossibility without any government economic intervention.

It is not easy to give a perfect definition of the term "cinema policy", since it is embedded with both economic and cultural concerns. Public intervention in the film industry is motivated by economic and cultural considerations. A country with a vital national film industry does not have to rely too much on foreign imports, which have a negative impact on the balance of payment.[9] Another economic reason for intervention is the need to protect the jobs of technical and artistic workers.

Cultural justifications for intervention are linked to the assumption that films are a powerful instrument of collective consciousness and have an importance that extends even beyond economic considerations. The government's ability to maintain viable, homegrown cultural industries that tell people about themselves is crucial to the sense of national identity. Public funding is then justified with the "cultural exemption theory"[10] that finds its latest expression and legal backing in the UNESCO Convention on Cultural Diversity signed globally by 148 countries in 2005.

Cinema policy is usually defined as a set of laws through which a government— with the support of trade unions—aims to regulate the sector directly or indirectly. On the one hand, the government has to guarantee competition on the market (in order to avoid a monopoly), and on the other hand it has to safeguard culture and national sovereignty. Thus, the main activities of a state in relation to the film industry are to guarantee the functioning of a free market, to favour international exchanges, to ensure that fiscal burdens are in proportion to the industry's real possibilities and market potential, and to attempt to improve the balance of payments.

The 1945 Legislative Decree did not impose the mandatory screening of Italian films that the producers wanted as defence against the invasion of US films; this was introduced by a private agreement with AGIS, signed on 10 January 1946, and was a move the cinema owners had not foreseen.

Once the initial enthusiasm abated, Italian cinema began to show the first signs of a crisis. The number of films produced began to drop and funding was unavailable. Despite the obligatory 60 days of Italian films introduced in the 1946 ANICA-AGIS agreement, Italian films found it increasingly difficult to make headway on the domestic market.

This situation highlighted the persistence of a series of structural difficulties in the Italian film industry. Not one single Italian production company had an integrated production process covering the entire country, and cinemas in the mid-1940s were still too few to ensure high earnings, since there were still entire municipalities without a cinema. Besides this, the production cycle was highly fragmented. In this situation, the only figure with the power to mediate was the Italian government, which needed to reconcile the opposing interests of the various professional associations, while avoiding direct conflict with US interests given the new political situation being shaped by the effects of the Marshall Plan (1947). In charge of government action regarding entertainment was parliamentarian Giulio Andreotti, who had become Under-secretary to the *Presidenza del Consiglio* one year before, and was to remain there until 1953. Andreotti had a leading role in cinema affairs for seven years: he shaped the rebirth of the national movie industry even though he chose to exercise his power in a latent way, so that he became labeled "The Great Invisible Man".[11]

Two years passed between the 1945 Legislative Decree and the new law. When the "Cappa Law" no. 379 (16 May) was introduced in 1947, it imposed 80 days of Italian films per year, and granted producers a subsidy equal to 10% of earnings over four years. The law also created a Central Office for the film industry, directly dependent on the *Presidenza del Consiglio dei Ministri*. The office implemented the measures in favour of the film industry; it promoted and maintained relations concerning international cinema exchanges, and controlled films and public bodies. In a circular dated 10 July 1947, Andreotti took over control of mandatory screening of Italian films from the police, and thereby gained the complete trust of the "American front" of cinema owners, distributors and the Italian branches of the major Hollywood studios.

Systematic law-breaking by cinema owners led to the formation of the *Movimento per la difesa del cinema italiano* (Movement in Defence of Italian Cinema), an association of directors, actors, technicians and journalists. Their demands were very precise, as shown by a manifesto published on 22 February: compliance with the cinema law and its revised version; introduction of a dubbing tax used to finance the production of Italian films; re-organisation of state and NGO cinema organisations; increased credit for the film industry; tax reduction; a democratic reform of film censorship. The governing parties saw this campaign as "electoral speculation", and the movement collapsed after a short time as it came under attack in the press and its supporters melted away.

In January 1949, Adriano Baracco began an editorial in *Cinema* with these words: "Order reigns in Warsaw: at present just one film is being made in our country, and it's a foreign film. There has never been such total stagnation Italian cinema from the time it came back to life in 1930".[12]

The seriousness of the situation and a legislative project that had been delayed for too many years, spurred the industry heads to action. On 14 February, Renato Gualino, President of the National Producers Union and of Lux Film, delivered a letter to the government, announcing that, "if the new law to help the cinema is not approved by the 30 April, the producers will automatically stop working".[13] Six days later, around 20,000 people demonstrated in Rome's Piazza del Popolo in support of Italian cinema. The most important figures in the film industry attended the event, with technicians and Cinecittà workers to hear Vittorio de Sica, Alessandro Blasetti, Anna Magnani and Gino Cervi. Film director Alberto Lattuada declared: "This shows that there is a perfect agreement—a rare thing—between capital and labour, and between manual and intellectual workers. What else do they want? It's only the government that doesn't seem interested in coming to terms with us".[14]

Andreotti came under accusation from several quarters, criticized that his was a policy of inaction and that he maintained "total freedom to import films for political reasons". His answer was to start working on two new laws.

The first, known by the diminutive form as the "*leggina*", was approved on 26 July 1949; it introduced a dubbing tax of two and a half million lire for foreign films in exchange for a voucher refunded after ten years. In order to make this bitter pill more palatable to the Hollywood majors, it was not actually called a dubbing tax, but a mandatory loan. The money went into a fund at the Banca Nazionale del Lavoro, "exclusively for financing the production of Italian films".[15] Distributors could count on a refund, and if they were also involved in production they could get money from the same fund they paid into; producers were under the illusion of being financed by American money. Italy chose to protect its film industry by attempting to satisfy everyone's interests, including the Americans.

After a lengthy debate, on 29 December 1949 Parliament finally approved the law placing the cinema definitively under state control and protection. Law no. 958, known as the *Legge Andreotti*, came into force on 1 January 1950. It guaranteed protection and funding to the film industry, but concentrated all power in the *Ufficio di cinematografia* (Cinema Office), which had the support of a technical committee and advisory commission. The *Federazione Italiana Lavoratori dello Spettacolo* (Federation of Italian Entertainment Workers—FILS) campaigned for a law that would not suffocate artistic freedom, and ANICA did the same. Andreotti sent them a clear message: too much inflexibility over a question of principle might delay or damage the approval of a law satisfying the producers' demands for increased subsidies and more relaxed enforcement of regulations on film nationality. Italian distributors were also ANICA members, but made big profits from distributing the American films not distributed directly by the Italian branches of the Hollywood majors. Similarly, cinema owners— whose association joined the newly formed AGIS (*Associazione generale italiana dello spettacolo*) in December 1945—were definitely in favour of US films because they made more money at the box office. The law seemed to reconcile all the different interests at stake without imposing any quota system on American films.[16]

This was possible firstly by giving producers 10% of their films' gross takings—to which a further 8% was added if the film had particular artistic features—and secondly by giving cinema owners a 20% tax refund, in exchange for screening Italian films on 80 days. The nationality of a film was verified by submitting the film synopsis in advance.

The members of the technical committee that made the decisions about state funding were mostly government representatives. The BNL administered both the state fund and the fund created from the mandatory loan imposed on foreign companies, and could grant credit only if the *Direzione Generale dello Spettacolo* agreed. This kind of control meant there was less need for stronger forms of ideological censorship because it imposed preventive censorship of screenplays, since producers would not propose a synopsis that was unlikely to meet with government approval. This is very similar to fascist film industry legislation[17] in its economic mechanisms and in the vast discretionary power of Government to decide on the allocation of funding: *historia non facit saltus*.

This gave tight control over film production, since production companies had to go through the Ministry's headquarters in Via Veneto to obtain

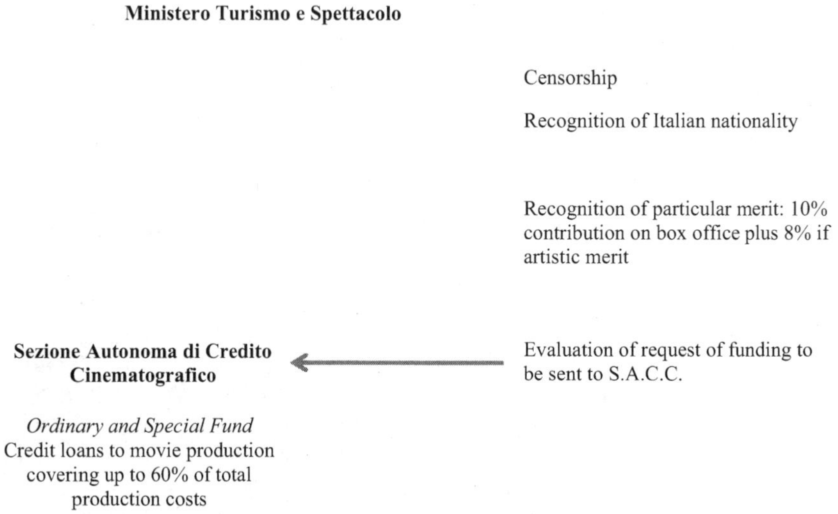

**Ministero Turismo e Spettacolo**

Censorship

Recognition of Italian nationality

Recognition of particular merit: 10%
contribution on box office plus 8% if
artistic merit

**Sezione Autonoma di Credito**          ⟵———————          Evaluation of request of funding to
**Cinematografico**                                                            be sent to S.A.C.C.

*Ordinary and Special Fund*
Credit loans to movie production
covering up to 60% of total
production costs

*Graph 5.2* Cinema Regulatory System in Italy, 1950–1960.
Source: personal elaboration.

funding and authorisation to distribute and export their films. They had
to have the screenplay approved in advance, along with the budget, work
schedule and film crew. Despite the problems connected with this strong
state control, the new law actually helped Italian cinema to recover and
marked an important turning point in film production. The situation obviously favoured recovery. New markets opened up in Europe, Africa and
the Middle East, and an intense relationship of co-production began with
France. American film imports fell as the backlog of old films gradually ran
out. In just a few years, the Italian film industry became the second in the
world for the number of films produced (from 25 in 1945 to 201 in 1954),
although its foundations remained fragile.

It is not easy to evaluate the effects of these measures,[18] also because of
the need to distinguish between questions of economics and ideology, meaning the forms of political control over Italian cinema. In addition, there are
also aesthetic questions, since (and this is the aspect stressed by previous
historians) the system of bonuses paid as a percentage of gross takings was
evidently a disadvantage for the cinema most appreciated by the critics,
since *neorealism* did not find the same favour with the public.

The Andreotti Law recalled the strategy of the Alfieri Law, but one of
the most important differences between the two laws was that there was no
longer a minimum share capital threshold, below which a production company lost all right to state help. Unlike fascism, *Democrazia cristiana* policy

did not apparently aim to encourage the formation of large companies, and actually allowed uncontrolled expansion.

If ideological and/or aesthetic judgements are avoided, it is possible to conclude for the moment by highlighting the short-term advantages given by the Andreotti Laws to a film industry that had grown up in mixed economy, where a private company could no longer exist without government aid. Essentially, the state production incentives—again excluding considerations about political control of the media—were not very different from those that other European governments gave to the various national film industries. The extraordinary growth of the following two decades occurred despite these measures and was the result of a particular situation in which Italian "otherness" was not just the weaknesses listed at the beginning of the chapter, but included positive elements, like a demand that—for years—seemed endless.

Law no. 958 should have expired in 1954 but was extended until 1956, when the new cinema Law no. 897 (31 July) came into effect. It consolidated Andreotti's approach to cinema policy, unifying the government subsidy at 16%, and increasing mandatory screening days for Italian films from 80 to 100. The *Democrazia Cristiana* government made sure it had control over film production: there were no longer two rates of state subsidy, one of which depended on a technical committee's judgement of the film's artistic quality. Now there was just one rate, meaning that a producer whose film synopsis was not approved would not obtain a subsidy equal to 16% of box office takings.

The law led to a rise in the number of films produced, and this meant increased box office takings for Italian films: in 1959, they accounted for 36% of total takings, and this was the start of a constant growth that lasted until 1970.

Between 1956 and 1957 Italian cinema experienced its first post-war crisis. A legislative vacuum lasting two years followed expiry of the 1949 Law. Panic spread among producers, and some of the most solid companies were paralysed: Gualino's Lux, and Minerva Film. Other factors contributed to this crisis: the advent of television, a new generation of spectators, increasing taxes, higher interest rates, the uncontrolled proliferation of improvised producers, and the growth of car ownership, which gave Italians other ways to spend their free time. The cinema was no longer their only source of entertainment, and Italians differentiated their consumer spending as incomes and lifestyles improved.

Unlike other economic sectors, the Italian film industry had to deal with a gradual slowing of production. In his introduction to the annual statistics report in 1956, SIAE Director General Antonio Ciampi spoke of a set of structural factors. These included shrinking credit, an excessive increase in investments, and production costs out of all proportion with the amount a film earned. He also mentioned that the excessive number of films in circulation reduced the amount each single film could earn, while the domestic market could not cover the production costs for big budget films, and there was also the difficulty of exploiting Italian films adequately abroad. Then there was speculation by some companies that had no capital but were given advance funding via secondary credit circuits.[19] In the spring of 1956, the cinema crisis reached its peak as Parliament discussed the text of the proposed reform of the law. The Rome Court declared the bankruptcy of Minerva Film, one of the largest production companies, and of Excelsa Film, Diana Cinematografica, Taurus Film, Fortezza and other regional distribution agencies. Renato Gualino, President of Lux Film, announced that he was no longer interested in production.

In 1956, *Oggi Illustrato* published a long letter by Angelo Rizzoli on the Italian film industry crisis, in which he talked about the causes and about some possible solutions. According to Rizzoli, the greatest problem of the Italian film market was the excessive discrepancy between production costs and earnings. Over 60% of Italian films made a loss in those years, and the producer would often lose almost all the capital invested. Rizzoli maintained that state intervention was essential in such a moment of crisis: "Is it really necessary to support the Italian cinema? I think so: our cinema must be helped for the sake of culture and for the sake of the national economy. It must be helped seriously, but in an enlightened way".[20]

However, except for this brief period of crisis, Italian cinema would continue to do well for many years in terms of total spending on entertainment by Italians.

At the end of the 1950s, came Law no.1097 (22 December 1959); it simply extended the measures of the 1959 law and would remain in force until Law no.1213 was introduced in 1965.

The successes of Italian cinema did not conceal the real base on which the system rested. Money flooded into the industry, and this artificially stimulated film production without encouraging consolidation of an industrial structure that had always been fragile and unstable. Funding was often in the form of non-repayable loans, and this deprived the industry of a sense of responsibility about rational management of financial resources, so that it was incapable of developing an independent strategy for surviving without the consolidated privileges that came under threat every time a law expired.

## ANICA-MPEAA Agreements

In the epic era of Italian cinema, from 1945 to the early 1950s, the policy of the big American production companies in the Motion Pictures Export Association of America (MPEAA) consisted of massive film exports, with an effective business strategy aimed at establishing lasting dominance, more at immediate profits or advantageous speculation.

Several factors favoured the invasion of US films. Firstly, the indisputable validity of American films meant that they were welcomed by the Italian public, hungry for American movies after years of deprivation due to fascist protectionism. The other factors were the practice of dubbing, the great number of cinemas, and the absence of laws limiting film imports or at least the duration of their circulation permit.

When film imports are mentioned, this means purchase of the right to commercially exploit a film in a certain country and for a certain length of time, usually five years. One measure to restore equilibrium to the Italian market would have been to set a limit on the duration of these contracts, since the American companies not only exported new films but also left old films in circulation for years. The majors used, and still continue to use, some typically oligopolistic sales techniques and rental contracts that fall into the categories of open and concealed dumping.

Dumping, or price discrimination, consists of selling a product abroad at a price lower than production cost. In the film industry, dumping can take stronger forms than in other industries, and despite some losses or missed earnings at the start, dumping can ensure a dominant position on foreign markets in the long run. Dumping is possible if the preferences of potential consumers and their geographical locations are different from the site supplying the product. In addition, there must be different price elasticities for the various segments into which the market can be divided: therefore, for the American film companies, the two markets were the United States and Italy. In order to carry out dumping, the different market segments must be separate from each other, meaning that an intermediary must not be able to buy in the segment where the price is lower and then re-sell the product where the price is higher. The Italian distributors could not buy films directly on the American market, but were forced to go through the Italian branches of the American majors, which offered them better prices than for the films actually produced in Italy. In addition to this form of direct dumping, there was an indirect or concealed form, i.e. the American Studios' Italian branches allowed Italian cinema owners to defer payments for film rental. This certainly helped the cinema owners, but did not leave a great deal of space for Italian films, since Italian producers had to cover their production costs and could not compete with the American rental conditions. Finally, the Americans allowed Italian cinema owners to use for free—or almost free—the anamorphic lenses that were essential for projecting the first cinemascope films; the Americans had exclusive rights to these lenses until the early 1950s. This was another kind of indirect dumping: a way of influencing or directing the cinema owners towards choosing Hollywood films by giving them an advantage that only the American film companies could offer.

Another aspect to consider is that Italian currency laws at the time prevented the export of Italian currency and therefore encouraged the so-called "cinema accounts". American films entered Italy on a franco valuta basis: Italian branches of the major studios imported films, but the profits they made were paid into special bank accounts, which constituted a currency debt. The American majors then used more or less legal systems to try and transfer the currency equivalent of these accounts back to the US. Another system was to produce films in Italy, either alone or as a co-production. MGM was the first major to launch this line by shooting *Quo Vadis?* entirely at Cinecittà. Other big budget films, like *War and Peace* or *Helen of Troy*, ushered in the Golden Age of Hollywood on the Tiber.

Those working in the film industry, especially ANICA members, were convinced that cinema was principally a matter of culture and ideas, as well as money, and that it was impossible to apply the same restrictions on the film industry that a government could impose on coffee or cotton or any other foreign goods. In addition to being protected by laws, the Italian film industry also engaged in international partnerships in the form of bilateral co-production agreements, initially with France, Germany and Spain. Italy also supported the creation of the European Film Union, which was supposed to guarantee the free circulation of people, capital and technology.

With regard to international partnerships, the agreement reached between ANICA and the MPEAA in May 1951 is especially noteworthy. Private agreements, subsequently ratified at the government level, regulated the film trade between Italy and the United States. The most important clauses were as follows: a) the Italian government would allow American companies in Italy to transfer 50% of their income to the USA; b) the MPEAA promised to pay 12.5% of the sums (converted into dollars) to an Italian company, Italian Film Export (IFE), to circulate Italian film in America; c) the MPEAA committed its member companies to invest 40% of their earnings on the Italian market in producing and distributing Italian films, while the remaining 60% was to be invested in other ways (hotels, ship building and other works of national interest); d) the Americans agreed to limit their exports to Italy to 255 films per year (205 reserved for member companies MGM, Fox, Paramount, Columbia, RKO, Universal, Warner Bros, Allied Artists, Republic, and 20 for United Artists), making a further 50 available to Italian importers; e) the American companies in Italy were to join ANICA.

When the American companies agreed to limit their imports into Italy, this was more a confirmation of the farsighted strategic vision of the big Hollywood majors than a diplomatic success for ANICA.

In 1953, talks began again on a new agreement between ANICA and MPEAA. The American organisation opposed funding IFE, while ANICA insisted on the importance of the subsidy, but was willing to reduce it from 12.5% to 10%. At the same time, however, the independent American distributors (IMPDAA, Independent Motion Picture Distributors Association of America) accused IFE of buying up the best Italian films for the American market and of distributing them at conditions the independents could not compete with. The agreement was renewed at 10%, but IMPDAA protested again, because IFE had created a subsidiary to distribute Italian films. The case came before the Federal Trade Commission, and IFE was accused of interference in free and fair market competition. The outcome was that the subsidies paid by MPEAA to IFE were declared illegal. When the subsidies were abolished in 1954, *Variety* reported the event as follows: "Elimination of the subsidy is a major victory for the Americans who have pointed out to the Italians that, due to a variety of circumstances including Federal Trade Commission pressure, they'll no longer be in a position to grant the aid".[21] In 1955 IFE closed its New York office and was replaced by a public body set up to promote Italian films abroad: Unitalia film.

## The European Dream of Italian Cinema

Reconstruction of Italian cinema after World War II took place in a climate of willingness to create international relations.

Some Italian producers, including Pittaluga, had been attentive to international collaboration since the 1930s; their aim was to put up a united front against the American invasion without harming chances of making opportunistic alliances with the same Americans.

The European studio heads were fascinated by the idea of a united front, but at the same time they demanded protectionist policies from their own governments in order to create partial—and often rather ineffective—national trade barriers against the Hollywood majors.

Leaving aside the Communist states, which opted for a state monopoly on production and imports, France and the UK are the countries that came closest to the Italian model. The British Labour government was initially concerned to protect its domestic film industry and avoid a leak of dollars caused by American film imports. It introduced a tax of 75% (Dalton Duty) on all earnings from foreign films. The United States reacted immediately by interrupting the flow of films: the 4,000 cinemas in the United Kingdom were hard hit, and the government was forced to repeal the law after seven months. Instead, it created a state bank to support the British film industry and to grant funding of up to 70% of production costs: the bank granted what the British call "end money", i.e. loans that are repaid last, so that the bank loses a substantial amount of money. In 1950, an extra tax on cinema tickets was used to create a state fund to grant non-repayable loans. At the same time, taxes were reduced to 20%, and improvements were made to the quota system requiring a certain number of screening days for British films; this could amount to as many as 120 per year for cinema circuits.

France created an even more extensive protection system, with a quota system for the distribution of dubbed films (no more than 110 American films), a screening quota (105 days per year reserved for French films), and *la loi d'aide* which provided aid to producers, calculated on the basis of a share of gross takings on the home market, and 25% of the currency transferred to France for the export of French films. This law and the quota system favoured French films, which were able to account for 50% of total box-office takings, but the excessive restrictions on the distribution of foreign films meant that the cinema owners saw their sources of supply dwindle.

The Italian producers were aware that protectionism could damage the film industry, which needed exchanges in order to flourish. However, the idea was that not only national economic interests were at stake in the competition with the American movie industry, but that the interests at stake were above all cultural: the European cinema versus the superficiality of the Yankee cinema.

Of all the dreams and utopias of grandeur in the history of ANICA, the united European front was probably the most profitable for Italian cinema. Although this front never actually came into being, co-production agreements made with the various foreign film industries helped the Italian industry to take off and play a leading role in European film production.

From the end of the war, ANICA put a great deal of pressure on the Italian government to include films in the trade agreements it made with many other European countries. The main aim was to favour the system of cinema exchanges as much as possible, in view of the imminent establishment of a single European market; this appeared the best response to the internal shortcomings of every single state and to the dangers from the other side of the Atlantic.

The first co-production agreement was made with France, on 26 October 1946. The meeting involved parliamentarian Alfredo Proia, head of film services of the Italian *Presidenza del Consiglio*, and Michel Fourré-Cormeray, Director General of the *Cinématographie Francaise*. Even before deciding on the co-production regulations, the keystone of a new reconstruction policy, it was necessary to resolve some administrative, technical and financial problems still outstanding between the two countries at the time of their Liberation. For this reason, there was a one-year trial period, during which the aim was to produce 15 full-length films: ten in Italy and five in France. The co-production system meant that financial risk was shared and this made it easier to deal with the cost involved in a big budget film. The intention was also to concentrate on quality products, as with *Fabiola* (1949), produced by the Roman company Universalia, directed by Alessandro Blasetti and featuring Michele Morgan, Michel Simon, Henri Vidal and Louis Salou. French participation involved French actors and collaboration on dialogues, while Italy supplied the artistic and technical crews. The film had a budget of about half a million lire and was part of a vast international co-production programme. Salvo D'Angelo, project head, stated: "The union of our forces must be fertile and effective. Our two markets can become one single market. If our experience is successful, French and Italian producers will find themselves with a market of ten thousand cinemas, guaranteeing their films much higher and more regular incomes".

The ambitious co-produced films were intended to be prestigious and took on the role of ambassadors for the countries involved. They were presented as the product of a dynamic and totally healthy industry, and the companies involved also had to be in good commercial and financial health. Co-productions were therefore subject to special authorisation from the

*Servizi Cinematografici della Presidenza del Consiglio* in Italy, and from the *Direction Generale de la Cinématographie* in France. Authorisations were granted only after the financial plans had been checked. In addition, according to the terms of the agreements and according to Italian and French law, co-produced films enjoyed the advantages (bonuses and quotas) given to films that were 100% national.

The balance sheet for 1949 showed that the system worked better in France than in Italy: nine of the ten films planned for Italy had been made, while not one of the French films had been completed. The new law providing temporary aid to the French film industry, the bonuses given to films produced in Italy, and revision of the regulations on admission and exploitation of foreign films led to a new co-production agreement in Rome on 21 February 1949. Film quality was still a priority, and in order to avoid the previous imbalance, it was decided that co-productions would be one-for-one: one Italian-French co-production for one French-Italian co-production. The co-production system was consacrated when the agreements were renewed in 1953, and the new agreements defined the French-Italian film co-production policy from then on. The co-production system seemed the best way to save Europe's national film industries. The success of the co-produced films confirmed the need for the system to be extended to all European countries, in order to define a successful European cinema that could compete with Hollywood.

In the 15 years following the first co-production agreement, Italy made many other similar agreements with the most important foreign film industries, either with cinema associations or else between governments. New agreements were signed with Germany in 1952, with Spain in 1953, Yugoslavia in 1954, Austria in 1955 and Argentina in 1957. Despite the definitely positive effects, the theoretical vacuum around the definition of the European cinema paralysed economic reflection; instead of creating a discussion, it was frozen in bureaucratic procedures and financial speculation that defeated the aims of the project. European film industries—especially the Italian, French and Spanish industries—developed their own production standard, whose presumed superiority to American film lay more in the reflected glory of the great literary and musical masterpieces than in narrative models really able to compete with the dynamic plots of the American movie industry.

European enthusiasm became bogged down in meetings and technical committees that went no further than announcements and declarations of intent. In 1955 the provisional committee of the European Film Union met in Cannes; it consisted of representatives of the producers' associations and Henri Frenay was the president. Despite the commitment of cinema industrialists, the union's problem was mostly political/economic, since trade liberalisation could not be separated from unification of laws on state assistance, and no film industry was willing to relinquish state help in order to leap into the uncharted territory of the European market.

The individual European countries therefore went ahead separately. ANI-CA's commitment in pursuing exchange and co-production agreements with other film industries allowed Italian production to grow rapidly and its films to circulate abroad, thus resolving the problem of its own limited domestic market, which was too small to allow the recovery of constantly rising production costs.

The co-production system soon degenerated: the project of real partnership between European producers was replaced by pure financial speculation aimed at obtaining state funding and avoiding customs barriers in other countries. The co-production system allowed a film to obtain two, three or even four nationalities, so that it could receive state subsidies in each country, and was included in the mandatory screening quotas.

Between 1950 and 1965, Italy co-produced around 1150 films, including 764 with France, 190 with Spain, 46 with Germany, and 141 three-way productions. Exports rose at the same time. In 1951, Italian films were distributed in 83 countries, from Belgium to Venezuela, from the United States to Turkey. Italian cinema grew in quantity and quality, but a more detailed analysis would show that box office takings must be re-calculated in order to divide the Italian producers' earnings from the American or other co-producers' earnings. This would make it easier to understand the reason for the resounding collapse of some important production companies like Minerva Film, Lux Film and Titanus, and also the constant instability of the Italian film industry, which never managed to balance its books in spite of state subsidies and its earnings from exports.

In any case, the positive aspect of these years was the re-definition of the relationship with Hollywood. The international success of Italian productions and co-productions took Italian cinema out of its provincialism, and made it a privileged representative of *italianità* in the world; this is true not only for films by the great directors, like Fellini, Rossellini, Antonioni and Visconti, but also of other types of film like the costume and peplum films. However, the Italian conquest of the foreign markets was also made possible by the American majors, and as Wagstaff recalls, "when President Johnson abolished the tax breaks for foreign investments and the American companies reorganised and merged in the 1970s, the European film industries collapsed".

## Notes

1 Dale, Martin 1995, *The Movie Game: The Film Business in Britain, Europe and America*, London: Cassell.
2 Zavattini, Cesare 25 August 1945, "Poesia solo affare del cinema italiano", in *Film d'oggi*, no. 10.
3 Nara, Italy, Motion Picture 865.4061, January 22, 1945 Confidential Report to the Secretary of State, Washington DC.
4 Deleuze, Gilles 1986, *Cinema 1: The Movement Image*, Minneapolis: University of Minnesota Press, pp. 205–215.

5 Declaration by Admiral Ellery Stone, quoted in Quaglietti, Lorenzo 1980, *Storia economica-politica del cinema italiano 1945-1980*, Rome: Ed. Riuniti, pp. 37–38.

6 Harry Spencer Truman, in Dyer, Richard 1973, *The People's Film*, New York: Hasting House, p. 175.

7 Data are based on statistics from S.I.A.E and are taken from *Cinespettacolo*, 10 April 1954.

8 ANICA had its own delegates in the following international organisations: BIC (Bureau International du Cinéma); FIAPF (International Federation of Film Producers' Associations); FIAD (International Federation of Film Distributors' Associations); CIITC (Confederazione internazionale industrie tecniche cinematografiche); Confederazione europea delle industrie tecniche; CICE (Comitato Industria Cinematografica Europea); Comitato dei Tre (made up of representatives of the Italian, French and German national producers' associations), INA (International Newsreel Association); ASIFA (Association International du Film d'Animation).

9 De Pirro, Nicola 1955, "Espansione all'estero del film italiano nel dopoguerra", *Lo Spettacolo*, Anno V (3): 1–34.

10 There are at least five rationales that are used to justify government's intervention in the cultural and creative industries. Firstly, investing in the arts now gives to current and future generations more cultural options and has a positive impact on the improvement of individuals' quality of life (Baumol-Bowen, 1966). The second rationale is that "fast industrial growth may have altered the preferences of the average consumer that is acquiring leisure faster than the preparation for using it (Scitovsky, 1972)". The third argument states that the government has to subsidise cultural and creative industries because these industries have a determinant role in shaping national culture and identity. The fourth rationale is linked to the positive externalities generated by the development of culture and artistic heritage. And, finally, the last justification is linked to the so-called Baumol disease that affects performing arts: industrial revolution has determined a dramatic increase in art production costs and government patronage is considered necessary.

11 Chiarini, Luigi 1954, *Cinema quinto potere*, Rome-Bari: Laterza.

12 Baracco, Adriano 15 January 1949, "L'ordine regna a Varsavia", *Cinema*, (6): 165.

13 From Gualino's letter, in De Agostini, Fabio Mida, Massimo 15 March 1949, "L'ordine non regna più a Varsavia", *Cinema*, (10): 297.

14 Alberto Lattuada, in "L'ordine non regna più a Varsavia", cit.

15 Art.3, Law 26 July 1949, n.379. The producers also have the right "to obtain authorisation to show one foreign film with Italian dialogues for every Italian film produced without paying the fee in the previous article"

16 In a speech to the Chamber of Deputies in April 1950, *onorevole* Andreotti reiterated: "The government is aware of the need for more precise import regulations, also regarding American companies. There are many reasons why we are opposed to legislation imposing a quota system. One reason is that this system compels Government bodies to be selective, and this is a difficult task, because the true choice should be made by the public who really like American films".

17 It is important to remember that Andreotti also worked with figures from the fascist era who had been reabsorbed into the political system. The "director general of entertainment is Nicola de Pirro, ex-director general of the theatre under fascism, ex- *squadrista* and fascist dignitary; division head Gianni de Tommasi is an ex-*squadrista*, and fascist dignitary who wrote for "Difesa della razza"; division head Annibale Scicluna is an ex-*irredentista*, writer for Popolo d'Italia and

Minculpop official responsible for reporting to the *Duce*; the head of the general affairs division Luigi Natale, the head of the import-export division Benito Orta and press office head Giorgio Nelson Page were all fascist dignitaries", in Guastini, Giancarlo, Restuccia, Bruno, Silvestri, Roberto (eds.), "Cronologia 1929–1964", in Various Authors 1974, *Politica e cultura nel dopoguerra*, Mostra Internazionale del Nuovo Cinema, Pesaro, Quaderno Informativo, no. 56, p. 138.

18 Cinema historian Zagarrio's embarrassment is evident when he offers an evaluation of the immediate post-war years:
When trying to reach a conclusion about economic policy between 1945 and 1948, historians encounter some important problems. Methodological problems, and questions about an overall judgement for which there is not an answer that everyone agrees on [. . .] Who is right? Those who highlight the crisis in the Italian industry of the time and the divide between intellectual output and industrial output, or those who view the industry of the time as a fertile period which laid the foundations for future strategies? [. . .] Does the period end with the nth defeat of progressive ideas, [. . .] or is it an incubation period for the "rebirth" of the flourishing Italian cinema of the 1960s? Should we accuse Andreotti the censor for the nth time, or should we thank him for being (perhaps unconsciously) the saviour of the nation's film industry? [. . .] These remain unresolved problems, and the debate is far from over".

19 Antonio Ciampi, "Introduction", in SIAE 1956, *Lo Spettacolo in Italia, Annuario statistico SIAE*, Rome: Pubblicazioni SIAE, p. x.

20 Rizzoli, Angelo 21 June 1956, "Una lettera sulla crisi del cinema", in *Oggi Illustrato*, n. 25, quoted in Della Casa, Stefano et al. 2003, *Capitani Coraggiosi. Produttori Italiani 1945–1975*, Milan: Mondadori Electa, p. 144.

21 Variety, 9 June 1954, in Ellwood, David, Kroes, Rob 1994, *Hollywood in Europe; Experience of a Cultural Hegemony*, Amsterdam: VU Press, p. 210.

# Bibliography

ARGENTIERI, Mino 1998, *Il cinema italiano dal dopoguerra ad oggi*, Rome: Editori Riuniti

AULENTI, Lino 2011, *Storia del cinema italiano*, Padova: LibreriaUniversitaria

BERNARDI, Sandro (ed.) 2004, *Storia del cinema italiano 1954–1959*, Venice: Marsilio / Scuola Nazionale del Cinema

BERTETTO, Paolo (ed.) 2011, *Storia del cinema italiano. Uno sguardo d'insieme*, Venice: Marsilio / Scuola Nazionale del Cinema

BIZZARRI, Libero 1987, *Il cinema italiano: industria, mercato, pubblico: raccolta di saggi*, Rome: Associazione Gulliver

BIZZARRI, Libero, SOLAROLI, Libero 1958, *L'industria cinematografica italiana*, Florence: Parenti

BONDANELLA, Peter (ed.) 2014, *The Italian Cinema Book*, London: Palgrave Macmillan for the British Film Institute

BONDANELLA, Peter 2009, *A History of the Italian Cinema*, New York: Continuum

BRUNETTA, Gian Piero 1996, *Identità italiana e identità europea nel cinema italiano dal 1945 al miracolo economico*, Torino: Fondazione Agnelli

CHIARINI, Luigi 1954, *Cinema quinto potere*, Rome-Bari: Laterza

COLOMBO, Fausto 1997, *L'industria culturale italiana dal 1900 alla seconda Guerra mondiale. Tendenze della produzione e del consumo*, Milan: Università Cattolica

CORSI, Barbara 2001, *Con qualche dollaro in meno: storia economica del cinema italiano*, Rome: Editori Riuniti

CORSI, Barbara (1986–87), *Scelte produttive dell'industria cinematografica fra la Legge Alfieri (1938) e la Legge Andreotti (1949)*, Pisa: Università di Pisa

COSULICH, Callisto (ed.) 2003, *Storia del cinema italiano 1945–1948*, Venice: Marsilio / Scuola Nazionale del Cinema

DALE, Martin 1995, *The Movie Game: The Film Business in Britain, Europe and America*, London: Cassell

DE GIUSTI, Luciano (ed.) 2003, *Storia del cinema italiano 1945–1948*, Venice: Marsilio / Scuola Nazionale del Cinema

DELEUZE, Gilles 1986, *Cinema 1: The Movement Image*, Minneapolis: University of Minnesota Press

DYER, Richard 1973, *The People's Film*, New York: Hasting House

ELLWOOD, David, KROES, Rob 1994, *Hollywood in Europe: Experience of a Cultural Hegemony*, Amsterdam: VU Press

FLIBBERT, Andrew 2007, *Commerce in Culture: State and Markets in the World Film Trade*, New York: Palgrave

LANDY, Marcia 2000, *Italian Film*, Cambridge: Cambridge University Press.

LIZZANI, Carlo et al. 1961, *Storia del cinema italiano*, Florence: Parenti

MAGRELLI, Enrico 1985, *Sull'industria cinematografica italiana*, Venice: Marsilio

MICCICHÉ, Lino 1995, *Cinema italiano: gli anni '60 e oltre*, Venice: Marsilio

PIRRO, Ugo 1998, *Soltanto un nome nei titoli di testa: i felici anni Sessanta del cinema italiano*, Turin: Einaudi

QUAGLIETTI, Lorenzo 1980, *Storia economico-politica del cinema italiano*, Rome: Editori Riuniti

SIAE 1956, *Lo Spettacolo in Italia, Annuario statistico SIAE*, Rome: Pubblicazioni SIAE

SQUIRE, Jason 1983, *The Movie Business Book*, London: Columbus Books.

TINAZZI, Giorgio (ed.) 1979, *Il cinema italiano degli anni '50*. Venezia: Marsilio

TORRI, Bruno 1972, *The Italian Cinema: From the Post-War Period to the Present Day*, Rome: Scalia

TREVERI-GENNARI, Daniela 2009, *Post-War Italian Cinema: American Intervention, Vatican Interests*, New York: Routledge

VARIOUS AUTHORS 1974, *Politica e cultura nel dopoguerra*, Mostra Internazionale del Nuovo Cinema, Pesaro, Quaderno Informativo, 56

VILLA, Federica 1994, *Materiali intorno al cinema italiano degli anni Cinquanta*, Milan: ISU, Università Cattolica

ZAGARRIO, Vito (ed.) 1988, *Dietro lo schermo. Ragionamento sui modi di produzione cinematografici in Italia*, Venice: Marsilio

# 6  Entrepreneurial Efforts in the Worldwide Race

> Technically I can explain to you what a producer does,
> but then it is a question of artistic inspiration . . .[1]

## Captains Courageous

Historians tend to offer different interpretations about the real conditions of the Italian film industry in the immediate post-war years. Quaglietti (1980)—also followed to some extent by Brunetta (1982)—insists above all on the industry's disastrous organisation, whereas Corsi (2001) insists on the speed with which film production started up again.

The Italian film industry started to slowly recover and, after a period of crisis during the '50s, it definitely boomed in the '60s when Italian films released beat out the Americans. The increase in national movie production was the result of the interactions among different factors: American investments,[2] the growth of European co-productions[3] and the effect of national cinema laws. Besides, box office of national films grew (from 8% on total box office in 1946 to 36% in 1954) while American ones dropped: from 80% in 1946 and then dropped to 70% in 1949, 63% in 1952 and 56% in 1954. This change in the lion's share was due to: the average quality of films, a more widespread use of colour, the re-creation of a star system capable of influencing collective imagination, the introduction of cinemascope. The boom was not registered only in the home market, but also internationally: in 1948, about 827 contracts were signed with 33 different countries for a total of 600 million lire. In 1956, contracts were over 2,000, Italian movies were exported to about 80 countries for a total of 8 billion lire.

Already, towards the end of the war, Italian producers willing to take risks had courageously begun working again. Twenty-five films were made in 1945: six by Lux, five by Excelsa-Minerva, three by Titanus, two by Manenti, one by Artisti Associati, one by Ceiad, two by Fincine, and five by various other companies. This list shows that over half of the films were either produced or financed by the three companies that were central to the development of the Italian film industry in the post-war years: Titanus, Lux and Minerva were production and distribution companies, and Titanus also had a chain of cinemas. The fragmented production system so characteristic of the Italian film industry meant that in 1946 there was a grand total of 48 production companies, of which only eight managed to make more than one film. Nevertheless, it was during this period, after the difficult and adventurous rebirth from the ashes of war, that Italian cinema seemed gradually to move towards industrial maturity. Gualino's Lux, Lombardo's Titanus and Rizzoli's Cineriz were much more rationally organised. The Italian producers of these years fall into two broad categories. There were the big production companies belonging to ANICA, and then there were small companies specialising in low profile films for the regional distribution circuits, which had, nevertheless, a certain continuity, like the companies of the Misiano brothers and of Roberto Amoroso.

Then there were a multitude of companies that were mostly short-lived companies created for speculation, which produced one film and then disappeared. This type of company, as we have already seen, had been a feature of the Italian film industry since the 1920s.

This meant that there were many different types of film on offer in the 1950s, ranging from the low profile films made for regional audiences to medium-high quality productions, up to the really big budget movies. Graph 6.1 shows the structure of Italian movie industry in terms of production companies from 1945 to 1965[4].

Despite the censorship, and despite the many film projects that never got off the ground, directors like Michelangelo Antonioni, Federico Fellini and Elio Petri could begin to establish themselves—albeit with a struggle. During this slow rise, which accelerated suddenly in the 1960s, box-office hits were produced by smaller film companies and by important industrialists, showing that everyone could make films, independently of their position

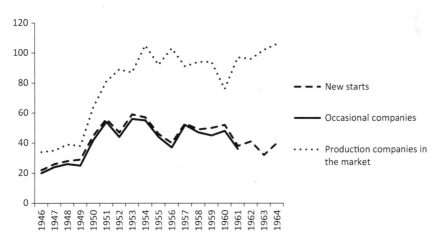

*Graph 6.1*  Italian Cinema Production Companies, 1945–1965.
Source: author's elaboration.

in the hierarchy of producers and distributors. The mechanism of state aid made it possible to get rich quickly, but at the same time stimulated entrepreneurial initiative and encouraged the type of medium-level production without which a film industry cannot survive.

However, there was also the other side of the coin, as shown by the worry expressed in the words of contemporary observers: "in one year we have produced about ninety films. There were 74 production companies working in 1951. This means senseless fragmentation. There aren't seventy-four producers in all Europe, so how on earth could they all be here. Out of 74, maybe there are 5 or fewer permanent companies with a continuous output. Only one is capable of doing what makes a production company solid, with producers, directors, artists and technicians under contract".

## Who the Producers Were

In the 1950s, all ANICA activities increased constantly: the number of films and the number of cinemas (in 1956 there were 15,700 cinemas with at least 6 million seats), the number of spectators and the help given by the state to the Italian film industry. This success depended on a set of factors: improved average quality, the use of colour film, the re-composition of a star system, and adoption of cinemascope. The distributors began to take more of a concerned interest in the national cinema and participated in the production of many Italian films, under the system of guaranteed minimum returns. It is interesting to understand the driving forces behind this "rebirth". As already said, the policy of protecting the industry led to a fragmentation that reached its peak between 1954 and 1955, when 200 production companies existed, and this meant that the production companies had limited bargaining power.

There was from the start, however, a clear distinction between the small group of stable companies working continuously, and a second group of sporadic producers. Natural selection in the second group was extremely difficult and became even more of a struggle when the introduction of colour film and other technical innovations meant that average production costs rose to a level beyond the reach of small businessmen.

The need to spread the risk over more than one film and the increase in average production costs made it essential for the industry to move gradually towards a more stable organisation centred on a few production and distribution companies. This process produced an articulated structure with companies grouped together, but they managed to remain sufficiently independent despite having co-production or distribution contracts with each other. This network structure had the advantages that it maintained a variety of projects, ideas and ambitions, without giving up the benefit involved in a more rational spread of investment risks across a sufficiently large number of films.[5]

Production is undoubtedly the most strictly financial and industrial stage of film-making. It involves a set of entrepreneurial, organisational, technical and administrative activities necessary for planning and making a film, and the film's success or failure depends on these. The creator of the film is not only the director, but is first and foremost the producer. Film production is ruled by pure speculation or can be based on serious industrial procedures and planning. The producer can put his own capital into the film or use other people's, but always keeps control of the finances. Or the producer becomes an *executive producer*, who organises the production schedule on behalf of others, controlling the finances and making studios, workshops and distribution agencies available. This means that there is a distinction between an *executive producer* and a *producer*, between the person who produces a film by assembling and coordinating the various stages of its production, and the person who manages a company, taking on the responsibility for the company's entire production policy.

The influx of American capital into a context like that of Italy, where the film industry was what we can define as proto-industrial, helped to consolidate the executive *producer* figure rather than the *producers*, i.e. the people working for the major studios to produce films that were Italian in name but were actually American.

But there were still plenty of *executive producers* who decided to become *producers*. Carlo Ponti and Dino de Laurentiis formed a company in the 1950s and made some ambitious films with the Americans: *Attila* (1953) by Piero Francisci, *Ulysses* (1953) by Mario Camerini, and *War and Peace* (1955) by King Vidor. The partnership ended with the last of these films. Both were tired of working as simple executive producers of other people's projects and had ambitions to become real producers. Taking different paths and with different outcomes,[6] Ponti and De Laurentiis invested their own money in film production in order to compete with the technical skill of spectacular Hollywood movies. These films, known as "super colossal films *d'autore*", gave a strong impetus to the development of the entire Italian production system.

It is interesting to read what foreigners thought about the Italian producers of the 1950s. In 1962, *Cinecorriere* published an article with the title "The Times on Italian Producers". The *Times* article said that: "Italian producers have discovered that quality is profitable". It drew attention to the fact that Italian films met with critical and public success in America; this was not only the case of directors like Antonioni, Fellini and Visconti, but also of the Italian producers, who were considered as gifted with "remarkable intelligence and breadth of vision".[7]

The *Times* gave the example of Lombardo's courageous decision to entrust Visconti with the job of directing *Rocco e i suoi fratelli*, although Visconti's films were not box-office successes. Dino De Laurentiis was compared with the big film magnates of Hollywood's Golden Age. Carlo Ponti had made *La Ciociara* and was planning to go ahead with *I sequestrati di Altona*, showing that he understood how important it was for films to be high quality. Franco Cristaldi had always used new talent, and the *Times* judged his

films *Salvatore Giuliano* and *Divorce Italian Style* two of the most interesting releases of the 1961–1962 season. For the *Times*, Alfredo Bini was
the ideal producer because his three films—*Il bell'Antonio, La Viaccia* and
*Accattone*—were successes with both critics and audiences: "Bini has all the
characteristics of contemporary Italian movie production: a good balance
between box office and critics acclaims".

For this second period of Italian cinema, which starts after the war, I built
a dataset that makes it possible to have a more complete analytical pro-
spective of the Italian film industry, at least for film production. From the
very beginning, the Italian film market was highly fragmented, with very few
examples of vertically integrated companies.[8] In the period under analysis,
we can distinguish between five different categories of movie production.
First, we have leading national producers (they produced 28 or more movies
in the overall period of analysis); next we have regular national producers
(14 to 27 movies) and third we have occasional national producers (one to
13 movies). A fourth category includes national collaborations, that is, movies produced by two or more Italian companies, and finally we have international co-productions which involved national and international companies.

From looking at single national productions, it is quite clear that the market consisted of many occasional producers. The leading companies had an
average market share of 21%, regular companies accounted for 9%, and
occasional companies for 70%. If we look at the types of company involved
in the film industry, we can see that 46% were limited companies, 38%
joint-stock companies, 11% family business and 5% were associations,
cooperatives and private institutions. Apart from some older companies
like Lux (founded in 1941) and Titanus (founded in 1932), the great majority of companies were founded after the Second World War. Organisation
and financial structure were strictly embedded. Broadly speaking, feature
film production was financed either using the resources of the production
company or by short-term loans. In some cases, money came from a combination of the two methods, but the majority of independent productions
were financed by loans, whereas the majority of films produced by the large
groups were financed by the companies' own resources—resources that
could of course be partly based on long-term loans. In the case of Italy, the
financial structure of both small-medium enterprises and big companies was
characterised by the dominance of credit loans over equity capital.[9] Banks
and distributors usually contributed with "first money"[10] (they had to be
reimbursed first), and covered about 50 to 60% of production costs.

The rate of new entries was extremely high immediately after the war:
an average of nearly 70% each year from 1946 to 1950, and during the
1950s new starts were about 49% each year. Most of these had a short life
cycle; they made a few movies and then disappeared. Financial resources
and organisational capabilities were needed for survival and competition
on a buoyant market, like the Italian market during the 1950s, and the
leading film companies usually followed a diversification strategy. Dino De

Laurentiis, for example, had two companies: Dino De Laurentiis Cinemato-grafica and DDL (De Curtis-De Laurentiis-Libassi). The first company was for ambitious projects like *La diga sul pacifico* (René Clément, 1957), *Le notti di Cabiria* (Fellini, 1957) and *La grande Guerra* (Monicelli, 1958), suc-cessful with critics and audiences alike and winners of prestigious awards. DDL, on the other hand, produced more popular commercial movies, like series featuring comic actor Totò. Franco Cristaldi, another movie tycoon, founded Vides Cinematografica in 1946. He invested in quality movies and young directors, but used co-productions with France and Spain as well as partnerships with other leading Italian companies like Titanus and Lux for more commercial movies.

The diversification strategy also helps to explain why not all occasional production ventures involved mere speculation, since some were dedicated to more specific and experimental projects. Directors Fellini and Lattuada founded Capitolium Film to produce *Luci del varietà*, while Arco Film pro-duced most of Pasolini's movies during the 1960s.

The number of national joint projects remained quite constant from the beginning of the recovery period until 1957, when the number fell, although it rose again in the following year. National joint projects mostly involved two companies (91%), and the most common partnerships were between two occasional companies (45%) and between a leading and an occasional company (32%). In the first case, the movies produced were commercial films with a more regional flavor, and for this reason they were handled by regional distributors (56%). It is interesting to notice that a handful of these movies (7%) were distributed by foreign companies, like Metro Gold-wyn Mayer, 20th Century Fox and Paramount; among these were Rossel-lini's *Paisà* (1947) and Visconti's *La terra trema* (1950). When not directly involved in making Italian movies, American companies had an incentive to distribute local productions to improve their position on the Italian market.[11]

The films made by a leading company in partnership with an occasional company were commercial, but with a more national flavor (like those fea-turing Totò), and very few of these can be categorized as art-house like *Francesco giullare di Dio* (1950) by Roberto Rossellini, *Accattone* (1961) by Pier Paolo Pasolini or *I Basilischi* (1963) by Lina Wertmuller. The pro-duction company itself usually distributed these joint projects when it had a distribution branch, as in the case of Titanus, Lux Film and Rizzoli. A joint project with a leading company gave the occasional company the chance to get into a distribution network of first-run theatres in big cities.

Joint projects between a leading and a regular company were quite rare—only 22 movies (7%)—and made in the early 1950s. Joint projects involv-ing a regular and an occasional company were a slightly more numerous (13%); these were made in the late 1950s and early 1960s, and were usually commercial productions, sometimes with erotic contents. During the period under study, the banks financed about 51% of total national joint projects.

## Financial Farces: Guaranteed Minimum Returns and Cinema Credit

Investing in a motion picture is risky. Unless a film is fortunate enough to garner sufficient advance sales to cover at least the movie's production costs, there is no guarantee that investors will recoup their investment or make even a small profit.

There are some features of the movie industry that are unlike other more traditional industrial sectors and that have an impact on financing methods. The best-known characteristics of movies are that every film is unique and the first copy is a prototype; demand is unpredictable; most production and distribution costs are incurred before a film can be released, and are thus sunk. A huge share of the investment takes place before circulation in cinemas. Cost structure has changed over time, and immaterial assets have acquired increasing importance. In the very beginning, movies were much more embedded with technical aspects, and this influenced the organisational structure: "the producers who emerged from the infancy of the film industry were hard-driving, competent and versatile. They took an active part in every department of movie making. These men were artisans as well as businessmen. They combined the talent of bankers and circus barkers".[12]

After the 1920s, when the movie industry became larger, more complex, specialized and content-driven, Hollywood began to dominate the world cinema.[13] Plots, stories and immaterial assets like actors, directors and scriptwriters became much more important. Stars became a long-standing feature of the movie business, and top performers began to command large salaries due to the positive impact they could have on box-office success.

These specific features influenced the organisational structure of the industry, and vertically integrated companies with an overall control of the value chain had an important competitive advantage. When we look at the histories of the different national cinemas, it is possible to distinguish between two main industrial configurations. On the one hand, there was the American way; the US film industry had an oligopolistic structure with high entry barriers and Hollywood was dominated by a few major studios, which were able to beat the competition with their distribution systems. Large-scale film release is not feasible without film distribution. The financial structure of these companies was no different from that of other industrial activities.[14]

Then there was the European configuration, with a very few large production companies and many small-medium film companies. The Italian film industry had always been fragmented, with a large number of small companies that produced only one or two movies and then disappeared. Some authors have argued that this particular configuration is coherent with the characteristics of movie production. According to Vogel (2007), "the feature-film business does not easily fit the usual moulds. Industries requiring sizable capital investments can normally be expected to evolve into purely oligopolistic forms: steel and automobile manufacturing are examples. But because movies—each uniquely designed and packaged—are not stamped out on cookie-cutter assembly lines, the economic structure is somewhat different".[15]

As many academics have argued, European film industries have not been able to develop a financially viable model, and production companies have relied on government support since the end of World War I. State intervention was seen as necessary after the war, since American movies flooded into European cinemas.[16] In addition, with the rise of nationalism and totalitarian governments, some countries adopted protectionist measures to guarantee the survival of their homegrown film industries.

There is a vast amount of literature about the creative industries, and specifically about the cinema, and it covers all the possible academic disciplines: from economics, to media studies, from organisation and management to sociology and so on. The complexity of production, the specificities of distribution and exhibition branches and the characteristics of demand driven by the "nobody knows anything[17]" principle make this industry worth investigation. In recent years, there has developed a growing body of macroeconomic and microeconomic research about the film industry, but there is still one specific feature that requires more investigation: film finance. There are two main reasons for the lack of academic research on this topic. One is the difficulty of obtaining data—especially historical data. The other reason is that film finance involves the problem of distinguishing between countries where the movie industry is mostly driven by market forces, like the USA, and those where there is government intervention and public subsidies. This is the case of Italy and other European countries like Germany, France and Great Britain.

Film production is a capital-intensive process and in most cases production companies do not have the scale of financial resources to finance their projects. Producers usually have to rely on external sources, but due to high risk and uncertainty, investment in film production is not very attractive for the majority of risk-adverse investors.[18] Although it is necessary to consider an inveterate weakness in the Italian financial system, it is impossible to overlook the fact that, in Italy, big business had always proved refractory to investing in the movie business.

Public subsidies are based on the assumption that market forces do not enable production companies to make enough money to cover their costs, and that this gap is not easily closed by industrial re-organisation or improved company efficiency.

From a purely economic point of view, this kind of aid influences producers' behaviour and is considered an obstacle to the functioning of market forces. Government intervention recalls Kornai's theory on soft budget constraint.[19] According to Kornai, public assistance is negotiable and subject to bargaining and lobbying. Consequently, there is no incentive for producers to act in an entrepreneurial way. A lack of box-office revenues can make producers even more dependent on public subsidies. According to some authors, the European film industry is trapped in a "self-confirming cycle of market failure and state intervention".[20]

Who provided the financial backing for a film if the producer did not have enough capital? In Italy, the most common mechanisms were the minimum guarantee system and cinema credit, together with state subsidies.[21]

The minimum guarantee system meant that the distributors took part in film production by investing capital in the form of cheques or bills of exchange, which they would recoup with box-office earnings. The minimum guarantee was, broadly speaking, an estimate of takings, at least on the Italian market. The producer's, distributor's and exhibitor's percentages were estimated on net takings—equal to gross takings minus government taxes and VAT. The distributor took a percentage of the net takings from the cinema, and then had to deduct the share that the producer had agreed to give him to cover the cost of distribution and risk. Here is an example. The distributor usually took a cut of 40% of net takings. The average share that the producer generally agreed to give the distributor for his agency expenses and the financial risk involved was 24%. Therefore, if a film took 100 at the box office, and net takings were 80, the shares were as follows: film rental gave 40% of 80, which is 32. Of this 32, the distributor kept 25%, which is 8. The remaining 24, is the producer's share. Each time a distributor paid a guaranteed minimum to the producer—i.e. he put his own money into film production—he had to consider these percentages in order to evaluate seriously the amount of his own investment. Therefore, if a distributor gave a guaranteed minimum of 50, the film would have to earn gross takings of at least 210 for the distributor to recoup the minimum guaranteed. If the film earned less than expected, there was a net loss for the distributor: this meant that the distributor had missed the real chance of making money at the box office. Regional distributors paid the guaranteed minimums either directly to the producer, or through a central distributor who acted as the financial and commercial intermediary. The guaranteed minimum tended to cover a more or less substantial share of the cost of making the film. Comedy films, dramas, and musicals had to cover much of their production costs with the guaranteed minimum for Italy, whereas other types of film, like peplum, adventure films and Westerns could also count on making money abroad. There is no doubt that this system required detailed understanding of market workings and extraordinary professionalism on the set. It is easy to imagine the difficulties faced by the producer if the film ran over its planned time and budget. In this case, the guaranteed minimum was not sufficient, and the producer would have to use his own money or else look for other capital. If no new capital was available, work on the film might grind to a halt or more commonly, the original plans were scaled down by cutting costs, meaning scenes and sequences, or else by selling shares. The material in the archives of the *Sezione di credito cinematografico* clearly reveals the role of distributors, who really guaranteed the credit that the bank granted to the producer. And this may be the reason why cinema legend has it that a Turin distributor's office had a notice on the wall that read "We would be real criminals if we signed more bills of exchange". The difficulties of recouping outstanding credit and the monthly rush when the bills of exchange were due to expire provide a first, although incomplete, explanation of the strategies behind film distribution in the cinemas. Distribution did not always follow any kind of rational logic, but more often than not was dictated by the need to recoup as much of the money advanced as possible.

As already mentioned before, during these years, the Italian producers could count on state funding and on credit provided by the *Sezione Autonoma di Credito Cinematografico* established under fascism. The Sezione (SACC) gained a wider scope with the 1947 Law, which added other activities besides that of funding film production: funding for distribution companies and cinemas, technological innovations in cinemas; purchase, editing and distribution of foreign films; advance payment of state subsidies introduced with the Cappa Law. The trend in the number of subsidies and the overall total for 1945–1965 is shown in Graph 2. 90% of the credit granted was funding for production. The special fund was formally separate from the ordinary fund (created in 1935), and requests for funding were evaluated by the bank but had to be authorised in advance by the Ministry's *Commissione Consultiva*, the real decision-making body.

As recalled in the previous chapter, SACC became a fundamental actor for sustaining national movie production with Law no. 448, July 26,1949, which aimed at reducing the number of foreign movies in the national market by obliging distributors to deposit 2,5 million lire[22] at the *Banca Nazionale del Lavoro* for every foreign movie imported and dubbed in Italy. The amount was used to create a special credit fund (*Fondo Speciale*)[23]. The law was revised in 1956 (no. 897, July 31) and the deposit was fixed at 5,5 million lire: 60% of the deposit was used for technical renovation of cinemas and

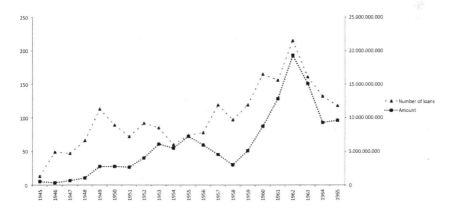

*Graph 6.2* Loans and Total Amount of Funding by S.A.C.C., 1945–1965.

Source: author's elaboration on Banca Nazionale del Lavoro archive.

the other 40% for sustaining national production and distribution of national movies.

The deposit was reimbursed after seven years. From 1945 to 1965, about 90% of loans were for movie production[24].

It is interesting to compare this with the ways in which credit was extended to the cinema in other countries. France adopted two methods of financing movies: a) a fund from an extra charge on tickets and with earnings from the *"taxe de sortie"* applied to every movie shot or dubbed in French;[25] b) the *Credit National* had a special section dedicated to financing movies (this fund covered only 30% of total production costs). In addition, producers could get a subsidy computed as a percentage of gross box-office takings in France. Britain had a bank fund that covered up to 70% of production costs; this method was abandoned in 1950 in favour of a public fund (from revenue taxes on tickets), which supported production companies with grants. German banks directly invested in production, distribution and exhibition companies. Spain used a method similar to Italy and France: taxes paid by importers of foreign movies went into a fund managed by the national movie industry association that gave loans covering 80% of total production costs. Mexico had an innovative system: the *Banco Cinematográfico* gave credit to producers (covering up to 80% of total production costs), and owned three different distribution companies responsible for the distribution of national production both on the Spanish-speaking market and worldwide.

To return to Italy: what requisites did a film project need in order to obtain funding from the credit institutes? The SACC archives (data available up to 1965) make it possible to give a first answer, although it is not complete. The archive data have been supplemented with data from other sources to create a database containing the following information for each film: the production company, co-production companies, distributor, nationality, film genre, director, year of release, amount of funding, box-office grosses, prizes won. The dataset gives a better understanding of the organisational structure of the Italian production and distribution branches of the industry, the emerging strategy of co-production with European partners and financing choices by the bank. We do not have information about movie budgets (these are not yet completely available) and therefore cannot infer the real effectiveness of this funding. Nevertheless, the dataset helps to understand what kind of "cinema" the bank and the state chose to support.

From 1945 to 1965, the total amount of funding increased each year: it grew constantly until 1955, fell between 1957 and 1958 due to the cinemagoing crisis and then rose again until 1961, before a final dramatic fall.

With reference to SACC funding, the bank gave loans to 53,7% of movies produced by leading Italian companies and 59% of movies by regular producers, while only 32.1% of movies by occasional producers were able to get funding. SACC financed 51.8% of national collaborations and 38.5% of international co-productions. Analysis of average funding gives the following figures: international co-productions received the highest average funding with 1,5 billion lire, followed by leading producers (1,48 billion), regular companies (1,34 billion), national collaborations (1,22 billion)[26] and finally the small companies (8 million). Larger companies were more likely to have access to funding. Big production companies were usually more financially reliable and could give more warranties to the bank. Was the bank more willing to finance the company or the movie project? Federico Fellini's experimental movie *Giulietta degli spiriti* that was produced by leading company Rizzoli and distributed by Cineriz (both these companies were founded by the tycoon Angelo Rizzoli) received the funding. *La dolce vita*, another great Fellini success, co-produced by small Italian company Riama Film and by two French companies (Gray Films and Pathé), and distributed by Cineriz also received SACC funding.

Another interesting case is that of Monicelli, a great Italian director whose projects were more commercial. He worked with all three types of producers. Small companies like Artisti Tecnici Associati, Cinematografica Distribution Indipendenti and Rosa Film produced his movies with famous actor Totò and the bank financed all these projects. When it came to movie genre, the Bank was more willing to finance dramas (30%), comedies (27%) and comic movies (15%).

Bank financing was connected to two major issues. The first was the length of the exploitation cycle that usually forced a locking up of capital, a high cost of credit and the necessity of considerably heavy current assets, even for small-medium enterprises. Producers usually found themselves unable to give the stocks of capital and real properties that were the regular warranties for credit access in other industrial sectors. Film producers could give only future box-office takings as a warranty, but for financial institutions, a movie was (and is) a "future good" subject to the risks involved both in fulfilment of the specific movie project and also in the exploitation cycle, since it is extremely difficult to predict demand.

As far as the Italian market is concerned, the exploitation cycle lasted about five years. The problem of exploitation was strictly connected to the credit period, which was an average of 18 months from first receipt. A production company usually spent the first 6 to 12 months shooting, editing and distributing its film. It would begin to reimburse investors about 8 to 12 months from the beginning of the exploitation cycle.[27] Consequently, when the company began planning a new movie project, it had to pay back loans before it receives any revenues for the first movie released. Besides this, in the first year, production companies covered an average of a third of their production costs with earnings from distribution. In the remaining four years, production costs were covered as follows: one-third with public funding and the remainder with profits from distribution on foreign markets. At the end of the first exploitation year, a company was usually able to cover only a quarter of its total production costs.

The second major problem connected to bank loans was represented by warranties. A production company had to offer guarantees with real property (whenever the company owned production or dubbing plants), future movie earnings, that is to say those coming from distribution and public funding (percentage on box-office results after four years), and real properties of the distribution company that assured the "secured minimum". This minimum consisted of very real means of payment: check of promissory notes to be recouped through the revenue, which is through the various rentals of the film to cinema operators in the agent's region.

One of my ambitions is to integrate the study of funding for the Italian cinema with information about state subsidies. At present the archive sources are difficult—if not impossible—to consult because the documents are divided between Rome and Oppido Lucano, a small town in the Basilicata Region of southern Italy. Many documents are not even catalogued. My hope is that in the not-too-distant future the public authorities will embark upon the process of storing and computerising the massive amount of data. This is fundamentally important to enable researchers to carry out the difficult task of assembling all the pieces of the complex jigsaw puzzle that is the history of the Italian cinema in the years following WWII.

## Together Is Better: The Big Deal of Co-Productions

From the mid-1950s, many European countries saw a rise in bilateral or multinational co-productions, which outnumbered purely domestic movies. This was as true for Italy as for West Germany and France. Co-productions represent an interesting topic because they represent examples of international joint projects, typically of short duration, which allows examining international activity not at level of parent firm, or even subsidiary, but at the project level—the movie. They were an increasingly common form of film-production in post-war decades that potentially enabled film producers to jump tariff barriers (especially within Europe) and sometimes enabled producers to overcome non-tariff barriers, the liability of foreignness. International co-productions were usually more successful at the box office if compared to foreign movies, as we can see from Graph 6.3. ITA/US co-productions were much more popular than US films. The same is true for France, Germany and UK.

Co-productions were the "European way" to reach international audience. The typical US approach was to bring foreign talent (and stories) to Hollywood, and to create films with wide international appeal. The European approach was based on international collaboration between production companies in different countries. A series of bilateral film co-production agreements were signed between national governments or official professional associations. Agreements typically required both countries to

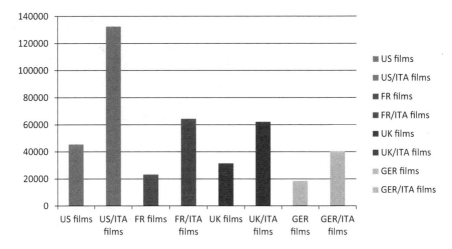

*Graph 6.3* Overcoming Liability of Foreignness: Average Box Office of Co-Productions and Single-Nationality Movies.

Source: Miskell and Nicoli, *International film co-productions in post-war Europe* (working paper). Data taken from Borsa Film.

contribute a minimum percentage of financial and creative resources. The rise of co-productions can be better understood in the light of the general market trends. The movie industry was facing major challenges: the overall levels of film-going were in decline; cinema no longer a weekly habit and there was a demise of neighbourhood cinema. On the other hand, audiences still flock to see big 'blockbuster' films and biggest 'hit' films continue to generate large profits. Small and medium budget films were being squeezed out, while big budget films had potential to make profits, but it was very risky and thus these movies typically needed an international audience to make money. Besides, in Europe and in the US there was a decline of vertically integrated firms and the rise of independent producers that needed to create major hit films to remain profitable. These can explain the success of co-productions as a strategy to face this new context of changes and challenges within the industry. Literature about co-productions is quite scant. We know that international co-productions were commonplace in Europe, and we know what motivated the firms. We know that producers of all sizes engaged in film co-productions, and they typically worked with wide range of international partners. But there are also some examples of stronger strategic partnerships. Still, there are a bunch of unanswered questions, worthy of being investigated: how did European film producers actually link up? what did the European production network look like? did producers look for long-term strategic partners or a series of one-off project collaborations?

The internationalisation strategy was strongly encouraged by ANICA. According to Eitel Monaco, head of ANICA: "Co-production has proven to be extremely useful. It has made a major contribution towards the internationalisation of our cinema, which over smug, risked being overwhelmed by Roman slang and pathetic melodies from the Gulf of Naples". ANICA's leaders realized that the broader the horizons grew, the greater the challenge became. In order to be competitive, Italian films had to achieve the technical standards of their American rivals, but most of all they needed to gradually eliminate their local flavour. The rising importance of co-production is demonstrated by the financial involvement of Italian companies; according to some official ANICA reports, from 1950 to 1960 Italian production companies invested about half of total cinema investments in bilateral or trilateral projects.[28]

This all began in Paris on 19 October 1949, when the *Direzione Generale dello Spettacolo* and the Centre *National de la Cinématographie* signed a bilateral co-production agreement. The aim was "to facilitate in all ways co-production of high quality films with high costs, which are easier to sustain if the expense is shared by several producers. The fundamental condition is that these films must be good enough to enable the expansion of French and Italian films in the world". Agreements to favour co-productions and exchanges were also signed with United States (the famous ANICA-MPEAA agreement[29]), Britain, Germany, Spain, and Argentina. Since the United States did not grant a "nationality" status to movies, co-productions were not possible, and movies made by an Italian and an American company were considered as *compartecipazioni*, i.e.financial collaborations.

Adventure and western movies were the most common genres of the European co-produced movies. Following the Hollywood crisis, those genres became rare on the European markets, which encouraged many European production companies to fill the gap.

The most important partnership was undoubtedly with France,[30] both in terms of number of movies co-produced and money invested: Italian companies usually contributed with 52% on the total budget. A similar cultural context, the dimension and consistency of both Italian and French movie industries favored collaborations among these countries. Co-productions with Spain were more problematic, since Spanish law had some restrictions on foreign artistic and technical personnel. Besides, the Spanish regime hasn't invested in the movie industry since it perceived movies as subversive and was particularly frightened by those influenced by Italian Neorealism.[31] The modest development of Italian-German collaborations was mainly due to some cultural differences: Italian productions companies tried to develop more international projects while German ones were more interested in fostering screenplays with a national flavor.[32] Graph 6.4 shows the number of co-productions released in three different period: Period 1 from cinema season 1957/8 to 1960/61; Period 2 from 1961/2 to 1966/7 and Period 3 from 1967/8 to 1970/71.

In the face of cinema-going crisis and American distribution supremacy, co-productions were considered a useful tool for entering new markets,

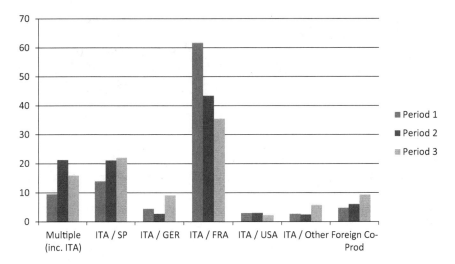

*Graph 6.4* Co-Productions Released per Period, by Nationality (%).
Source: Miskell and Nicoli, 2015 (working paper).

enlarging exploitation cycle, sharing competences and finding new alternatives to the problem of funding. If, for example, a movie was financed jointly by an Italian and a French company, and if the movie was recognized to have domestic privileges in both countries (recognized as national; included in the screen-quota regime; worthy to get public grants and subsidies), then the market would be increased and both companies could work to increase its technical and artistic quality. If, on the one hand, movie professionals welcomed this new strategy, on the other, the Communist political party criticized co-productions because it was against an idea of European cinema: "we are tired of this idea of community and integrated pool. We do not want to sacrifice our national independency in the name of European cinema".[33]

The co-production system allowed co-produced films to enjoy all the advantages that each country's government gave to its nationally produced films: mandatory screening, cinema credit, refunds and quality awards in Italy; *loi d'aide*, cinema credit and exemption from import quotas in France.

The problems raised by co-productions are well explained in this document taken from *Cahiers du cinéma* in 1957:

> As far as production is concerned, we can identify two different periods: a first period in which the aim was the co-creation of a film. Teams had to be carefully selected at the industrial, technical and artistic level, which often meant that they produced uninspired films, cosmopolitan commercial products which in the end eroded the artistic talents of the two or three countries involved in their production. At the moment, we are seeing a second period, in which we have gone beyond the original

conception, especially in Franco-Italian co-productions. We decided that it was important for France to help Italy make films tailored to Italian talents and artistic traditions, and vice-versa. This system, which really comes down to financial co-productions, seems to be bearing fruit. . . . This new approach is definitely a step forward, and allows two cinema industries to help each other without upsetting the technical and artistic conditions of production".[34]

The treaty naturally contained certain conditions for enjoyment of these benefits. Excluding films financed 50–50, production had to reciprocal, meaning that an Italian-French film shot in Italy had to be followed by a French-Italian film shot in France. Secondly, the minority participant could not contribute less than 30% of the estimated budget. Finally, the artistic cast was sub-divided into "screenplay" and "performance", and these had to alternate between the French and the Italians.

This last condition was intended to prevent fictitious co-productions and unleashed a protest by film industry workers. The French actors' union rose up, claiming to defend national identity: "what we see as an injury and betrayal is the production of purportedly French films whose actual content would convey foreign-inspired ideas, opinions and tastes".[35]

The same tone is found in a letter sent by René Clair and Vittorio De Sica, president and vice president of the International Film Academy, to film directors in France and Italy. The document underlined that the "contamination" imposed by the agreement endangered the quality and originality of the respective productions, with repercussions at the box office. Adriano Baracco, director of *Cinema*, commented that

> the current regulations for Italian-French co-productions are a masterpiece of bureaucracy and seem more suited to the wine industry than to the cinema; it is well known that mixing different types of wine together sometimes gives good results, but it should be just as well known that mixing up a worker from Bologna with a Parisian troupe only produces rubbish. Whoever organises a co-produced film these days has to use a pharmacist's scales more than a producer's intuition.[36]

But the film producers had a different opinion. Salvatore Persichetti, vice president of the ANICA *Unione Nazionale Industrie Tecniche*, wrote:

> Art has no borders, and any nationalistic concept wrapped up in nostalgia for autarchy would be absolutely contrary to that ideal bridge that Italian genius has built in order to launch its messages of beauty to the world. We need European partnerships which we hope will lead as soon as possible into a European film community . . . the chances of recouping money invested in production on one single market are lessening.[37]

Aside from the controversies, Italian film companies lost no time in taking advantage of the opportunities offered by the agreement. Nevertheless, alongside increasingly widespread co-production, film industry speculation also revived. As time went by, fewer and fewer co-productions involved the careful balancing of investments and parity. In the end, the unspoken rule was that a minority producer contributed 15 or 20% of the film budget. This was the equivalent of the share paid by a film distributor to import a film, but with the difference that in this way the film enjoyed the advantages of a national film and received state aid based on a certain percentage of box-office takings.[38]

This type of co-production was widespread mainly in the 1960s, whereas "financial co-productions" were legalised from the early 1950s. These were productions in which one of the partners invested only a certain amount of capital: "this type of co-production allows a foreign producer to use an Italian co-producer (who is theoretically obliged to contribute, but does not, and is paid for the use of his name) and in this way he can obtain the Italian State film subsidy for a French film which is formally co-produced (at the same time there is an Italian producer who does the same damage to the French taxpayer)".[39]

Among the first to invest in the co-production business was Angelo Rizzoli: *Don Camillo, Fanfan la Tulipe, Lucrezia Borgia, Le belle di notte, Puccini,* and *Il ritorno di Don Camillo* were all produced between 1951 and 1952 based on the Italian-French production treaty. Over a period of 20 years, Rizzoli co-produced 62 films with France, out of a total of 144. Less important relations were established with Germany, Spain, Yugoslavia and Bulgaria. There were also some co-productions with Great Britain and the United States, but these were sporadic partnerships. Rizzoli did not actually like the Americans a great deal: he was used to being the leader and could not bear to find himself in the role of a poor relation. In this respect, his activities were very different from those of the other Italian producers like De Laurentiis and Lombardo, ready to look for partners in America. Rizzoli looked to Europe, and adopted different strategies: partnerships with the most important French and German production companies (Les Films Ariane and Bavaria Filmkunst), but also co-productions with dummy companies and dummy "producers". One of these was Robert Chabert of Francinex, Rizzoli's French counterpart in the production of *Don Camillo*. Francinex was initially a part of the Filmsonor-Cinedis group, and then passed under Rizzoli's direct control in 1951. Another satellite company was Franco-London Film, represented by Henry Deutschmeister. In 1963, Rizzoli decided to create a real branch in France: Francoriz. Under the cover of these different names, Rizzoli succeeded in exploiting all the vast opportunities that were explicit and implicit in the cinema agreement: majority and minority shares in joint ventures, camouflaged imports, triangular co-productions, co-productions *in proprio.*

If we look at the overall situation of the Italian cinema industry at the beginning of the 1950s, co-productions accounted for about 21% of total output, and by the end of the decade this had risen to 62%. Most movies were produced in collaboration with France (72%) and Spain (16%), and a very few with Germany (3%), Great Britain (2%), the United States (3%) and other countries like Yugoslavia, Egypt and Japan (4%). About 38.5% of co-produced movies were financed by S.A.C.C. Co-productions with France were among the biggest box office hits: *Don Camillo* by Julien Duvivier (1952), *La grande Guerra* by Mario Monicelli (1959), and the world-famous *La dolce vita* by Federico Fellini (1960) were hits at the Italian box office. The other important co-productions were made in triple partnerships involving Italy, France and Spain (9% of total tripartite productions) and Italy, Germany and Spain (7%), especially for movies with a Western flavour. The Italian company *Produzioni Europee Associate* was formed specifically to develop these projects. The motto of its founder, Alberto Grimaldi was "the movie industry improves thanks to co-productions".[40] In triangular collaboration, Italy was usually responsible for technology and the development of creative inputs, while its foreign partners were in charge of money, services and location.[41]

Co-productions turned out to be particularly successful at the box office: at the beginning of the 1950s, their market share was 17.2%, rising to 60% by the end of the decade.[42] Italian producers used co-productions not only as a means to make bigger profits but also as a way to increase their competitive advantage and improve the quality of their films. We know from the literature that big companies were used to co-production: Titanus, Rizzoli, Cino del Duca and Dama were some of the major Italian companies that followed this strategy. In the dataset, 37% of co-productions were made with the involvement of Italian leading companies. It is extremely interesting to see that 47% of co-productions were made with occasional companies, while only 16% with regular companies. Joint projects usually involved two (50.8%) or three companies (31.1%). Only 13.6% of projects involved four companies, and only 4.5% involved more than four. If we focus on co-productions involving two companies, we can see that all three types of Italian producer had privileged relations with France and Spain, since 43% of co-produced movies were made with these countries. The banks were more willing to finance co-productions involving two (19%) or three companies (12%). Financed co-productions were handled by national distributors (50%) and—interestingly—by regional ones (37%). One remarkable example is *Matrimonio all'Italiana* (1964), a hugely successful comedy by Vittorio De Sica, starring world-famous actors Sophia Loren and Marcello Mastroianni. The film was co-produced by a leading Italian company Compagnia Cinematografica Champion and French company Films Concordia, and distributed by Interfilm, an Italian regional company.

The average funding for co-productions was about 1,49 billion. If we break down information about number of companies involved, we see that

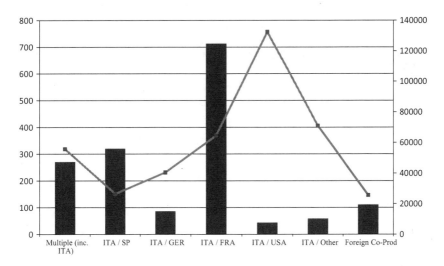

*Graph 6.5* Number of Co-Productions and Average of Box Office Performance.

Source: Miskell and Nicoli, *International film co-productions in post-war Europe* (working paper). Data taken from Borsa Film.

international projects involving: two companies got 1,41 billion; three companies 1,54 billion; four companies 1,73 billion and five companies 1,36 billion lire. The nationality of the partner company could change the amount of average funding. Being in partnership with a French company meant that the average funding was about 1,5 billion lire. Collaborations with Spanish and German companies had respectively an average funding of 8 and 9 million lire. The average funding with British companies was 1,19 billion and that with American companies was equal to 1,42 billion lire. According to the literature, projects with American companies cannot be categorized as pure co-productions since the reciprocity principle was not working. It would be more correct to speak about co-partnership: American capital was in most cases necessary to cover high budget and to guarantee with the secured minimum. Carlo Ponti, Dino De Laurentiis, Goffredo Lombardo, Alberto Grimaldi and Franco Cristaldi are some of the major Italian tycoons that were able to work with American majors. *Guerra e Pace* by King Vidor was produced in 1956 by Ponti-De Laurentiis with Paramount and *Il Gattopardo* by Luchino Visconti was produced in 1963 by Titanus and Fox. Even though it was easier to collaborate with European countries, thanks to a favourable legislation that fostered movie co-productions, Italian companies continued to prefer American partners. In the view of Carlo Ponti:

> The American film industry produces less films and needs more than ever before the cooperation of internationally minded producers, in

order to fill the gaps in their home and international markets. We in Italy can no longer produce films for the Italian markets. We can't get our money back at the Italian box office alone. We need American capital, we need the American market, and we need American companies to distribute our films globally.[43]

## Film Genres

After the 1956 crisis, the Italian film industry developed in different directions with regard to film genres. One was a genre influenced by Hollywood: the epic film shot in Italy but with American actors in the leading roles. "Big films that tend to get the best showing dates and attract more public interest".[44]

These super-productions included *Ulysses* directed by Mario Camerini (1953) and *War and Peace* directed by King Vidor (1956). *Ulysses* was a Lux-Ponti-De Laurentiis co-production starring Kirk Douglas, and its first-run takings were a record 280 million lire.[45] *War and Peace* was produced by Ponti and De Laurentiis and starred various internationally famous actors and actresses like Audrey Hepburn, Henry Fonda, Vittorio Gassman and Anita Ekberg; its first-run takings were 700 million lire. In 1957–1958 two more super-epics made 400 million lire in first-run showings: *La Tempesta*, directed by Alberto Lattuada and produced by De Laurentiis, starring Silvana Mangano, Van Heflin and Geoffrey Horne; and *The Naked Maja*, directed by Henry Kostner and produced by Titanus, starring Ava Gardner, Anthony Franciosa and Amedeo Nazzari. Other epics were released in the 1960s: *Barabbas, El Cid, Sodom and Gomorrah*. What these productions had in common was the choice of a storyline evoking universally known and very spectacular events and personalities, like epics, and international stars in leading roles.

Alongside this type of film, a more prestigious tendency developed: the epic film *d'autore*, representing a more mature production partnership with the United States. Among the most important examples of this genre are *La dolce vita, La grande Guerra, Rocco e i suoi fratelli, Boccaccio 70, Otto e mezzo* and *Il Gattopardo*.

These productions contributed to the growth of the Italian film industry, but another genre was even more important, also in terms of the number of films produced: the historical-mythological films, the "peplum" and "swashbuckler" movies. These were B-movies, in other words, they were low- to medium-budget films but guaranteed box-office hits, and they led the way for improvements in production standards of a whole series of genres and sub-genres, like the Spaghetti Westerns and Italian gothic horror movies; types and sub-types of film that enjoyed a huge boom in the Italy of the late 1960s.

The big budget films made at Cinecittà by the major studios created a working production system that could be used by dozens and dozens of

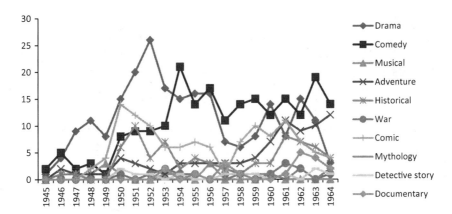

*Graph* 6.6 Movie Genres, 1945–1965.
Source: author's elaboration.

small and very small production companies, like Galatea Film, Donati and Carpentieri's Panda Film, Misiano's Romana Film, Oscar Film, Achille Piazzi's Spa Cinematografica, Italgamma, Majestic and Diamante. These were all production companies making B-movies. The production model for this genre of film was more or less the same, whether the production company was big like Titanus, medium like Galatea, or one of the many small companies that sprang up and then died straight after making one film. Big companies like Titanus took advantage of the opportunities offered by the genre films; these low-budget movies required small investments, but guaranteed big profits. Production costs could be kept low because costumes, situations, actors and sets were the same.

The boom in production of the historical/mythological and romantic neorealism genres, mostly by Titanus, meant that Italian cinema began to come out ahead in the eternal struggle with Hollywood. A study of film genres between 1945 and 1965 shows that 30.22% are drama, 24.66% comedy, 15.06% adventure and 11.43% comic. When single Italian producers (excluding national collaborations and international co-productions) are considered, they are seen to have a very similar production strategy, with drama and comedy as the most important genres. Did producers specialize in certain genres? Occasional producers focused on one genre but this does not mean that they were more specialized, since these companies had a very short life cycle and produced very few movies before abandoning the market. Leading and regular companies, on the other hand, were quite similar in their entrepreneurial attitude, focussing on an average of three genres. The bank was more used to financing drama (30%), comedy (27%), comic (15%) and adventure (12%) films,[46] but the two genres that obtained the

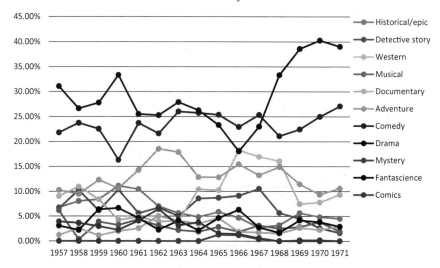

*Graph 6.7* Film Genre Popularity in First-Run Italian Market.
Source: Miskell and Nicoli, 2015.

highest average amount of funding were the mythological films (1.78 billion lire) with stories of Hercules and other Greek heroes, and the historical films (2.61 billion lire) with stories about the Roman Empire, the Three Muske-teers and Napoleon. These genres also did extremely well at the box office, averaging takings of 4 billion and 5 billion lire, respectively. Both genres were usually co-produced with French companies.

## Notes

1  Dino de Laurentiis, quoted in Della Casa, Steve, 2003, *Capitani coraggiosi. Produttori italiani 1945–1975*, Milan: Mondadori Electa.
2  In 1951, after long negotiations, the first ANICA-MPEAA agreement was signed. A positive effect for the Italian movie industry was the reduction of American movies imported thanks to a sort of auto-contingent system: from about 500 American movies imported in Italy in 1949 to about 200 movies, on average each year, from 1951 to 1961. Another major effect was to bind 50% of all the revenues of American movies in Italy to the financing of production and distri-bution of Italian movies (in Italy and abroad) or to the production of American movies in Italian production plants. During the entire period of the above agree-ment, about 50 million dollars (30 billion lire) have been invested by American companies in Italian movie production branch.
3  The co-production policy was strongly fostered by ANICA. The first agreement was signed in 1946 with France and was the followed by West Germany, Spain and Argentina. In 1950 another international agreement was signed with Great Britain and in 1955 with Russia. Co-producing was seen as a winning strategy for European movie industries to compete with the powerful Hollywood.

4 Data analysis is the result of personal data mining. The dataset contains the overall production of Italian movies from 1945 and is based on different sources: historical archive of Banca Nazionale del Lavoro (for movie funding), Annuario del Cinema Italiano and Catalogo Bolaffi del Cinema Italiano. For each movie, information provided are the following: movie production company, co-production companies, distributor, nationality, film genre, director, year of release, amount of funding, box office grosses, prizes won. The dataset helps having a deeper understanding of the organizational structure of Italian production and distribution branches, the emerging strategy of co-production with European partners and financing choices by the bank. We do not have information about movie budgets (it is not yet completely available) and for this reason we cannot infer the real effectiveness of such funding. Nevertheless, the dataset helps to understand which was the idea of "cinema" the bank and the state have chosen to sustain.

5 Zambetti, Sandro 1978, "Cinema e pubblico in Italia negli anni Settanta. Gli indirizzi produttivi, i generi, il film popolare", in Ferrero, Adelio et al. (eds.), *Storia del cinema*, III, Venice: Marsilio, 56–78.

6 After the company broke up, De Laurentiis financed important films like *La Grande Guerra* and *La Dolce Vita*, often in co-production. In1962 he created a complex of film studios called Dinocittà, where he alternated big budget epics with cultural films, like Visconti's *The Stranger (Lo straniero)*. The box-office flops of some of his super productions led De Laurentiis to sell Dinocittà in 1971 and move to the USA. Ponti moved to the USA after the split with De Laurentiis. Ponti produced all the films of his wife, Sophia Loren, with his own companies or on behalf of American companies, but also entered into very prestigious production partnerships, like Godard's *Contempt (Le Mépris)*.

7 Della Casa, Steve, 2003, *Capitani coraggiosi. Produttori italiani 1945–1975*, Milan: Mondadori Electa.

8 According to Vogel, this is a characteristic of the feature film business: "Industries requiring sizable capital investments can normally be expected to evolve into purely oligopolistic forms: steel and automobile manufacturing are examples. But because movies—each uniquely designed and packaged—are not stamped out on cookie-cutter assembly lines, the economic structure is somewhat different. Here, instead, we find a combination of large oligopolistic production/distribution/financing organizations regularly interfacing with and being highly dependent on a fragmented assortment of small, specialized service and production firm", in Vogel, Harold 2014, *Entertainment Industry Economics*, Cambridge: Cambridge University Press, p. 71.

9 Ottavi, Nino 1959, *Il finanziamento della produzione cinematografica*, Florence: Cursi.

10 Sanders, Terry 1955, "The Financing of Independent Feature Films", *Quarterly of Film, Radio, and Television*, 9 (4): 380–389.

11 Miskell, Peter, Nicoli, Marina 2016, "From Outsiders to Insiders? Strategies and Practices of American Film Distributors in Postwar Italy", *Enterprise and Society*, 17 (3): 546–590.

12 Rosten, Leo 1941, *Hollywood: The Movie Colony. The Movie Makers*, New York: Harcourt, p. 244.

13 Many researchers have dealt with the historical dominance of United States in the film trade and have proposed a wide variety of cultural, political, economic and sociological factors to explain this pre-eminence. Some (Wildam and Siwek, 1998, Hoskins, McFayden and Finn, 1997) have stressed the importance of a large and wealthy home market where production costs could be recouped easily. Others have considered a tenar fascination with America and American

consumer products (Sorlin 1991, Tunstall, 1977). Guback (1969) and Seagrave (1997, 1998) have emphasised the role of the Motion Picture Association of America, with its aggressive lobbying to promote American movies abroad.

14  "The financial structure of the motion picture industry today is no different from that of any other established and stable business. The companies are capitalized through issuance of common and preferred stocks, listed on stock exchanges, and additional financing is provided by the usual means of bonds, notes, debentures, mortgages, and so forth", in Glover, John, Cornell, William 1951, "The Motion Picture Industry", in Glover, John, *The Development of American Industries*, New York: Prentice-Hall, pp. 745–761.

15  "Here, instead, we find a combination of large oligopolistic production/ distribution/ financing organization regularly interfacing and being highly dependent on a fragmented assortment of small, specialized service and production firms", in Harold Vogel, 2007, *Entertainment Industry Economics: A Guide for Financial Analysis*, Cambridge: Cambridge University Press.

16  Thompson, Kristin 1985, *Exporting Entertainment: America in the World Film Market 1907–1934.* London: BFI; Higson, Andrew, Maltby, Richard (eds.) 1999, *"Film Europe" and "Film America": Cinema, Commerce and Cultural Exchange 1920–1939.* Exeter: University of Exeter Press; Trumpbour, John 2002, *Selling Hollywood to the World: US and European Struggles for Mastery of the Global Film Industry, 1920–1950*, Cambridge: Cambridge University Press; De Grazia, Victoria 2005, *Irresistible Empire: America's Advance through Twentieth-Century Europe*, Cambridge, MA: The Belknap Press of Harvard University Press.

17  Goldman, *Adventures in the Screen Trade*, New York: Grand Central Publishing.

18  Morawetz et al., "Finance, Policy and Industrial Dynamics", *Industry and Innovation*, 14 (4): 421–443.

19  Kornai, Janos 1979, "Resource-Constrained versus Demand-Constrained Systems", *Econometrica*, 47: 801–819.

20  Eberts, Jake, Illot, Terry 1990, *My Indecision if Final: The Rise and Fall of Goldcrest Films*, London: Faber and Faber; Finney, Albert 1996, *The State of European Cinema: A New Dose of Reality*, London: Cassell; Moran, Albert 1997, *Film Policy: International, National and Regional Perspectives*, London: Routledge.

21  While empirical studies on factors that can influence the film market are abundant, the literature on the impact of regulatory factors on the film industry is surprisingly scant.

Economists have approached the issue of public intervention and of its effectiveness on industry dynamics. Bagella and Becchetti demonstrated that the net impact of public funding on box office performance of Italian movies (between 1985 and 1996) was insignificant mainly because there has been a poor investment—by production companies—on immaterial features (directors, actors, and so far). Jansen analyses the German movie industry, the determinants of movie performance and the impact of subsidies (committee and reference subsidies). The empirical analysis suggests that subsidies, specifically the committee system, distort producers to make movies suited to audience preferences. The author concludes that, even though the subsidy reference system has a positive impact on movie performance at the box office, the government should not subsidise the movie industry. Teti, Collins and Sedgwick have recently analyzed the effectiveness of public funding on box office performance of Italian movies. The result of their study shows that, from 1999 to 2003, "the public grant regime was clearly not able to assure the development of the industry as intended, since in an overwhelming number of cases, production losses exceeded subsidy". Other contributions have evaluated the direct impact of screen-quotas on box office performance of movies, finding a negative correlation.

22 This amount corresponds to about 47 million lire (1990).

23 The Special Fund could be used to finance production, distribution and export of national movies, to buy technical materials and to furnish cinemas in small cities.

24 Author's elaboration using data from the Historical Archive of the *Banca Nazionale del Lavoro*.

25 This first method aimed to stimulate national movie production, since profits made from the exploitation of each movie had to be re-invested in the production of new movies; but in most cases those sums were grants. In fact, once they had shown that they had re-invested, the producers did not have to reimburse the state.

26 The presence of a leading company raised the level of average funding. In the case of regular plus occasional companies, average funding was 9,7 million lire; for leading plus occasional companies it was 1,14 billion; and 1,88 billion lire for leading plus regular companies.

27 The bank was usually the first to recoup its investment once money flowed in from the box office. According to Tavares (Tavares et al. 2003) "Investment in a film can be described as an aristocracy of deal money where the further down you sit in the pecking order, the higher the risk of non-recovery and/or net profit participation". See Tavares, Elspeth 2003, *The Dream Catcher Goes Back to Basics to Re-Define the Weaves of Co-Production Deal Making!*, Cannes: The Business of Film, Finance Cannes.

28 ANICA 1961, *Sommario Statistico 1960–1961*, Rome: SAET.

29 The agreement was signed in 1951. American majors agreed to a voluntary import quota of 225 films annually (50 were reserved to Italian distributors). This agreement also aimed at finding a solution to difficulties faced by Italian movies in the American market. Part of American movie profits in the Italian market were unblocked (they have been blocked by currency restrinctions): MPAA companies could export 50% of their Italian earnings; 12,5% was used for the creation of a fund administered by a state company called I.F.E. (Italian Film Export) that promoted Italian films in the United States (I.F.E. was responsible of dubbing and distribution). Since I.F.E. was perceived by MPAA as a tool to promote foreign films in the US market, after a few years it started reducing the sum to be paid for the fund.

30 French partners were usually big companies like Franco London Film, S.G.C., CFPC, Cinetel, Les Films Marceau and Francinex.

31 Rossi, Umberto 2004, "Il mondo delle coproduzioni", in Various Authors, *Storia del Cinema Italiano*, Venice: Marsilio Editori, p. 439.

32 ANICA 1962, *L'industria cinematografica negli anni 1960 e 1961*, Rome: SAET.

33 Chiaretti, Tommaso 6 May, 1953 "La sconfitta di Cannes", *L'Unità*, quoted in Corsi, Barbara, "Eutanasia di una visione", in Brunetta, Gian Piero 1996 (ed.), *Identità italiana e identità europea nel cinema italiano dal 1945 al miracolo economico*, Fondazione Giovanni Agnelli: Turin.

34 *Cahiers du cinèma*, 71, May 1957, pp. 14–15, cited in Wagstaff, Christopher 1995, "Italy in the Post-War International Cinema Market", in Duggan, Christopher, Christopher Wagstaff (eds.), *Italy in the Cold War: Politics, Culture and Society, 1948–58*, Oxford, England and Washington DC: Berg Publishers, pp. 89–116.

35 From the Manifesto of the French actors' union, in *Cinema*, no. 33, 28 February 1950, p. 100.

36 A. Baracco, Roma-Parigi (senza controllore), in *Cinema*, no. 76, 15 December 1951, p. 317.

37 Letter by Salvatore Persichetti, in Anonimo, 13 May 1953, "Perché le coproduzioni convengono al cinema italiano", *Cinemundus—Araldo dello Spettacolo*, (78).

38 The role of the minority co-producer ended up as being the same as that of the pure distributor once it was established that money could be provided even

when the film had been completed. In this case, it was no longer possible to claim that the minority co-producer was sharing the entrepreneurial risk of producing the film.

39  Bizzarri, Libero 1979, "L'economia cinematografica", in Fasoli Massimiliano (ed.), *La città del cinema: produzione e lavoro nel cinema italiano*, Rome: Napoleone, p. 43.

40  Savino, Paola 2009, *Alberto Grimaldi: l'arte di produrre*, Rome: Centro Sperimentale di Cinematografia.

41  Venturini, Simone 2005, "Spettacolo e tecnica nelle coproduzioni degli anni Cinquanta e Sessanta", in Manzoli, Giacomo, Pescatore, Guglielmo (eds.), *L'arte del risparmio: stile e tecnologia*, Roma: Carocci, pp. 68–77.

42  Rossi, 2004, p. 437.

43  Bergfelder, Tim 2006, *German Popular Cinema and European Co-Productions in the 1960s*, New York-Oxford: Berghahn Publishing, p. 53.

44  Rossi, Umberto 1966, "L'americanizzazione del cinema italiano", *Cinema 60: mensile di cultura cinematografica*, VII (59): 55.

45  First-run takings refers to takings in the most important Italian cities over the first weekend of release.

46  These genres on average received this amount of funding: drama 1,1 billion lire, comedy 1,32 billion, adventure 1,40 billion and comic 1,26 billion.

# Bibliography

ANICA 1962, *L'industria cinematografica negli anni 1960 e 1961*, Rome: SAET.

―――――. 1961, *Sommario Statistico 1960–1961*, Rome: SAET

BAGELLA, Michele, BECCHETTI, Leonardo 1999, "The Determinants of Motion Picture Box Office Performance: Evidence from Movies Produced in Italy", *Journal of Cultural Economics* 23: 237–256

BARLOZZETTI, Guido et. al. (eds.) 1985, *Modi di produzione del cinema italiano: La Titanus*, Rome: Di Giacomo Editore

BERGFELDER, Tim 2006, *German Popular Cinema and European Co-Productions in the 1960s*, New York-Oxford: Berghahn Publishing

BERNARDINI, Aldo, MARTINELLI, Vittorio (eds.) 1986, *Titanus: la storia e tutti i film di una grande casa di produzione*, Milan: Coliseum Editore

BIZZARRI, Libero 1979, "L'economia cinematografica", in FASOLI Massimiliano (ed.), *La città del cinema: produzione e lavoro nel cinema italiano*, Rome: Napoleone, pp. 37–47

BRUNETTA, Gian Piero 1982, *Storia del cinema italiano: dal 1945 agli anni Ottanta*, Rome-Bari: Laterza

BRUNETTA, Gian Piero, FANTINA, Livio 1992, *L'Italia al cinema*, Venice: Marsilio

CORSI, Barbara 2001, *Con qualche dollaro in meno: storia economica del cinema italiano*, Rome: Editori Riuniti

DE GRAZIA, Victoria 2005, *Irresistible Empire: America's Advance through Twentieth-Century Europe*, Cambridge, MA: The Belknap Press of Harvard University Press

DUGGAN, Christopher, WAGSTAFF, Christopher (eds.), *Italy in the Cold War: Politics, Culture and Society, 1948–58*, Oxford, England and Washington, DC: Berg Publishers

EBERTS, Jake, ILLOT, Terry 1990, *My Indecision if Final: The Rise and Fall of Goldcrest Films*, London: Faber and Faber

GILI, Jean 2014, "European Co-Productions and Artistic Collaborations: The Italian Response to the Hollywood Studio System", in Bondanella, Peter (ed.), *The*

*Italian Cinema Book*, London: Palgrave Macmillan and the British Film Institute, pp. 211–218

GLOVER, John, *The Development of American Industries*, New York: Prentice-Hall.

GOLDMAN, William 1983, *Adventures in the Screen Trade*, New York: Grand Central Publishing

GUBACK, Thomas H. 1969, *The International Film Industry*, Bloomington, IN: Indiana University Press

HIGSON, Andrew, MALTBY, Richard (eds.) 1999, *"Film Europe" and "Film America": Cinema, Commerce and Cultural Exchange 1920–1939*, Exeter: University of Exeter Press

HOSKINS, Colin, MCFADYEN, Stuart, FINN, Adam, JACKEL, Anne 1997, "Evidence on the Performance of Canada/Europe Co-Productions in Television and Film", *Journal of Cultural Economics*, 21 (2): 129–138

JANSEN, Christian 2005, "The Performance of German Motion Pictures: Profits and Subsidies", *Journal of Cultural Economics*, 29: 191–212

KORNAI, Janos 1979, "Resource-Constrained versus Demand-Constrained Systems", *Econometrica*, 47: 801–819

LEE, Shi Y., KIM, Eun-mee, KIM, Young II 2008, "The Effect of the Korean Screen Quota System on Box Office Performance", *Journal of World Trade: Law, Economics, Public Policy*, 42 (2): 335–346

MISKELL, Peter, NICOLI, Marina 2016, "From Outsiders to Insiders? Strategies and Practices of American Film Distributors in Postwar Italy", *Enterprise and Society* 1 (6): 1–45

MORAN, Albert 1997, *Film Policy: International, National and Regional Perspectives*, London: Routledge

MORAWETZ, Norbert et al. 2007, "Finance, Policy and Industrial Dynamics: The Rise of Co-Production in the Film Industry", *Industry and Innovation*, 14 (4): 421–443

OTTAVI, Nino 1959, *Il finanziamento della produzione cinematografica*, Florence: Cursi

QUAGLIETTI, Lorenzo 1980, *Storia economico politica del cinema italiano*, Rome: Editori Riuniti

ROSSI, Umberto 2004, "Il mondo delle coproduzioni", in Various Authors, *Storia del Cinema Italiano*, Venice: Marsilio Editori, pp. 431–441

_____. 1966, "L'americanizzazione del cinema italiano", *Cinema 60: mensile di cultura cinematografica*, VII (59): 53–56

ROSTEN, Leo 1941, *Hollywood: The Movie Colony. The Movie Makers*, New York: harcourt

SANDERS, Terry 1955, "The Financing of Independent Feature Films", *Quarterly of Film, Radio, and Television*, 9 (4): 380–389

SAVINO, Paola 2009, *Alberto Grimaldi: l'arte di produrre*, Rome: Centro Sperimentale di Cinematografia

SEAGRAVE, Kerry 1998, *American Television Abroad: Hollywood's Attempt to Dominate World Television*, Jefferson, NC: McFarland

_____. 1997, *American Films Abroad: Hollywood's Domination of the World's Movie Screens from the 1890s to the Present*, Jefferson, NC: McFarland.

SORLIN, Pierre 2014, "How the Italians Happened to Cherish and then to Disdain the Cinema", in Bondanella, Peter (ed.), *The Italian Cinema Book*, London: Palgrave Macmillan and the British Film Institute, pp. 219–225

_____. 1991, *European Cinemas, European Societies 1939–1990*, New York: Routledge

TAVARES, Elspeth 2003, *The Dream Catcher Goes Back to Basics to Re-Define the Weaves of Co-Production Deal Making!*, Finance Cannes: The Business of Film

TETI, Emanuele, COLLINS, Alan, SEDGWICK, John 2013, "An Offer They Couldn't Refuse (But Probably Should Have): The Efficiency of Italian State Subsidy to Moviemaking, 1995–2003", *Public Money & Management* 34 (3): 181–188

THOMPSON, Kristin 1985, *Exporting Entertainment: America in the World Film Market 1907–1934*, London: BFI

TRUMPBOUR, John 2002, *Selling Hollywood to the World: US and European Struggles for Mastery of the Global Film Industry, 1920–1950*, Cambridge: Cambridge University Press

TUNSTALL, Jeremy 1977, *The Media are American*, London: Constable

VENTURINI, Simone 2005, "Spettacolo e tecnica nelle coproduzioni degli anni Cinquanta e Sessanta", in Manzoli, Giacomo, Pescatore, Guglielmo (eds.), *L'arte del risparmio: stile e tecnologia*, Roma: Carocci, pp. 68–77

VOGEL, Harold 2014, *Entertainment Industry Economics: A Guide for Financial Analysis*, Cambridge: Cambridge University Press

_____. 2007, *Entertainment industry economics. A guide for financial analysis*, Cambridge: Cambridge University Press

WAGSTAFF, Christopher 2014, "Production around 1960", in Bondanella, Peter (ed.), *The Italian Cinema Book*, London: Palgrave Macmillan and the British Film Institute, pp. 149–162

WILDMAN, Steven and SIWEK, Stephen 1998, *International trade in films and television*, Cambridge: Ballinger

ZAMBRETTI, Sandro 1978, "Il cinema italiano negli anni Settanta: le strutture, il pubblico, il mercato", in Ferrero, Adelio (ed.), *Storia del cinema. Italia anni Settanta e le nuove cinematografie*, Venice: Marsilio

# 7 Drawing the Crowds
## Box Office Miracles

Some years I went to the cinema nearly every day, maybe even twice a day. In those years, the cinema was my world. It was a different world from the one around me, but I felt that only what I saw on the screen was complete, necessary and coherent, while off the screen I saw just masses of unrelated elements that seemed thrown together haphazardly.[1]

## Limelights: Cinema Audience

The cinema-going public was another element that influenced the dynamics of the Italian movie industry in the post-war years. There have been many studies of film consumption habits, but these have mostly dealt with the question in terms of *reception studies* (Taylor 1989, Bobo 1988,), *cultural history* (Sorlin, 2001, Casetti, 1999, Brunetta, 1993) and making meaning (Barker and Austin, 2000, De Berti, 2000, Mayne, 1993). In Italy, too, debate and principal theoretical contributions have mostly concerned the viewing experience, the rituals and the places where consumption takes place (Morreale, 2011, Casetti and Mosconi, 2006, Mosconi, 2006, Spinazzola, 1985). Very few publications use consumption data to analyse spectator preferences or attempt to explain the reciprocal influences between consumption choices and production strategies (Fanchi and Mosconi, 2002). Researching film consumption habits is difficult because data are not easy to find: the first data collection took place during the Fascist era, but the method was not perfected until the 1950s.[2]

In Italy, the cinema has always been the popular form of entertainment *par excellence*. According to the official statistics for 1924, Italians spent as much on the cinema as they did on all theatre shows. In the following ten years, cinema earnings doubled. Consumption rose continually, and at the end of the 1940s, the cinema accounted for two-thirds of the total Italians spent on recreation/entertainment. Unlike the rest of Europe, Italy saw a constant rise in consumption and numbers of new cinemas. In the 1950s, interest in understanding audiences and their tastes led to the appearance of the first studies, reports and surveys. In addition, the cinema boom raised

the problem of criticism of consumption and products of the movie industry for the first time. In the 1920s and '30s, it was possible that commercial films were never even reviewed, or else were commented on only very
briefly. Therefore, intellectuals had the problem of understanding why films
they did not value were actually popular, and why the public did not like
progressive films (Bernardi 2004). The debate that began in the years of the
Italian cinema boom, and which would influence many subsequent analytical studies (Farassino 1989, Spinazzola, 1985, Micicchè 1974), arose
less from a desire to understand the market and production strategies than
from a problem related to teaching methodology. Critics and intellectuals
usually define *a priori*, according to their own sensitivity, what the public
should see and appreciate. When public tastes do not agree with them, they
will say that films are merely "crowd-pleasers", accusing producers of being
interested primarily in making money and blaming them for a decline in
film quality.

The situation was naturally much more complex than can be evinced
from an essentially critical analysis of this kind. Since the end of World War
II, many factors have influenced the relationship between the public and
the film industry. These include the attitude of the Centre-Right government towards *neorealist* cinema, the massive presence of American films,
and the Italian distributors' preferences for films that were easy to place on
the market.

## Overtaking: Italy vs. America

It is often said that a film exists only when it is projected in a cinema,
and that one of the most important yardsticks of success is the box office:
"Apart from all its artistic qualities, which deserve absolute consideration
and respect, the success of a film, can only be measured in one infallible
way: the lines of people waiting to buy a ticket at the box-office". This
period witnessed both an economic miracle and a cinematographic miracle.

What had always been just a dream was finally coming true: the Italian
cinema was able to compete with Hollywood and, in some cases, even came
out ahead in the contest. While the buoyant Italian film market became an
increasingly attractive location for US film companies in the 1960s, it was
also an increasingly competitive market. As Hollywood studios scaled back
production in response to declining audiences at home and in other areas of
the English-speaking world, Italian film production boomed.[3] In 1958, Italy
produced 141 films, but by 1972 (the peak year) this figure had doubled
to 280. Here was a clear contrast with the declining numbers of American
films distributed in Italy: down from 233 in 1958 to just 127 in 1967.[4] Film
historians tend to agree that it was not just the volume of Italian film production that was increasing in this period, but also its quality.[5] Graph 7.1
shows the average box office performance of Italian and foreign films, as
well as of co-productions.

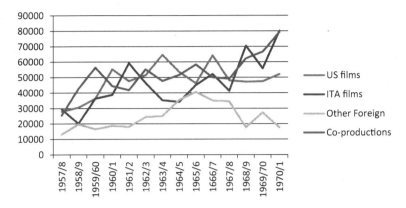

*Graph 7.1* Average Box Office Performance of Film Releases in the Italian First-Run Market, 1957–1971.

Source: Miskell and Nicoli, 2015.

Directors such as Rossellini, Fellini, Di Sica, Visconti and Leone attracted international acclaim, while stars like Sophia Loren and Marcello Mastroianni achieved success in both Europe and America.[6] While film-makers of the immediate post-war years had achieved international critical acclaim for *neorealist* classics such as *Rome, Open City* (1945) and *Bicycle Thieves* (1948), by the mid-1950s, the focus of Italian cinema had shifted from "films *of* the people" to "films *for* the people". The 1960s saw the emergence of popular genres like the spaghetti Western, and the establishment of a lasting tradition of *commedia all'italiana*, which provided the basis for some of the best-loved films of the day and has remained popular ever since.[7] As Peter Bondanella argues: "The decade between 1958 and 1968 may in retrospect be accurately described as the Golden Age of Italian cinema, for in no other single period was its artistic quality, its international prestige, or its economic strength so consistently high".[8] Gian Piero Brunetta identifies the emergence of an "Italian style" in the post-war period that "would help to shape international cinema, influencing directors like Scorsese, Coppola, Ivory, and Campion".[9]

The Italian film market may have become increasingly important for the major US distributors by the 1960s, but it was a market in which Hollywood films were far from dominant. American pictures accounted for over half of all box-office revenues in Italy in 1958 (with Italian films earning just over 30% of the total), but by 1972 the share of box-office earnings by US films had dropped to just over 15%, while Italian productions (or co-productions) accounted for over 60% of the market.[10]

The number of US films released onto the first-run market fell from 326 in the 1957–1958 season to 151 in 1970–1971. Italian releases over the same period rose from 140 to 210 per year. The turnaround in the market shares of US and Italian films was particularly evident in first-run cinemas, as well as on the wider market. The data shown in Graph 7.2 confirm the rapid decline in the number of US films released in the late 1950s, and the growth in domestic production from the mid-1960s. The lines in the chart (relating to the right-hand axis), illustrate that the turnaround in market shares of US and Italian films was evident in first-run cinemas and also on the wider market.

Data have been elaborated from an original dataset. The dataset was compiled primarily from information contained in the trade weekly *Borsa Film*, which has made it possible to obtain data on box-office revenues generated by every film that went onto the Italian first-run market between the 1957–1958 and 1970–1971 cinema seasons, together with its allocated screening period. Using the records it is possible to track where and when films were first released, and to disaggregate data on revenues and screening days for each film at a regional level. *Borsa Film* records each film's distributor, genre, director and leading actors. This information has been supplemented with information about the production companies behind each film.[11]

Did the growing market share of Italian films simply reflect the increased number of Italian films released, or were they genuinely more popular than Hollywood movies? Most surveys of the Italian film industry do not directly address the question, yet it is crucial to understanding the strategies of firms operating in this market.

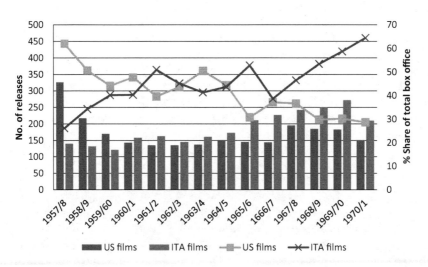

*Graph* 7.2 Number of Italian and American Films Released in the First-Run Market and Their Market Shares, 1957–1971.

Source: Miskell and Nicoli, 2015.

For much of the period under study, the popularity of Italian and American films was broadly comparable. The shift in the overall market share towards Italian pictures (and away from Hollywood) was largely determined by the numbers of Italian films released, rather than by any decisive change in consumer preference for domestic products. The sharp decline in the market share of US films in the late 1950s was almost entirely due to the declining number of Hollywood pictures produced at the tail end of the studio system.

It is only towards the end of the period that a preference for Italian films seems to appear (although it is impossible to say how long this lasted), and this explains the shift in market shares towards domestic products at the end of the 1960s. The most popular American films released in Italy during this period include a large proportion of "sword-and-sandal" epics, such as *The Bible/La Bibbia* (John Huston, 1966), *The Ten Commandments/I Dieci Comandamenti* (Cecil B DeMille, 1956), *Cleopatra* (Joseph Mankiewicz, 1963) and *Ben Hur* (William Wyler, 1959). The most popular Italian releases included the comedies *Matrimonio All'Italiana/ Marriage Italian Style* (Vittorio De Sica, 1965), *Per Grazia Ricevuta/Between Miracles* (Nino Manfredi, 1971), and *Il Medico della Mutua/Be Sick . . . It's Free* (Luigi Zampa, 1968), as well as Sergio Leone's *Per Qualche Dollaro in Piu/For a Few Dollars More* (1965) and *Il Buono, Il Brutto, Il Cattivo/The Good, The Bad and the Ugly* (1966). Fellini's *La Dolce Vita/The Sweet Life* (1960) was also among the ten most popular films released during the period.

## A Popular Phenomenon

From the end of World War II, Italy had a mass cinema. When the numbers of spectators are compared with the number of cinemas, it is seen that the cinema had reached heights of popularity that it would never achieve again. 1955 was the year when the highest-ever number of tickets was sold in the history of the Italian cinema: a total of 819,424,000 lire. Going to the cinema became a weekly ritual, one of the most popular leisure activities. In any case, the cinema should be seen within the wider context of a media transformation during this decade; the post-war years also saw rising numbers of people flocking to variety shows and reviews, as well as the constant growth of radio. When Italian television broadcasting began in 1954, going out to watch television became a collective ritual, and TV took on a central role in recreation and socialisation.

When Italian figures on cinema spending are analysed in the context of spending on shows and entertainment in general, it can be seen that the percentage spent on the cinema grew until mid-decade,[12] reached its peak in 1955 and then settled back down to more or less the same percentages as in the first few years.

The rising number of cinema-goers corresponds—as already seen—with an increase in film industry output: from 98 films produced in 1950 the number rose to 132 in 1959 (with a peak of 191 films in 1954), giving a

*Table 7.1* Entertainment Expenditure in Italy, 1949–1959

| Year | % of entertainment spending |
| --- | --- |
| 1949 | 75.4 |
| 1950 | 74.8 |
| 1951 | 76.3 |
| 1952 | 77.0 |
| 1953 | 77.6 |
| 1954 | 78.4 |
| 1955 | 79.0 |
| 1956 | 78.6 |
| 1957 | 76.9 |
| 1958 | 75.0 |
| 1959 | 75.2 |

Source: SIAE, *Lo spettacolo in Italia.*

total number of 1,212 films in the entire decade. After the end of the war, there was also a boom in the number of cinemas; from the 5,000 still operating during and after the war the number of cinemas increased to 6,551 in 1948, and this was followed by an even steeper rise in the following years, up to a peak of 10,500 in 1956 (not including the 5,449 church halls).

Cinemas were organised in three distinct circuits. The first-run cinemas were in the centres of the most important cities, and were followed by the second-run cinemas in the outskirts of the big cities or in the medium-sized towns. Last of all came the third-run cinemas of the "deep market" (as it is usually defined) in the small towns, and these suffered more than the other circuits from competition with the large number of church halls that had sprung up since the end of the war. From a film's release to the final withdrawal of the copies from the market, its life cycle passed through these three circuits. Its debut in the more remunerative first-run cinemas was followed by release onto the second-run circuit, with its the low-middle class audiences, and as many as four years might pass before the film arrived at the final stage of its commercial exploitation on the lowest-level cinema circuit. Of course, there was no obligation for a film to debut in city cinemas, and many films made by companies with a strong regional identity often opened directly in the second-run and third-run cinemas of Southern Italy.

Towards the end of the 1950s, some important changes took place in the film industry and in international audio-visual systems. The film industry had to start reckoning with the competition from television, which was causing a steep decline in cinema audiences in many Western countries. Since regular television broadcasts in Italy began only in 1954, the Italian cinema did not yet feel the effects of competition, at least not to the same extent as in the United States and other European countries.

Italians continued going to the cinema, but it is important to recall that public viewing habits changed during these years. From the end of the war until 1955, viewing habits were quite undifferentiated, but changes took place in the end late 1950s; the public began to take more care in its choice of Italian films, and this meant that quality films were successful at the box office.

In any case, there were many different types of film on offer in the 1950s. These ranged from the very low-profile productions aimed at the provinces to medium-high level productions, and the big super-productions aimed at capturing public attention and repeating the success of *Fabiola* by Alessandro Blasetti (1949, prod. Universalia).

In 1957, the box office was dominated by Dino Risi's *Belle ma povere* and Bragaglia's *Lazzarella*, whereas the 1959 hits were Rossellini's *Il generale della Rovere* and Monicelli's *La grande Guerra*. These films were produced by a solidly professional cinema and appealed to the consolidated values of Italian culture. The *film d'autore* had its big year in 1960, with Fellini's *La dolce vita*, Visconti's *Rocco e i suoi fratelli*, and Antonioni's *L'avventura*. This showed that the average spectator had changed, and was now a literate city-dweller, no longer attracted by sentimental popular taste—as certain film critics contemptuously defined Matarazzo's movies—but by the kind of mid-cult cinema that would find best expression less in the *cinema d'autore* than in the *commedia all'italiana*. This would bring popular *neorealism*, romance and comedy together into one single genre that would revive the Italian cinema of the 1950s. The spaghetti Western would take over the adventure genre from the peplum and swashbuckler movies.

The four big box-office hits in 1960—*La dolce vita*, *Rocco e i suoi fratelli*, *La Ciociara* and *Tutti a casa*—were *films d'autore*, but with features that appealed to a general public. As Giuliana Muscio observed (1995):

> If you think about *Rocco e i suoi fratelli*, which is definitely not an easy film, you realise that it's talking about Italian conditions during those years, about emigration, social exclusion, and about the clash of two cultures. It does all of this by depicting situations that are not too far from *fotoromanzi*-style drama, so that the general public can identify with the story and the characters. It was able to communicate both with intellectuals and the general audience of the time by combining sex and violence with social and family problems. If you have a product with a strong stylistic content, something like a *film d'autore*, but at the same time you tell a story that fits into the social context we all live in, and uses cultural models we all share, then you make both a quality film and a film for the public.

Faced with sociological changes involving its public, a new era heralded by television, and the availability of new leisure alternatives, the cinema should have taken steps to consolidate the artistic quality of its products, and at the same time it should have made big budget films that could also arrive on the international market.

In the words of Gustavo Lombardo, the Italian cinema should have developed a new plan. "The risks and costs cannot be faced if well-balanced plans for high-level big budget productions are not formulated in time. An industry like ours cannot live without forward planning. Consolidated worldwide industrial practice dictates that film companies absolutely need long-term plans. These require tiresome re-drafting and study, but pre-suppose the continuity of a stimulating and constructive policy". Lombardo was fully aware that the Italian movie industry needed to aim at unifying its audiences by producing commercially successful films of great quality. These films, as seen with production company *Titanus*, knew how to captivate the spectators in the first-run cinemas, but were also successful on the second-run and third-run circuits, on the so-called "deep market" in the outer cities and rural areas.

Catholic organisations and non-religious groups played a central role in developing the mass cinema: both areas of society helped to spread the cinema as a means of education and socialisation

> As Giovanna Grignaffini has justly remarked, it became a ritual during these years: Going to the cinema was above all a group habit. The cinema was the centre of social life, the place to appear in public and meet the opposite sex, and was where different generations mingled. Even the ritual of effectively seeing a film varies surprisingly from the theoretical model of spectatorship . . . the public was constantly moving and people changed places in communication rituals that took place while the film was being projected.[13]

Cinema was an extremely popular form of entertainment that had acquired an important role in everyday life; it was often mentioned in conversations and used as a benchmark. Cinema clubs had an important role in educating the public about film choices and viewing.

The large number of parochial cinemas showed that the Catholic community, beginning with its religious hierarchies, saw the cinema as an educational tool. Communists and Catholics alike understood that the cinema had to be the central sphere of cultural action, especially in a moment when spectator numbers were growing. The Catholic associations had created a specific organisation, the *Centro cattolico cinematografico*, which evaluated a film's morality according to Christian ethics. The main target of Catholic censorship was American films, considered responsible for showing a society without rules, where the celebration of consumerism and free and easy morals were the common thread of the narrative. This hostility to Hollywood films was shared, on the opposite front, by the communists: "The Party did all it could to mobilise public opinion in support of the national film industry, encouraging people to choose films that were not those offered by the ever-present Hollywood industry".[14] Communists were uneasy about films celebrating American values, since the US was viewed as the homeland of capitalism. Togliatti himself was aware of this danger, warning young communists that the "tendency to escapism" was like "stepping outside the reality of life", stigmatising "the illusory solutions presented by the American cinema". These deceptive dreams should be countered by "a new collective and realistic behaviour" based on "clarity and simplicity".[15] Communists advocated an Italian cinema that gave a more realistic view of life than the American cinema.

After the war, measures like the creation of a genre system were adopted in order to encourage the recovery of the film industry, attract bigger audiences and oppose the domination by American films. Until the mid-1950s, the Italian cinema was organised with a genre system that reflected public tastes according to social class and geographical location. The so-called *films d'autore* were for the wealthier public in the cities and first-run cinemas, while comedies and musicals, melodramas and historical dramas were for the lower classes flocking into the second-run and third-run cinemas in the suburbs and smaller urban centres. And there was also the local market, especially in the South, where Neapolitan musicals and melodramas were very successful. In this phase, "the great success of the mass consumption cinema was due to a typical post-war need for escapism, but also sprang from the entertainment tradition"[16] that had already existed before the war.

The genre system lasted up to the mid-1950s, when an "average" product began to gain ground. This was the comedy film, whose task was to standardise public tastes and guarantee the box-office takings necessary for the survival of the film industry. Plots and themes of comedy films actually came to represent "those middle classes that had not experienced a group identity based on belonging to associations, not even during the fascist era".[17]

By constructing the storyline around the mutual adaptation of the individual's needs and those of the society into which the individual was attempting to integrate, the comedy film portrayed the aspirations and values, moods and mentalities of these classes. Usually "aimed at the expectations of an average public", the comedy film expanded its audience, especially in the first few years, before it incorporated elements of "popular *neorealism*"; "the genre is attuned with the daily life of wider audiences and by embracing lower and middle class audiences, the cinema offered a foretaste of the standardisation that would take place in society".[18]

The same period also saw changes in the cinema-going public. Lower-middle class and lower class adults in the provinces and the South, especially women, turned to television, while the cinemas attracted more young people from all social backgrounds, and also middle- and upper-class adults, especially in the cities. The comedy films also took these changes into account and offered stories featuring more young and more middle-class people.

The merit of the post-war Italian cinema is that it "went out to discover a country and its collective history, starting from the bottom, preferably attempting to concentrate on the petty bourgeoisie's becoming proletarian and the proletariat's becoming bourgeois".[19] The corpus of fiction films "does not completely correspond to all of the country's history or reflect it all, but it does succeed in portraying an important segment, and in capturing the (noticeable or almost imperceptible) short-, medium- and long-term economic and social, ethical and ideological, cultural and anthropological, urban and environmental macro or micro-transformations, oscillations and variations. [. . .] Basically, all post-war Italian cinema is like a gigantic hyper-text that can be analysed, broken down and navigated following a variety of approaches".[20]

## Italian Comedy Films in the Fifties

In the 1950s, there was a noticeable increase in the number of comedies produced in Italy. In 1950, there were 30 comedies out of a total of 98 films produced (30.6 %), while in 1959 58 of the 132 films made (43.9%) were comedies. The data on box-office takings of Italian films show that comedy gradually, and then definitively, replaced melodrama as the most popular film genre towards the mid-1950s. When 1949–1959 takings are broken down by genre, they show that 41% of total takings came from comedies, comic-comedies and comic films, 17% from melodramas, 15% from historical films, 6% from minor *neorealism*, with the remaining 21% belonging to various genres. In the following decade, comedy would maintain and further consolidate this dominant position.

According to Vittorio Spinazzola, it was romantic *neorealism*'s use of growing numbers of women in leading roles that allowed this genre to replace melodrama in the public's affections. The condition of women in Italy was presented in a new and no longer punitive way when it came to relationships between the sexes and family ethics, and this became romantic *neorealism*'s "supreme strength", underlining its "vocation as the cheerful champion of female emancipation".[21]

It must be noted that "*neorealism* neglects women and—except for the odd unimportant female portrayal—concentrates above all on 'male' problems and experiences and focuses on a 'political sphere', whereas the popular cinema deals above all with the 'private sphere' by focusing on romantic problems".[22]

The comedy film in this period perfectly summarised the modern conflicts taking place in Italy, in particular the semi-humorous or humorously dramatic aspects involved in the birth of a consumer society. These were the years of transition from rural society to life in the industrial cities, and large segments of the female population were involved in this process. Female employment opportunities diversified and increased; women were not only the dominant motif of cinema narrations, but also discovered that they were consumers. The film that launched the "romantic neorealism" genre is *Due soldi di speranza* (1952) by Renato Castellani. It also launched a narrative model based on episodes, and this stylistic model made it possible to show the rapidly changing features of the new mass culture, the transformations caused by industrialisation, and their effects on the social fabric.

This type of comedy and narration expanded with the *"Don Camillo"* series to embrace political themes, moving into the city and into the inner city neighbourhoods with the Dino Risi series *Poveri ma belli* (1957), *Belle ma povere* (1957) and *Poveri milionari* (1959), and also with *Le ragazze di Piazza di Spagna* (1952) by Luciano Emmer, *Siamo tutti inquilini* (1953) by Mario Mattoli, *Le ragazze di San Frediano* (1954) by Valerio Zurlini, and *Le signorine dello 04* (1954) by Gianni Franciolini. These comedies had a social background of transformation; Italy was making the difficult transition from agriculture towards industry before the economic boom at the end of the decade. Although it was not the immediate vehicle of an ideology, romantic *neorealism*, and comedy in general, is the most apt expression of this climate: "Far from limiting itself to portrayal of new stories and new behavioural codes, comedy itself became a promoter of change, disseminating it in society, and accustoming the public to change and instability as new ways and styles of life".[23]

Another tendency that comedy developed from the early 1950s was choral narration in interconnected episodes, starting with *Altri tempi* (1952), collective films *L'amore in città* and *Siamo donne* (1953), and *Tempi nostri* (1954) by Alessandro Blasetti. Since the public appreciated this narrative structure, it was re-used several times. In a series of films directed by Luciano Emmer (*Domenica d'agosto*, 1950; *Parigi è sempre Parigi*, 1951; *Le ragazze di Piazza di Spagna*, 1952; *Terza liceo*, 1954) and by Gianni Franciolini (*Villa Borghese*, 1953; *Le signorine dello 04*, 1954; *Racconti romani*, 1955; *Racconti d'estate*, 1958), screenwriter Sergio Amidei tried out a new type of narrative: multiple or interconnected narration, the precursor of episode narration. In these films, the narrative structure was broken down into parallel stories against the background of a unifying framework consisting of a place (the beach, the tourist area, the city neighbourhood) or a time (Sunday, a national holiday). "The different narrative situations are not presented diachronically (i.e. one after the other), but in a way that makes them seem simultaneous, an effect obtained by alternating them when editing the film".[24]

Alongside this type of *commedia di ambiente*, another type of comedy took its inspiration from the same social fabric, but revolved around a strong character. Some of these comedies came close to the French model of comedy model or sophisticated American comedy—like *La fortuna di essere donna* (1955) or *Amore e chiacchiere* (1957)—or else they concentrated on describing and recounting a single character, attempting a deeper psychological exploration in the case of leading female roles, for example *Il segno di Venere* (1955) by Dino Risi, *Guendalina* (1957) by Alberto Lattuada or *Nata di Marzo* (1958) by Antonio Pietrangeli. On the other hand, when it came to male characters, this intimism gave way to a more ironic or sarcastic approach, with films like *Lo scapolo* (1955) by Antonio Pietrangeli, *Il marito* (1958) by Nanni Loy and Gianni Puccini, *Il vedovo* (1959) by Dino Risi, and *Il moralista* (1959) by Giorgio Bianchi.

## The Great Italian Cinema of the Sixties

The 1960s began with two epic films *d'autore*: *Rocco e i suoi fratelli* by Luchino Visconti and *La dolce vita* by Federico Fellini, while Vittorio de Sica brought *La Ciociara* to the screen. 1963 is the year of *Il Gattopardo* and *Otto e mezzo*. Critics all over the world greeted these films with interest, and they were also successful at the box office: *La dolce vita* held the record for takings in 1960, and marked a kind of aesthetic and conceptual dividing line of the decade. In 1960 Rossellini finished his two-part series on the Resistance with *Era notte a Roma*, which followed *Il generale della Rovere*. Another director who emerged in this period was Michelangelo Antonioni. His trilogy consisting of *L'avventura* (1960), *La notte* (1961) and *L'eclisse* (1962) showed Antonioni's capacity for innovative cinema language and the films were also successful with the public: *La notte* grossed 470 million lire, *L'avventura* 340 million and *L'eclisse* 305 million.

Production company Titanus is emblematic of this process of change. Gustavo Lombardo was careful to keep abreast of the times, to meet and anticipate new audience needs. From 1959, Titanus's production strategy was based on the interconnection of films of different quality levels (which could be distinguished manneristically as high-level and low-level production), but almost always with a stylistic note *d'autore*, like the three Lattuada films, *Il bidone* by Fellini, *Il tetto* by De Sica, *Uomini e lupi* by De Santis, *I magliari* by Francesco Rosi and *I magistrati* by Luigi Zampa. In the wake of the French *nouvelle vague*, Titanus also launched a "youth operation", giving young artists the chance to make films cheaply and in relative freedom; young directors made around 100 first and second films for Titanus between 1960 and 1965. Ermanno Olmi, Marco Ferreri, Pier Paolo Pasolini, the Taviani brothers, Lina Wertmüller, Elio Petri and Damiano Damiani are just some of the new directors who emerged in this period. Lombardo wanted to make an important contribution to the generational turnover in the Italian cinema: "I am grateful to Visconti for including some youngsters just starting out in the studios in his cast of newcomers. At a time when film production is a race for projects worth billions and billions of lire, and there are those who believe a film can give certain guarantees only if it has hugely expensive performers, Visconti's choice of actors for his extremely difficult characters can be a positive example. I think it's self-evident that to give really valid and concrete contribution to the cinema, a film needs to have something new to say in terms of its structure, and in the way its various different elements are distributed".

It is important to stress that there was no real *nouvelle vague* in Italy. This was mostly due to the absence of a central focus for it to form around, like the French journal *Cahiers du Cinéma* that was linked with many of the leading figures in the French cinema revival. In addition to this, the *neorealism* that had inspired the Italian *nouvelle vague* was now difficult to present to a greatly changed cinema audience. Another factor was that the aid the French Ministry of Culture gave to French film-makers was not a possibility in Italy, because the Italian state had always viewed any form of innovative cinema with suspicion. Some producers, like Franco Cristaldi or Alfredo Bini, launched isolated attempts to recruit new directors, trying to keep production budgets low. This was often a rather expensive production policy compared with the artistic and commercial results, and therefore defeated the aim of keeping to a small budget. Lombardo's strategy culminated in the two epic films *d'autore*: *Rocco e i suoi fratelli* and *Il Gattopardo*.

"The production of *Rocco e i suoi fratelli* is based on detailed and objective research into a social and historical context of our country. It was not easy to bring Rocco's family to life . . . we hope we have succeeded in rendering Visconti's idea. We also needed to describe the social context of the Southern Italians in Milan, not from the outside like regretful folklore, but with all of its inherent drama. This has been the difficulty of producing Visconti's film. If today someone asked me about the total cost of my production, I would answer that I owed this film to the Italian cinema and that I'm happy to have made it—even before the public has judged the film".[25]

Italian producers feared Visconti more for his Communist Party sympathies than for the huge production costs of his films, often disproportionate in comparison with the modest box-office takings. Lombardo fought hard for *Rocco*. When the film was shown, it was confiscated by the Milan State Prosecutor, and the critics at the Venice Film Festival did not appreciate it at all. *Rocco e i suoi fratelli*, *La dolce vita* and *Il Gattopardo* ushered in the season of the grand films *d'autore*. This formula was created to ensure greater exploitation of the first-run cinemas: if the film was a success, the first-run cinemas—with their higher ticket prices—ensured more rapid recovery of production costs. According to Lombardo's concept, the epic *d'autore* was aimed at expanding the market, not only via the first-run cinemas. The success of the movies he produced was also—and mostly— entrusted to provincial audiences. The Titanus project was created in three years, from 1960 to 1963, coinciding with one of the most successful periods of the Italian film industry. Lombardo was well aware of the difficulty of sustaining a production policy involving only big budget movies: "The big actors with the names that draw audiences demand crazy figures. We need to be brave enough to pay more for the value of creative ideas and to rely less on the attractiveness of a star, even one we have under contract; we should always depend on a lively and interesting story for success, which is just what today's public prefers". Titanus had produced two big budget films: *Maja desnuda* by Henry Koster and Mario Russo in 1958 and *La sposa bella* by Nunnally Johnson in 1960; it was working on the epic film *Sodom and Gomorra*, and Visconti's *Il Gattopardo* was showing in the cinemas.

Visconti's film was released in March 1963, and for Lombardo it was an investment that he needed to acquire legitimacy as a producer and achieve equal status with his American counterparts. For this reason, he set no limits on the budget and concentrated on intensive distribution in the first-run cinemas in the most important cities. By the end of the 1963 season, the film had brought in 776 million lire just from these cinemas, accounting for 90% of its overall takings of 856 million lire by 30th September.

During the 1963–64 season, intensive exploitation of the first-run cinemas carried on, and the film totalled 1 billion lire. No other Italian film had ever managed to make so much money.

According to Lombardo, the Italian market needed more than epic films *d'autore* but also required "films by young people, meeting the need for interest and human warmth that make them a guaranteed success, even with every kind of mass audience". These were low-budget films, an average product focused on the director's own issues and on the typical experimental expressive techniques of avant-garde art. Despite its praiseworthy intentions, this project did not have actually the desired effect. The new directors were given the difficult task of renewing the Italian cinema at a time when television and the economic boom—with its implications for cultural consumption—perhaps required the industry to change with the times.

Alongside his young director policy, Lombardo also opened up to collaboration with the Americans, changing his mind about his initial intention to remain independent. Titanus took care to establish a system of collaboration with the American majors after some good experiences of dual and triple co-productions with European partners, like Spain and France for *Rocco e i suoi fratelli*. Being a partner in a co-production meant firstly that production costs were reduced by at least 30%, and this was important at a time when production costs were beginning to rise. Italian film companies tried to sign agreements with the Americans in order to open up the US market to Italian movies and to be able to use American money for ambitious projects. The 1961 Titanus-MGM agreement had these same objectives.

MGM signed a production agreement as a minority partner (49%) with Titanus, plus an agreement to distribute Italian movies in the United States.

The new company planned to produce at least six films, and made *L'isola di Arturo* by Damiano Damiani, *Le quattro giornate di Napoli* by Nanni Loy, *Cronaca familiare* by Valerio Zurlini, *Ti-kojo ed il suo pescecane* by Folco Quilici and *Smog* by Franco Rossi. The sixth film was never made, partly because the US public was not particularly interested, and the films never took advantage of the widespread distribution promised in the agreements.

The shift in big box-office returns from the US to the Italian cinema, and from low-profile to quality films is an undisputable fact and it allowed the larger film companies to concentrate on the first-run circuit, meaning that they recovered their production costs more rapidly and reduced the company's exposure to financial risk. This strategy also rewarded the small companies, which decided to invest in quality films with long-term earning potential, as did Franco Cristaldi's *Vides* and Alfredo Bini's *Arco Film* in its early days.

The genres also underwent a renewal during this same period; it was increasingly a question of film series (*"filoni"* for the Italian critics), with a huge number of films produced by a multitude of small companies in a relatively limited period of time. So, while first-run cinemas showed medium-high quality films like the cinema *d'autore* and the new *commedia all'italiana* of the 1960s—which differed from that of the 1950s in its forms and in its target audience—there were also less sophisticated products, like the sensationalist documentary, a genre launched with *Europa di notte* (Alessandro Blasetti, 1959). The new *commedia all'italiana* was particularly successful with audiences; the films were well made and there was always an element of fashion. The cinema is both a shaper and a product of the country's *modus vivendi*. It is a shaper because it is always slightly ahead of events, and it is also a product of people's instincts, moods and inclinations. The public liked comedies, even if they tended to finish on a pessimistic note. From the producer's point of view, these comedies earned prestige and praise from the critics, but were not so successful in economic terms. The returns were not very high; although there many cinemas and large audiences, tickets were cheap. In addition, producers did not have the same opportunities as to exploit films as they do now, for example selling broadcasting rights to TV companies. Profits came mostly from the box office, but even films now recognised as landmarks in the history of Italian cinema did not bring in huge amounts of money when they were first released. *Il Sorpasso* was first shown at the Cinema Corso in Rome; it was a Friday, the day when film premieres were held. The night's takings were low, and on the following night the film took in only 400–500,000 lire, which was not very much even then, since a ticket cost 500 lire. The cinema owner was about to take the film off the programme, and it was only on Monday that box-office takings rose as the word spread that the film was worth seeing. It is also interesting to note that the first reviews of *Il Sorpasso* were lukewarm, and that the film did not receive one single award.

It was difficult for Italian-style comedy films to break into foreign markets, although they did quite well in Spain and South America. Italian producers tried hard in the United States, along with Joseph Levine who had distributed the neorealist films on the other side of the Atlantic. In the US, these films were well received by the critics, but takings were low. Only *Il Sorpasso* (released as *The Easy life*) did well at the box office, while others did badly; one of these failures was *I Mostri*, but it consisted of episodes and was not cinematographically outstanding.

On the other circuits—which would not disappear altogether until well into the 1970s—there was a real boom of the peplum genre, which was common from approximately 1957 to 1963, or the Western, which was at its height of popularity between 1964 and 1970. These films easily found their way onto the minor cinema circuits in other European countries and

North America. State funding meant that production of these genres continued to flourish, independently of their market results.

In the long term, the policy of producing films for the first-run circuits, which the Italian film companies pursued from the late 1950s, did not appear to favour the largest companies. Since there was no other force regulating the market, state funding turned out to be a two-edged weapon in that it increased the competition, while the most spectacular movies involved high-risk investments that were not always recouped rapidly. Between the mid-sixties and the end of the decade, the companies that had concentrated most decisively on quality films and on the international market went out of business. Titanus closed down its production branch in 1964, and Galatea followed suit in 1965, while the Rizzoli film companies did not survive the death of the editor (1970), and even De Laurentiis moved to the United States in 1971 following the failure of his "Dinocittà" studios.

In the 1970s, everything changed. In the first place was society, whose metamorphoses no longer inspired Italian-style comedies. Producers changed and so did screenwriters, directors and the actors. "When all is said and done, the Italian-style comedy has had its day. It has worn itself out, just like any genre if it is exploited intensely".[26]

## Notes

1  Calvino, Italo 2010, "Autobiografia di uno spettatore", in Fellini, Federico, *Fare film*, Torin: Einaudi, p. X.
2  See SIAE (Società Italiana Autori Editori) publications: *Il Giornale dello Spettacolo* and *Borsa Film*.
3  Brunetta, Gian Piero 1993, *Storia del cinema italiano*, Rome: Editori Riuniti.
4  Bondanella, Peter 1983, *Italian Cinema from Neorealism to the Present*, New York: Continuum, pp. 142–144.
5  Nowell-Smith, Geoffrey 2008, *Making Waves: New Cinemas of the 1960s*, London: Continuum, pp. 152–162; Wood, Mary 2005, *Italian Cinema*, Oxford: Berg, pp. 14–21; Sorlin, Pierre 1996, *Italian National Cinema 1896–1996*, London: Routledge, pp. 115–143.
6  Small, Pauline 2009, *Sophia Loren: Moulding the Star*, Bristol and Chicago: Intellect Book; Reich Jacqueline 2004, *Beyond the Latin Lover: Marcello Mastroianni, Masculinity and Italian Cinema*, Bloomington: Indiana University Press; Burke, Frank, and Marguerite Valler (eds.) 2002, *Federico Fellini: Contemporary Perspective*, Toronto, Buffalo, and London: University of Toronto Press; Wagstaff, Christopher 1998, "Italian Genre Films in the World Market", in Geoffrey Nowell-Smith and Steven Ricci, *Hollywood and Europe: Economics, Culture, National Identity*, London: BFI, pp. 74–85.
7  Wagstaff, Christopher 1992, "A Forkful of Westerns: Industry, Audiences and the Italian Western.", in Dyer, Richard, Vincendeau, Ginette, *Popular European Cinema*, London: Routledge, pp. 245–261; D'Amico, Masolino 2008, *La commedia all'italiana. Il cinema comico in Italia dal 1945 al 1975*, Milan: Il Saggiatore; Grande, Maurizio 2003, *La commedia all'italiana*, Rome: Bulzoni; Pintus, Pietro (ed.) 1985, *La commedia all'italiana. Parlano i protagonisti*, Rome: Gangemi Editore.
8  Bondanella, *Italian Cinema*, p. 142.
9  Brunetta, *The History of Italian Cinema*, p. 10.
10  Ibid., p. 143.

11  A more detailed analysis is contained in a recently published paper by Miskell, Peter, Nicoli, Marina 2015, "From Outsiders to Insiders? Strategies and Practices of American Film Distributors in Post-War Italy", *Enterprise and Society*, 1 (6): 1–45.

12  Società Italiana Autori ed Editori SIAE, in Storia del cinema Italiano, Marsilio, Bianco & Nero, vol. VIII e vol. IX.

13  Grignaffini, Giovanna 1998, "Female Identity and Italian Cinema of the 1950s", in Bruno, Giuliana, Nadotti, Maria, *Off Screen: Women and Film in Italy*, London-New York: Continuum, p. 125.

14  Gundle, Stephen 1995, *I comunisti italiani tra Hollywood e Mosca. La sfida della cultura di massa (1943–1991)*, Florence: Giunti, p. 138.

15  Togliatti's article was published in "Vie Nuove", A ciascuno i propri sogni, 16 aprile 1950. For the Catholic approach to the cinema, cf. at least Brunetta, "Cattolici e cinema", in Tinazzi, Giorgio (ed.) 1979, *Il cinema italiano degli anni '50*, Venice: Marsilio, pp. 305–321.

16  Colombo, Fausto 1998, *La cultura sottile. Media e industria culturale in Italia dall'ottocento agli anni novanta*, Milan: Bompiani, p. 230.

17  Lanaro, Silvio 1992, *Storia dell'Italia repubblicana. L'economia, la politica, la cultura, la società dal dopoguerra agli anni Novanta*, Venice: Marsilio, p. 112.

18  De Giusti, Luciano 2003, "Disseminazione dell'esperienza neorealista", in Id. (ed), Storia del cinema italiano, vol. VIII 1949/1953, Rome/Venice: Bianco & Nero/Marsilio, p. 18.

19  Brunetta, Gian Piero 1995, "Il cinema legge la società italiana", in Barbagallo, Francesco, *Storia dell'Italia repubblicana, vol. II, La trasformazione dell'Italia: sviluppo e squilibri, tomo II "Istituzioni, movimenti, culture"*, Turin: Einaudi, p. 786.

20  Ibid., p. 784.

21  Spinazzola, Vittorio 1985, *Cinema e pubblico. Lo spettacolo cinematografico in Italia 1945–1965*, Milan: Bompiani, p. 119.

22  Carrano, Patrizia 1988, *Malafemmina: la donna nel cinema italiano*, Florence: Guaraldi, p. 66.

23  Canova, Canova 2003, "Forme, motivi e funzioni della commedia", in Bernardi, Sandro, *Storia del cinema italiano 1945–1954*, Rome/Venice: Bianco&Nero/Marsilio, p. 260.

24  Rossitti, Marco 2005, *Il film a episodi in Italia tra gli anni Cinquanta e Settanta*, Bologna: Hybris, p. 71.

25  Lombardo, Goffredo 1960, *Dovevo farlo*, in Aristarco, Guido, Carancini, Gaetano, *Luchino Visconti, Rocco e i suoi fratelli*, Rocca S. Casciano: Cappelli

26  Pintus, Pietro 1985, *Commedia all'italiana. Parlano i protagonisti*, Rome: Gangemi.

## Bibliography

BARBAGALLO, Francesco 1995, *Storia dell'Italia repubblicana, vol. II, La trasformazione dell'Italia: sviluppo e squilibri, tomo II "Istituzioni, movimenti, culture"*, Turin: Einaudi

BARKER, Martin, AUSTIN, Thomas 2000, *From Antz to Titanic: Reinventing Film Studies*, London: Pluto Press

BERNARDI, Sandro 2004, *Storia del cinema italiano 1945–1954*, Rome-Venice: Bianco &Nero/Marsilio

BOBO, Jacqueline 1988, "The Color Purple: Black Women as cultural readers", in Pribram, Deidre (ed.), *Female Spectators: Looking at Film and Television*, New York: Verso, pp. 90–109

BONDANELLA, Peter 1983, *Italian Cinema from Neorealism to the Present*, New York: Continuum

BRUNETTA, Gian Piero 1993, *Storia del cinema italiano*, Rome: Editori Riuniti

BRUNO, Giuliana, NADOTTI, Maria (eds.) 1988, *Off Screen: Women and Film in Italy*, London-New York: Continuum

BURKE, Frank, VALLER, Marguerite (eds.) 2002, *Federico Fellini: Contemporary Perspective*, Toronto, Buffalo, and London: University of Toronto Press

CALVINO, Italo 1974, "Autobiografia di uno spettatore", in *Romanzi e racconti*, Milan: Mondadori, pp. 27–49

CARRANO, Patrizia 1988, *Malafemmina: la donna nel cinema italiano*, Florence: Guaraldi

CASETTI, Francesco 1999, *Theories of Cinema, 1945–1999*, Austin: University of Texas Press

CASETTI, Francesco, MOSCONI, Elena (ed.) 2006, *Spettatori italiani. Riti e ambienti del consumo cinematografico in Italia 1900–1950*, Rome: Carocci

COLOMBO, Fausto 1998, *La cultura sottile. Media e industria culturale in Italia dall'ottocento agli anni novanta*, Milan: Bompiani

D'AMICO, Masolino 2008, *La commedia all'italiana. Il cinema comico in Italia dal 1945 al 1975*, Milan: Il Saggiatore

DE BERTI, Raffaele 2000, *Dallo schermo alla carta*, Milan: Vita e Pensiero

FANCHI, Maria Grazia, MOSCONI, Elena (eds.) 2002, *Spettatori italiani. Ritti e ambienti del consume cinematografico*, Milan: Vita & Pensiero

FARASSINO, Alberto 1989, *Neorealismo cinema italiano 1945–1949*, Turin: EDT

GRANDE, Maurizio 2003, *La commedia all'italiana*, Rome: Bulzoni

GUNDLE, Stephen 1995, *I comunisti italiani tra Hollywood e Mosca. La sfida della cultura di massa (1943–1991)*, Florence: Giunti

LANARO, Silvio 1992, *Storia dell'Italia repubblicana. L'economia, la politica, la cultura, la società dal dopoguerra agli anni Novanta*, Venice: Marsilio

MAYNE, Judith 1993, *Cinema and Spectatorship*, London: Routledge

MICCICHE, Lino 1975, *Cinema italiano degli anni '60*, Venice: Marsilio

MORREALE, Emiliano, 2011, *Così piangevano. Il cinema melò nell'Italia degli anni Cinquanta*, Rome: Donzelli

MOSCONI, Elena 2006, *L'impressione del film. Contributi per una storia culturale del cinema italiano 1895–1945*, Milan: Vita e Pensiero

MOSCONI, Elena, FANCHI, Maria Grazia 2002, *Spettatori. Forme di consumo e pubblici del cinema in Italia 1930–1960*, Rome/Venice: Bianco & Nero/Marsilio

NOWELL-SMITH, Geoffrey 2008, *Making Waves: New Cinemas of the 1960s*, London: Continuum

PINTUS, Pietro (ed.) 1985, *La commedia all'italiana. Parlano i protagonisti*, Rome: Gangemi Editore

REICH, Jacqueline 2004, *Beyond the Latin Lover: Marcello Mastroianni, Masculinity and Italian Cinema*, Bloomington: Indiana University Press

ROSSITTI, Marco 2005, *Il film a episodi in Italia tra gli anni Cinquanta e Settanta*, Bologna: Hybris

SMALL, Pauline 2009, *Sophia Loren: Moulding the Star.* Bristol and Chicago: Intellect Book

SORLIN, Pierre 2001, *European Cinemas, European Societies*, London: Routledge
_____. 1996, *Italian National Cinema 1896–1996*, London: Routledge

SPINAZZOLA, Vittorio 1985, *Cinema e pubblico. Lo spettacolo cinematografico in Italia 1945–1965*, Milan: Bompiani

TAYLOR, Helene 1989, *Scarlett's Women: Gone with the Wind and Its Female Fans*, New Brunswick, NJ: Rutgers University Press

TINAZZI, Giorgio (ed.) 1979, *Il cinema italiano degli anni '50*, Venice: Marsilio

WAGSTAFF, Christopher 1998, "Italian Genre Films in the World Market", in Nowell-Smith, Geoffrey, Ricci, Steven (eds.), *Hollywood and Europe: Economics, Culture, National Identity*, London: BFI, pp. 74–85

_____. 1992, "A Forkful of Westerns: Industry, Audiences and the Italian Western", in Dyer, Richard, Vincendeau, Ginette, *Popular European Cinema*, London: Routledge, pp. 246–261

WOOD, Mary 2005, *Italian Cinema*, Oxford: Berg

# Part IV

# "Shooting the Miracle"

# 8   Towards Obscurity

Italian cinema is dead.
Who has been the killer?[1]

## Can Politics Affect the Industry's Development?

Some historians trace the roots of the Italian cinema industry crisis in the 1970s and '80s back to the Corona Law of the mid-1960s, "the anti-cinema law".

Law no. 1213, approved by Parliament on 4 November 1965, contained "new" measures in favour of the cinema industry, aimed at encouraging the quantitative and qualitative development of Italian films via a complex set of state interventions. Section I stated: "The State considers the cinema to be a means of artistic expression, cultural education and social communication, and recognises its economic and industrial importance", specifying that "production, distribution and screening schedules are considered to be of important general interest" (Art. 1). Respecting these principles, "the State: a) encourages consolidation in the different sectors of the national film industry; b) promotes an industrial structure with state participation, ensuring that it integrates private industry and operates to keep costs low; c) encourages and helps initiatives to enhance and disseminate Italian cinema, especially films of particular artistic and cultural interest; d) guarantees the conservation of Italian films for educational and cultural purposes in Italy and abroad; e) trains professional managers, and promotes study and research of the film industry " (Art. 2). The subsequent sections contained regulations about full-length films, short films, current affairs, children's films, production, cinema funding, exhibition and distribution.

This Law aimed to provide a series of interventions that would (at least this was the intention) provide incentives to the film industry by creating an implicit distinction between productions that would benefit from its measures, and productions that—for various reasons—would not benefit. It became evident that the new regulations were not aimed at all film production companies, but only at those whose films corresponded to the abstract framework outlined by this law.

The film industry crisis began to have an effect in the late 1960s in Italy and in Europe. The states had begun taking an interest in the health of the Italian cinema industry in 1956, when the advent of television had caused declining audience numbers. From then on, the trade press had published a series of alarmist articles about the damage done to the cinema by competition from television.

At the end of the 1960s, cinema audience numbers fell in all European countries. In France, for example, audiences were 400 million strong when the cinema was at the height of its popularity, but by 1969 the figure had fallen to just 95 million. Higher ticket prices were unable to compensate for the declining numbers of cinemagoers, and total box-office takings had fallen to the equivalent of just 89 million lire, which was less than 50% of Italian box-office takings. This decline in what had been for years continental Europe's most lively and dynamic film market not only affected the number of films made in France, but also affected exports of Italian films to France, and French investments in co-productions.

An even more drastic decline took place in West Germany, where ticket sales fell from 830 million in 1955 to just 175 in 1969: a drop of 80%. The crisis of the German film industry was due to the improved quality and increasing numbers of television channels, the enormous number of films shown on television (400 full-length feature films in 1969) and the lack of strong state support for the industry.

The British film industry was similarly affected, and registered a decline in ticket sales like West Germany: a drop of 80% compared with the early 1950s. Production slowed to just 90 films a year, with state funding reduced by 90%.

The European situation was aggravated by the crisis in the US movie industry. In the early 1960s, Hollywood was hit hard by the television boom, and experienced a drop in ticket sales, takings and film production. This was followed by a slight upturn in audience figures, and the majors found a profitable new source of earnings from selling the rights to show their films on TV after they had been shown in the cinemas. Nevertheless, the US movie industry in the late 1960s soon found itself in a crisis caused by a number of factors: rapid saturation of the TV market, continually changing audience tastes, a series of box-office flops, rising production costs, the Republican administration's first measures aimed at curbing an overheated economy, and the consequent credit crunch. All of these factors created problems for some of the major Hollywood studios, and the US crisis had both positive and negative effects on European film industries. Although it meant that European films had more market space, it also meant that the majors were less willing to invest in Europe, in joint ventures and in purchasing the rights to exploit European films.

## The Crisis and the Successes

Explanations of the crisis that hit the Italian film industry in 1977 have often been superficial. Since the decline in audience numbers took place at the same time as the first independent TV channels began broadcasting,

ANICA immediately saw this as the second most important cause of the crisis after the increase in ticket prices.

In order to understand what happened in 1977, it is necessary to understand that major changes were taking place in the US majors, in Italian production and cinema management, and in television. Each of these elements influenced the change in the cinema's reference public. Ten years earlier, the Americans had experienced a crisis of the same entity as that now affecting Italy. It did not take much to realise that the cinema-going public had changed, that audiences had matured and now chose their films more carefully, distinguishing quality films from more commercial productions. Cinemagoers chose the films they wanted to see and they also had the option of watching TV, which offered plenty of entertainment and varied programmes. The Americans established "the commercial policy of market concentration"[2] and exported this across the Atlantic via the major studios' subsidiaries; they distributed films, imposing high prices on exhibitors and obliging them to keep films on screens for long periods. While film showings became concentrated in the first-run cinemas as the other cinemas were eliminated, the reduction in American investments and the credit crunch meant that Italian film production became concentrated in the hands of just a few companies; they produced films that were either "big-budget productions" on a par with US blockbusters, or low-quality films that were often pornographic.

In the Italy of the early 1970s, the public changed and shrank as the masses were replaced by mature spectators. This process ended with the advent of private television channels, which showed the lowest-quality films that had finished their life cycle in the cinemas. The real decline in cinema audiences mostly involved audiences for this kind of film. Other spectators continued going to the cinema; takings increased, but viewing figures fell because cinema programmes were longer.

It is interesting to look at the changes in the Italian public during the 1970s as seen by ANICA, with a concern expressed in the cinema magazine *Cinema d'oggi*. In 1967 and early 1968, international collaboration, the good number and quality of films, and agreements with television meant good prospects for the Italian cinema.[3] In 1968, came the first awareness that audiences were falling, but film production was still at a relatively good level.[4] The problems began to hit hard in 1972, when in addition to the credit crunch and tax burden, industry exponents criticised increased ticket prices; there was a 10% drop in audience numbers compared with 1968, which meant around 530 million lire in lost takings.

Some producers appeared to be fully aware of what was happening: "No one can deny that there is a crisis involving audiences, but they have definitely not fled. The truth of the matter is that a good film is no longer enough for them; films need to be outstanding. There is a public is available for this type of film".[5]

Takings actually rose between 1968 and 1972 from 170 to 230 billion lire, and quality films were seen by a large public. Nevertheless, ANICA was not satisfied with this increase in takings because it was accompanied by rising production costs: "box-office takings may suggest that our industry is in excellent form, but a more detailed analysis reveals the serious deficit between costs and earnings. Last year, Italian films took in 118 billion lire, but the producers only get back a fifth of this, i.e. around 26 billion, which is hardly enough to cover production costs".[6]

Despite the losses, audience numbers were still high in the early 1970s. Italy's 500 million spectators made it the world's second largest market, and cinema tickets were cheap compared with other leisure activities like the theatre or sporting events.

Articles in *Cinema d'oggi* reiterated that only commercially valid films could stay on cinema screens a long time and attract a large public. Although these films did bring in spectators, the crisis was held to be the direct result of TV programmes, thought to attract even the segment of the public that followed quality films. ANICA's main concerns were that the increased cinema ticket prices would make it impossible for the whole family to go the cinema, and that the wide variety of films shown on TV would lead to a further drop in audience figures.

## The New Cinema Audience

In 1977, numbers fell sharply from the previous year: audiences were down by 20% and takings plunged from 454 to 373 million lire. In an attempt to understand the reasons for this decline, ANICA and AGIS commissioned DOXA research institute to do a statistical study on Italian spectators. The results were published in *Cinema d'oggi*, together with a similar study by DOXA in 1972.

There were two stages to the survey. In the first stage, 8,000 people over the age of 15 were interviewed in order to quantify the numbers of regular and occasional cinemagoers and of non-cinemagoers and to evaluate their social and demographic characteristics. Questions were also designed to find out who watched the films shown on TV. The second stage of the survey interviewed 40 people who went to the cinema at least once a month and 2,500 who went at least twice a year, to acquire data about their attitudes, motivation and expectations about the type of films on offer.

The survey revealed that 57% of Italians had not been to the cinema at all during the 1970s: the cinema had lost its typically ritual nature of the '50s and '60s. Of the 43% who still went, the survey revealed that 20% had gone less often during the 1970s, while 12% actually went more during the period (mostly the 15–24 age group), and a further 12% had not changed their habits. Of these spectators, 25% went frequently (once or more times a week), 43% went with an average frequency and 32% went infrequently. It was also found that there were more cinemagoers in larger cities than in smaller centres.

These data revealed three important trends. One was the large number of young cinemagoers, due to the market segmentation policy pursued by the film industry in order to meet the falling demand for family entertainment. A second trend was that spectators in the large cities went to the cinema more often, meaning that they were willing to travel in order to have more choice and more comfort in cinemas. Thirdly, when the new survey was compared with DOXA's 1972 survey, what emerged was not so much the drop in the absolute number of spectators as much as the frequency with which the public went to the cinema. DOXA attributed the reasons for this decline in frequency above all to increased ticket prices; this made the cinema more expensive, so that audiences became more selective and demanded better-quality films. It is also important to consider that the public made better-informed choices about what to see, and that the smaller number of films in circulation meant that films had a longer run in the cinemas. All of these factors explained the decline of cinema ticket sales.

When it came to the issue of competition between cinema and television, 80% of the cinemagoers interviewed said that they watched films on television at least once a week. Compared with the 1972 data, this reveals a growing interest in the new form of communication, due also to technical improvements, like the use of colour in RAI broadcasts. With the advent of private TV stations, the number of hours dedicated to films shown on TV increased (from 230 in 1976 to 329 in 1977), but the offer differed from the cinemas in that the films shown on TV were of poor quality, so that it was mostly a case of competition between television and the second- and third-run cinemas.

The survey also revealed that the public was fully aware of the specificity of the cinema, so that "when cinemas offer the public new films that stimulate their interest and expectations, audiences have shown that they are ready to prefer the cinema to television and other leisure time activities, but when cinema films are mediocre, the competition with films and TV programmes becomes more intense".[7]

In addition, demand for the cinema was stimulated by different needs according to the public involved. For adult spectators, the cinema was associated with the idea of isolation and silence, while young spectators saw an outing to the cinema mostly as a way to socialise and to share the experience of watching the film. Going to the cinema was a real ritual: spectators watched in silence, waited in front of the screen for images to appear, and experienced emotions.

The new cinema public also seemed to want more information on which to base the choice of films. The demand for spectacular technical effects and originality grew. The decision to see a film was planned in advance, and if it had always been the actors or film genre to influence the public's choices, the DOXA report now revealed that the director's reputation was an important factor.

The Italian public had changed a great deal. Television was just one factor that had brought about the decline in cinema audience figures. It was not that Italian cinema was dying, but there was a profound change in its relationship with the public. This did not necessarily mean a drop in consumption, but did mean a change in the way it took place. ANICA seemed aware of this change, as shown by *Cinema d'oggi*: "the home market can still produce a quality films at reasonable prices. The national cinema can still produce a considerable number of films and aspire to earnings that are mostly remunerative".[8]

Armed with this new understanding of the cinema-going public, the film companies thought it would be possible to relaunch the industry, and set their primary objective as the production of films that would attract international interest, on which to invest most of their human and economic resources. Without neglecting Italian production, which would, in any case, pursue quality.

1977 was the year when Italian producers realised what was needed, but this was also the year when some hugely successful American films arrived on the screens: Star Wars, Taxi Driver, Saturday Night Fever, King Kong, Rocky, and Close Encounters of the Third Kind. These films accounted for 46.5% of total box-office takings. US films began once again to dominate the most important cinema circuits and also to invade TV screens. Once again, the biggest worry for Italian exhibitors was how they could obtain enough American films to keep the cinema circuits working at full capacity.

## Crisis and Reform

The crisis of the Italian cinema led to a debate about the possibility of new legislative interventions aimed at a reform.

One of the most significant problems of the Italian film industry is certainly a cultural problem, as is evident from the very first pages of this book. This basically means an inability to understand that the cinema has an artistic dimension, but cannot exist without its economic dimension. Faced with declining audiences, critics inevitably reacted by accusing the public of superficiality. But it is impossible to overlook the fact that offer and distribution influence demand, i.e. the public response. Of course, these mechanisms influence each other.

Discussion of film industry reform revealed the desire to remain doggedly anchored to the atypical industrial nature of film as a product. The Italian film industry has always been able to count on direct state funding, as much in terms of bailouts as in terms of pure and simple multiplication of earnings. Despite its constant presence in the dynamics of the market, the state has never invested in improving the movie industry or in protecting the good quality and socially concerned cinema. The figures showing the total amounts of aid (over 45 billion lire between the BNL fund and state aid to production and exhibition) absorbed by the film industry in the period 1971–75, show that 80% went to support the private cinema, while the remainder went to the public cinema.

What attracted most criticism was the refund system, i.e. state aid consisting of 13% of a film's gross takings. The situation in other countries was quite similar. The refund system was the general rule in all EEC countries, under different guises but with no real differences. The same was true for the aid-providing image of governments that intervened to support the cinema with easy credit and a continual reduction in tax levels. All Italian reform projects tended towards abolition of refunds and an increase in special credit for the cinema. 1977 and 1978 saw the introduction of two new laws increasing the special BNL fund to 20 billion lire and reducing tax to just 2% of the gross ticket price.

Only the Socialist Party (PSI) had an organic project for reform of cinema legislation, while Communist Party (PCI) and the Christian Democrats had more generic plans. The first point of the democratic proposals (PCI and PSI) was the transfer of responsibility for the cinema industry from the Ministry of Tourism and Entertainment to the Ministry of Cultural Assets, which would then be renamed the Ministry for Cultural and Environmental Assets and Entertainment. This was sufficiently indicative of the left-wing attitude towards the cinema, seen as a sector needing protection in the cultural interests of society, rather than as an economic and industrial sector to redevelop. The other left-wing proposals involved reshuffling the central film industry commission to increase the number of representatives from the professional associations, workers (unions) and SACC board of directors, the creation of a central body to control the *Centro sperimentale di cinematografia*, *Italnoleggio*, the *Cineteca nazionale*, *Istituto Luce*, and *Cinecittà*, and the regional decentralisation of some aspects of film industry administration and organisation via the creation of special committees. The democratic parties also agreed on the abolition of the refund system, which worked as follows: 26% of gross box-office takings usually went to the state as VAT and entertainment tax, and 13% of this percentage was then returned to the producer/distributor for five consecutive years as aid (i.e. a refund).

Since state aid was a percentage of takings, the highest-earning films benefitted most. Secondly, if cinema managers or the state increased ticket prices, the 13% rose automatically.

Therefore, the Socialist Party proposed a reform of the incentive system alongside elimination of the refund system. The BNL's ordinary fund would remain (increased from 700 million to 6 billion lire), and they also requested the creation of a special cinema fund of 20 billion lire for the first year and 15 billion for the following two years, through an annual state grant from the tax on films on television and on films shown in cinemas. A third tax, intended to feed the special fund, was a tax on dubbed foreign films, consisting of 2% of the rental quote. This tax did not apply to films with a majority production share held by EEC countries. The objective was to tackle the progressive increase in the Italian box-office takings of American films. The special fund would provide economic support for both the "industrial" cinema (a minimum of 35% of the fund was for this) and the cultural cinema (a minimum of 30%). The greatest problem lay in defining cultural cinema. The Communist Party proposed that funding for artistic films be allocated according to the verdict of a committee of "artistic experts". The Socialist Party, on the other hand, proposed evaluating the cultural validity of a film once it had been shown: in this case, funding would be granted only when a film had already been on the cultural circuit (in at least five regions) in the year following its first screening, for a number of days decided annually.

One further and fundamental point of debate concerned film rental reform. The previous law (the 1965 Corona Law) established that the Minister could intervene to define the rental percentages (according to the film's nationality) in the absence of any such agreement between the professional associations. This article was always ignored, and the reform did not alter it in any radical way, but established the maximum rental tariff only for the distribution of films on the cultural and school circuits. The reappearance of this article—albeit with a minor adjustment—showed that even at the political level it was not considered possible to overturn the balance of power that distribution had imposed on the market. A further point on which the political parties agreed was the tax shelter system, which the USA had abolished in 1975.

The Italian tax shelter project envisaged that 70% of the income earned by film production companies was not considered taxable income if this were re-invested in the production of subsequent films. The aim was to introduce into the Italian market a mechanism that would stimulate re-investment.

Another topic of debate concerned relations between the cinema and television. In this case, the political parties advanced a range of different proposals: a tax on film broadcasting, obligatory screening of Italian-made films, a ban on repeatedly showing the same films, a ban on showing films on a public holiday and on the day before a holiday.

The reform projects never went any further and show the main defects in tone of the debate about the Italian cinema: the idea that a film is first and foremost a cultural entity—at the expense of its economic and industrial dimension—and that the problems of the Italian film industry are completely divorced from the wider international context. So the response to the tyranny of the American blockbusters was to re-launch the quality cinema; the response to the concentration of investments was state aid for film production; the response to the concentration of cinemas was the regionalisation of the weaker circuits. Therefore, the proposed solutions involved traditional state support, without any change in the balance of power and the economic mechanisms underlying the workings of the film market.

## The Eighties

At the beginning of the new decade came the first symptoms of a crisis that would explode in the second half of the 1980s, and then continue with ups and downs until the start of the 1990s.

In this period, Italian cinema lost its identity, so that somehow it would have to start over again, retrieve its quality, and most of all it would have to achieve recognition outside Italy. The 1980s saw some good films and directors, but did not produce any great world-class films. This was a decade in which the Italian cinema "lost its bearings", in terms of searching for new contents, new poetry, a project that was valid and possibly not provincial, and hopefully some attempts at reform. To give an idea of the extent of this industrial crisis, it is sufficient to know that only 80 films were made in 1985 (the post-war minimum) and that the total number of spectators fell inexorably from 525 million in 1970 to 123 million. This physiological process at the same time also affected other countries with a grand cinema tradition like Japan, Great Britain and France. The crisis had an especially devastating effect on the Italian genre cinema, which lost most of its public with the growth of commercial TV. The Italian genre films made in the 1980s were just cheap imitations of Hollywood blockbusters, and the resulting B movies went straight onto the home video circuit. This meant that Italian cinemas were monopolised by films from the wealthy Hollywood studios, and these became increasingly dominant from now on. During these years, the *commedia all'italiana* also faded away, as its greatest exponents gradually ran out of creativity, although directors like Monicelli, Scola, Fellini and Bertolucci, and performers like Sordi, Gassman, Tognazzi, Manfredi and Mastroianni were still able to conjure up their last great exploits, leaving a lasting impression on the last two decades of the twentieth century, at least until the first half of the 1990s. In the early 1980s, *maestro* Monicelli created around Alberto Sordi one of the most important characters in the great actor's career, the "marchese Onofrio del Grillo" of *Il marchese del Grillo/The Marquis of Grillo* (1981). The film is set at the beginning of the nineteenth century, when Rome was still under papal rule, and the *marchese* is a noble prankster, one of Pope Pius VII's guards. The film's extraordinary success made the *marchese* into a well-known figure of popular culture. The role was created entirely around the great Roman actor's ability to play characters that were popular stock figures, poised between contrasting feelings and impulses. The film is a *commedia popolare*, pure theatrical entertainment with all the humour of the situation created by the witty dialogues, flavoured with plenty of Roman dialect, paradoxical situations and mistaken identities.

In a depressing scenario, with television literally ransacking the stores of film producers and broadcasting an excessive number of films, leading to deserted cinemas and a crisis in the film industry, the film market crisis also turned into a creative crisis. Once the impetus of innovation and research ended, film producers aimed to make easy money as fast as possible. The defunct *commedia all'italiana* was replaced by farces with lewd dialogues, like the *"cinepanettoni"* (Christmas films) and similar products that were at their height of popularity in the early years of the new century: films like *"Natale sul Nilo"* (Christmas on the Nile) or *"Natale in India"* (Christmas in India).

Fellini's film *Ginger e Fred/ Ginger and Fred* (1986) contains an emblematic depiction of this period of crisis. All agree unanimously in recognising the potency of Fellini's prophetic vision. With his fleshy and curvaceous portrayals of women and the lively, colourful gaudiness of the world his characters inhabit, Fellini seems to predict much of the superficiality and showy opulence of what was to come at the end of the century. The film's female lead is played by Giulietta Masina, Fellini's favourite actress and wife for almost 50 years, while the male lead is once again Marcello Mastroianni, Fellini's favourite actor and alter-ego. The film tells the story of Amelia (Masina) and Pippo (Mastroianni), two ex-dancers with a modest but exciting past career as a warm-up act specialising in Fred Astaire and Ginger Rogers numbers. After a long absence from the stage, the two aging dancers accept a private Italian TV channel's offer to take part in a show. When their dance number is just about to start, it is interrupted by a power cut: in the darkness of the TV studio Amelia and Pippo realise they have nothing in common with this kind of show business. The pair decide that the best finale for Ginger and Fred is to leave the stage while the spotlights are off, but the electricity returns just when they are about to go, and as their dance number continues, their magic momentarily takes over from the vulgarity of the adverts and sponsors. The film is a savage satire of consumer culture and the private TV stations, which Fellini especially hated for their bad habit of interrupting films with advertising. The overweening importance of publicity messages eliminates all the poetry, putting at centre stage an insipid TV presenter, savagely portrayed by Fellini. Television game shows and advertising are depicted as the dominant and alienating forms of the new mass culture. The film is sometimes dream-like and sometimes unsettling in its expression of a dark underlying pessimism, softened only by the two leading characters and their love story, and it seems to predict the salient features of the communication forms dominating contemporary mass society. Fellini's criticism of commercial TV (the barely concealed reference is to Silvio Berlusconi's TV, which at the time of the film was tightening its grip) is interwoven with the personal affairs of the two aging dancers, as they re-live their nostalgia for the good old days and regret for a love affair that never came to anything. The film is also a delicate love story, perfectly poised between sentiment and irony, with two actors whom it would be reductive to call sublime. Aside from Golden Globe and BAFTA nominations in the Best Foreign Language Film category, the film won many prizes, the most important being the *David di Donatello* and the *Nastro d'argento* awarded to Marcello Mastroianni, both in the "Best Actor" category, and the *Nastro d'argento* awarded to Giulietta Masina as the "Best Actress".

The creative and economic crisis that emerged in the 1980s began to ease during the 1990s, but the 1992–1993 and 1993–1994 seasons marked an all-time low in terms of the number of films made, the Italian market share (15%), total spectator numbers (under 90 million per year) and number of cinemas. The effect of this industrial decline was the definitive establishment of television as the entertainment medium *par excellence*, so much so that it absorbed all the types of genre cinema, no longer fit to compete with the great Hollywood blockbusters. However, despite this stagnation, some new cinema personalities quickly achieved international fame and recognition. The first to emerge was the Sicilian director Giuseppe Tornatore. His feature film debut in 1986 with *Il camorrista/The Professor* was followed two years later by *Nuovo cinema Paradiso/ Cinema Paradiso*, a huge success with public and critics alike, which gave him a vast appeal, also due to a sublime performance by French actor Philippe Noiret, who actually played his best film roles in Italy. A moving and nostalgic flashback to a bygone era of Italian life revolving around a provincial cinema, and above all to the way that audiences experienced the cinema, to a time when priests censored onscreen kissing, and the public laughed and cried with the films of Totò, John Ford or Raffaele Matarazzo. After some unforeseen difficulties (including cuts by censors), the film won the *Grand Prix du Jury* at the Cannes Film Festival and the Oscar for the Best Foreign Language Film. In 1995, Tornatore directed Sergio Castellitto in *L'uomo delle stelle/The Star Maker*, which won the *David di Donatello* and the *Nastro d'argento* for Best Director, as well as the *Gran Premio della Giuria* at the Venice Film Festival.

Plenty of Italian directors emerged during this period, but there was no specific type of Italian cinema that spread across international cinema screens, thus leaving the idea that the great season—when Italian cinema was exported and the great Italian directors were imitated and copied abroad—was now over. What is evident is that the crisis does not only involve the film industry, but is a wider crisis involving an entire country: an economic crisis and a political crisis. This shows how the cinema is inevitably embedded in, and deeply affected by, its specific social, economic and cultural context.

In the early 1970s, the Italian cinema industry still held a prominent position on the world market, in terms of both production and consumption. However, the following two decades were marked by a strong tendency on the part of the Italian market to become a mere consumer of films and TV products made in the USA. The cinemas were no longer the privileged temples of secular life's most important ritual, and the influence of the cinema on film consumption diminished considerably.

The national cinema industry's productive space and international market position changed completely. American cinema emerged from a period of crisis and began a comeback that was destined to give it to a newly dominant and almost exclusive position on the world market. Italian producers disappeared from the scene, or emigrated, or laid down their arms, leaving television as a major producer of films. In a period of growing consumption and rising living standards, the cinema seemed to have lost its position as a central social ritual. Producers gradually lost their trust in the film industry as a viable source of income. Encouraged and protected by the state, more for "humanitarian reasons" than for any other reasons, Italian producers were structurally weak, narratively fragile, and incapable of making an impact on the general viewing public or finding a place on the world market. The classical producers of the 1950s and '60s had now become more akin to mediators or agents, and the Italian film industry was even more fragmented than ever before. In 1980–81, 67 companies produced 87 films; two years later 84 different companies made 112 films and at the beginning of the 1990s the number of production companies was almost the same as the number of films.

Public TV and all private networks began to realize that it was more worthwhile to buy foreign products, the cost of which had already been recovered, than to produce their own and risk not being able to sell them abroad. Carmine Cianfarani, ANICA's third chairman, defined the 1980s as the era of "accelerated transition" from a business model to a model dominated by technological development. Contemporary ANICA analyses and forecasts emphasized that the future belonged to were interactive networks, television, virtual reality, informatics in every sphere of life, the globalisation of information and integrated audio-visual systems; this is precisely the present situation. During an official ANICA meeting in the mid-eighties, Cianfarani recalled a principle that had always been a kind of commandment for the association: "Individual capacities, however great, can never hope to overcome the worldwide challenge".

Since the 1970s, when Pier Paolo Pasolini released his scandalous *Salò o le 120 giornate di Sodoma* (1975), Italian cinema has alternately been identified, critically and commercially, as paralysed by crisis or on the verge of a "renaissance". Italian cinema has experienced and continues to experience many "life crises"—to paraphrase Pasolini—in which economic, political and cultural features have always been inextricably involved.

## Italian Cinema and the Digital Revolution

In 2001, Alberto Abruzzese, in the introduction to the book by René Baravjel[9], wrote, "cinema has now entered the new millennium but no one has thought about what the cinema could be in the future. For example, if the cinema could continue its paths without calling itself into question. On the other hand, do we have to consider cinema as an old language as well as literature and the theatre? Again, can we think about new possibilities for cinematic language? Can we imagine finding for it a new semantic space?" Whenever cinema has lived a technological leap forward, professionals have always be skeptical about future possibilities. Since the digital revolution has appeared, cinema professionals have spoken about it as a "technological abuse" full of virtual scenery and nothing more: "technology for technology's sake". Italian directors declared that what is badly needed is technology for ideas and new contents and not vice versa. Other foreign directors have been less catastrophic. Cinema has always been something made of a material space and environment: directorial choices made on the set, editing choices made in the editing room. As film-making becomes more and more digital, it is inevitable that new challenges has to be faced. Digital technology has affected primarily the way of directing and organizing work on sets. Nowadays, many professionals speak about "workflow". When Soderberg was asked about digital technology, he responded: "I can tell you now that if I had this technology earlier in my career, the work would have been better. I would've been able to see my ideas quicker and been able to respond and make adjustments faster. Now, I'm cutting scenes the same night they were shot and I can go back and make adjustments or do the whole thing over again. The ability to error-correct quickly is so much more pronounced".[10] As for the coming of sound and colour, the transition to digital technology opens up debates and mixed feelings.

The near-total cessation of celluloid projection has been perceived as a symbolic end-point. On the other side of the barricade, other professional voices insist that the prospects for audio-visual expression have never been brighter, given the vast amount of new platforms and setting. Yet, the act of seeing a feature film in a theatre has changed. Digitized cinema delivery and projection allows the exhibitor to program their cinemas more flexibly—as it means no expensive 35mm print is needed—to respond to the needs of their local audience.

Digital technology has undoubtedly changed the rules of the games, in the production, distribution and reception of cinema contents. In 2012, for the first time, 35mm film became the minority cinema format after nearly 90,000 screens went digital worldwide. According to the IHS Screen Digest Cinema Intelligence Service, cinema has moved from what once was a technology-free zone to one driven by technology.

Digital technology has brought about democracy—digital camera can be easily bought—as well as industry concentration. In the cinema industry, the digital revolution has meant aesthetic changes as well as deep economic consequences. Digital production is cheaper than analog, but not every production company has moved towards this new technology. Reasons are varied and many. There is still the need to define a unique technological standard. Cinema halls are still adapting: in Italy only 50% are equipped for d-cinema. Independent and traditional cinema-makers have approached digital technology in different ways. Young film-makers prefer d-cinema because they feel free to experiment, because it is affordable and they can use different distribution channels where image quality is not imperative. The digital revolution has opened many opportunities: it has brought new products; it offers the possibility to experiment and to change traditional economic industry structures. On the other hand, the danger is "a new paradox, where everyone produce for anyone". Another important consequence is that the digital has determined a new conceptualisation of debut film, which reverberates on the access to public funding. The digital revolution has profoundly changed Italian cinema in all its features, artistic, technical and economic. No one knows what is going to be the cinema of the future, but what is needed is to "be prepared to radically change our conceptual and theoretical maps".[11]

## Notes

1 Valerio Jalongo, director of the documentary *Di me cosa ne sai* (2009) about Italian cinema industry crisis from 1960s.
2 Wagstaff, Christopher 1999, "Il nuovo mercato del cinema", in Brunetta, Gian Piero, *Storia del cinema mondiale: Europa*, Turin: Einaudi, p. 863.
3 "Prospettive", in *Cinema d'oggi*, 18 December 1967, no. 12, p. 1 and Eitel Monaco, "L'Anica per il cinema italiano", *Cinema d'oggi*, 1 January 1968, no. 1, p. 1.
4 Monaco, Eitel 23 December 1968, "Prospettive favorevoli ma condizionate", *Cinema d'oggi*, (49): 1.
5 "Il pubblico c'è, non è fuggito", *Cinema d'oggi*, 21 January 1972, no. 3, p. 8.
6 "Azione incisiva", in *Cinema d'oggi*, 4 December 1972, no. 46, p. 1.
7 "Il film ha sempre un grande pubblico", *Cinema d'oggi*, 4 October 1977, no. 34, p. 4.
8 "Il mercato interno è ancora valido per una produzione selezionata", *Cinema d'oggi*, 8 November 1977, no. 38, p. 3.
9 Barjavel, Renè 2001, *Cinema totale. Saggio sulle forme future del cinema*, Rome: Editori Riuniti.
10 Vishnevetsky, Ignatiy February 2013, "What is the 21st Century?: Revising the Dictionary", *MUBINotebook*.
11 Montini, Franco 2002, *Il cinema italiano del terzo millennio*, Turin: Lindau.

## Bibliography

BARJAVEL, Renè 2001, *Cinema totale. Saggio sulle forme future del cinema*, Rome: Editori Riuniti
BRANCATO, Sergio 2001, "Italy in the Digital Age: Cinema as New Technology", *Modern Italy* 6 (2): 215–222
BRUNETTA, Gian Piero 2007, *Il cinema italiano contemporaneao*, Rome-Bari: Laterza
FLICHY, Patrice 1994, *Storia della comunicazione moderna*, Bologna: Baskerville
GRECO, Michela 2002, *Il digitale nel cinema Italiano. Estetica, produzione e linguaggio*, Turin: Lindau
MICCICHÈ, Lino 1998, *Schermi opachi: il cinema italiano degli anni ottanta*, Venice: Marsilio
MONTINI, Franco 2002, *Il cinema italiano del terzo millennio*, Turin: Lindau
ZAGARRIO, Vito 1998, *Cinema italiano anni novanta*, Venice: Marsilio

# 9 Conclusions

"To create and equip a national cinema industry is a serious challenge".[1]

## Italian Cinema: The End?

"Italian cinema lacks means and lives as it can. But, is it possible that it continues living on the margins of life?"[2]

"We need to abandon this idea of Muse aided by the State. We need more entrepreneurial attitude and less moaning. We need to create products suitable for new audience tastes and new business models. We need creativity and most of all courage".[3]

The first statement dates back to 1929 when Italian cinema was trying to find solutions to compete with Hollywood. The second statement is from 2005, a year that professionals described as one of deep crisis for national cinema.

This book has shown how different "forces" (structural and contingent, as well as general and particular) have interacted along time—from the very beginning of the twentieth century to the end of the 1960s—and have profoundly influenced structural changes in the Italian movie industry and have determined its peculiar trajectory, both in terms of economic and cultural features. Cultural legitimacy, economic and financial forces, government intervention, foreign relations and patterns of consumption have strongly interacted and their relations have changed over time and in their intensity. For instance, cultural forces have influenced both political forces—in formulating theories of the role of the cinema within the state—and economic forces, in propounding theories on the cinema as an economic sector. For many years, cinema was seen as an exclusively speculative sector: this influenced any inclination the financial system or private operators might have to invest in cinema, limiting the amount of capital invested. Economic forces, here seen as operators of the value chain, mainly interacted with political forces especially by lobbying associations connected to the category. The political forces on their part acted on the economic forces by carefully regulating the sector and by opting for protectionist/free trade policies. By tracing the story of an industry "rise and fall", this book has explored some questions that rise whenever an economic historian approach the analysis of the Italian cinema, especially from an economic point of view: what has been the institutionalisation process of the Italian film industry? What happens to the making of a creative industry in a country where government and institutions play such a relevant role? Which factors have shaped the policy-making process in the creative industries?

The history of the Italian cinema is one of decline and revival, of films and actors that have become part of our collective imagery. It has been the story of directors able to renew the aesthetics and style of movies, of ambitious and daring entrepreneurs, and at the same time of producers, films and actors who appear overnight on the screen and equally quickly are forgotten. It is a type of cinema characterized both by the presence of a mania for what is foreign and by an impelling desire for self-identity: Italian audiences watched American films to dream and to escape and watched Italian films because they saw themselves reflected in them.

The history of Italian cinema is extremely interesting because it is the story of an "in between" industry, full of contradictions. It is the story of a movie industry that tried to "institutionalise" itself (Burch 2001, Casetti 2002 and 2005), continually defining and negotiating its own nature and identity as to economic, political and cultural institutions.

When we think of successful film-making able to make a name for itself on international markets, we immediately call to mind American movies that since the 1920s have established their competitive superiority over European films.[4] From that moment onwards Italy, like France, Germany and the United Kingdom, have tried to bridge the gap with the United States, adopting mechanisms to defend themselves from the American film industry and in support of their national film industry. Italian cinema was then the follower, which managed to recover fully during the 1950s, and '60s, actually reaching second place in world markets for the number of films produced and the number of box-office takings.

When the history of Italian cinema is analysed, we must not imagine a tardy or unsuccessful approach (Contaldo and Fanelli, 1986). Italian cinema must then be analysed as a case with its own distinguishing features, the study of which is useful for understanding which processes govern the institutionalisation[5] of a sector of creative industries, its transformation into an independent and qualified field, the formation of its productive structures and its own specific language, the ways in which production practices, artistic aspirations and movie consumption are interconnected. The processes of institutionalisation affect why and how the cinema determines for itself specificity and legitimacy: its own personality and identity (Gaudreault 2004, Odin 2004). Although the transition from a pre-cinematographic field to what is known as classic cinema has been amply studied, (Grievson and Kramer, 2004, Elsaesser and Barker 1990) little attention has been paid instead to the compromises and changes that the cinema as an institution has had to tackle. These changes have been determined as much by elements within the system as by external forces. The different combination of state laws, entrepreneurial skills, intellectual ferment and artistic personalities has determined the degree of originality that marked Italian cinema at least until the end of the 1960s.

## Business Structure: Mushroom Producers and Courageous Captains

The analysis of the first 60 years in the life of Italian cinema has been carried out by subdividing the span into three periods: the early making of the Italian film industry (1900–1924); the Fascist period (1925–1943); the period under a democratic government (1945–1965). This division in time enables us to understand one of the characteristics of the Italian movie industry. The sector does not in fact follow a classical type of evolution in which an initial furore of productions, designed to make the most of the opportunities presented by an emerging technology, is followed by a selection of the most efficient enterprises. From 1924, the Fascist dictatorship takes control and uses cinema as an instrument of propaganda and thus profoundly influences economic forces. At the end of the Second World War, the advent of democracy, together with the new vigour of reconstruction restores to the sector a more market-oriented approach that enables it once again to compete on an international level. The relationship established between industry and state during the fascist period continues without registering any conspicuous discontinuity with the past.

These are three distinct moments in which the forces that influenced the dynamics of the sector interacted in different ways and with different results determining what was the characteristic trajectory of Italian cinema. These forces are related to the productive structures and to the value chain as a whole (production—distribution—exhibition), to the political and cultural forces, to the reaction of audiences, to international dynamics and especially to the relationship with the United States.

After a brief promising period from 1911 to 1914 when Italy won acclaim on international markets—Cabiria (1914) was very successfully screened in New York, Buenos Aires, Paris and Tokyo—the Italian cinema stagnated, worsened as much by exogenous factors, the First World War, as by endogenous ones, for example the want of stylistic innovation, the absence of financial capital, production houses' organisational improvisation and the lack of coordination within the value chain.

If we observe Italian cinema from the early twentieth century to the 1970s, prior therefore to the transformations brought about by television, we can note that organisational models did not undergo particular changes. Alongside the few small to medium-sized enterprises and the very few vertically integrated ones, the mushroom productions continued to survive.

During the 1920s and '30s, the amateurish characteristics, the scarce attention paid to international changes and the sluggish renewal of production houses slowed down modernisation and growth. If, on the one hand, the "amateur touch" was able to offer more varied products of a higher quality, the Italian cinema enterprises demonstrated that they did not possess the necessary drive to upgrade themselves from a technological point of view or to be open to international commerce, where, due to competition, the quality of the product had become vital. Nor were the reduced commercial contacts between Fascist Italy and the rest of the world—autarky was on the Fascist manifesto—an encouragement to pursue the path of international engagement.

In the post–Second War period, no particular changes in the configuration of the sector are to be seen, not even from the point of view of proprietors or personnel. The small-medium sized firms continue to prevail and there is only one, Lux, which has a vertically integrated, American-style structure, able, that is, to control all the phases of the value chain, from production to cinemas. In this period, there were numerous examples of production run on entrepreneurial lines. Peppino Amato, Carlo Ponti, Dino De Laurentis, Angelo Rizzoli, Goffredo Lombardo are only a few of the "courageous captains" who produced successful films, able to leave a mark both on public imagery and on the evolution of cinematographic technology and lexis. So the change was to be seen above all in the capacity to make films that were appreciated not only by national but also by international audiences. It is plausible to imagine that such a change in productive skills was the consequence of the evolution in audiences' tastes. The cinema market during the 1920s and '30s was a captive market (Sedgwick and Pokorny, 2010): people went to the cinema mainly to enjoy themselves, and the demand for films was probably influenced by the offer. For a business, therefore, it was important to guarantee a continuous offer of products. After the Second World War, the massive arrival of American films increases the offer, audiences become more demanding and companies' survival on the market is connected to their ability to offer films in line with the tastes of a more mature audience, one which differed from that of the 1930s.[6] It is not enough merely to be present on the market, as what is required are above all human, technical and artistic resources, able to work together to realize specialized products and addressed to a variety of audiences.

## Cultural (mis-) Perception: Institutionalising a Creative Industry

All in all, the history of the Italian film industry highlights what happens to the development of a creative industry in a country where political and institutional factors have a strong impact and role in the definition of economic and cultural features of the movies. The book has highlighted the role played by some specific institutions in the foundation of a new industry, how they nurtured it and how they made it competitive on both national and international levels. These institutions influenced the "thinkability" (Casetti 2005) of Italian cinema and the legitimacy it would have as an art form and as business. Building from this particular case study, the book has offered more general insights on how the specificities of creative goods can impact their development paths. It sheds light on the economic and cultural context to which policies promoting and protecting these industries have responded, and, ultimately, assesses the effectiveness and impact of these policies on industry dynamics.

In the post–Second World War period, cultural debate took on different extremely ideological characteristics, centred around the possibility of having a cinema free in its subject matter but subsidized by the state. The problem was no longer one of style, but regarded the importance and the role of movies within a democratic state. If this role had been determined a priori by Fascism, in this new phase, it was the result of on-going negotiation involving individuals, the government and professional associations. Cinema was now accepted by intellectuals as an art form, but it was necessary to understand how it could elude market laws. The difficulty in reconciling the needs of actors and producers permeated the debate in specialist magazines. Producers were accused of accepting the thraldom of money and of being willing to modify their own productive strategies—for example when constrained by censorship—consequently humiliating the artistic reasons of the cinema as a form of expression. The vehement tones used to accuse producers denied what should have been their role as popularisers of subject matter, delegitimizing it. The analysis of economic problems was shelved in favour of a purely qualitative or often ideological reflection, making it impossible to imagine a cinema that was different from the one traditionally subsidized by the state. Certainly Italian cinema as an industry has always suffered from the problem of being marginalised by high culture. In the early 1900s, cinema was seen as a celluloid industry, "the dishonest and lucky daughter, a powerful and over-powering industry like money".[7] In the 1920s and '30s the judgement passed by the philosopher Benedetto Croce,[8] who had ruled out that it could be considered an art form, weighed heavily on cinema. If the general public appreciated cinema because it was able to provide entertainment and offer an escape valve, intellectuals, men of letters and philosophers considered it a form of entertainment best suited to maids and office girls. Even in 1956, at a time of lively debate on the legislation that the government was to have passed for the cinema (remember that 1955 was a year of vacatio legis), Montanelli in the newspaper *Il Corriere della Sera* wrote "the crisis of the cinema is welcome if it serves to free us from those dodgy businessmen who mistake improvisation and imprecision for talent, and whose debts the country is fed up paying, only to leave them as owners of villas and swimming pools".[9] This cultural context certainly did nothing to help cinema to be regarded as an industry.

## The Powerful Visible Hand: The State

Undertaking the study of the history of Italian cinema from the point of view of cinema policies means both understanding what were the consequences on the industry of certain political choices and understanding the history of the institutions and the mentalities that influenced those policies. Cinema, then, has to be collocated historically in the more general history of the society which that cinema formed. The relationship between the Italian government and cinema has always been one of love and hate. Analyzing the reasons for state intervention in cinema and understanding the economic and cultural objectives implies, in the first place, understanding the importance and the role of cinema in defining and negotiating its own existence within a political system and the way this was achieved.

The Italian state "discovers" cinema in 1913, during its golden years. The steps taken envisage supervision, censorship and taxation, with a series of taxes often increased especially during the war and in the years immediately following it.

The advent of Fascism does not initially change the situation. The first steps taken were on taxation and censorship. The timing and modality with which Fascism intervenes in the governance of the sector go hand in hand with the evolution of the regime. The debate on the influence of Fascism on cinema is still open today. There are scholars who are of the opinion that the sector was totally dependent on the regime, especially as far as subject matter was concerned, while some more recent studies try to depoliticize the relationship between cinema and Fascism, maintaining that cinema was relatively free both in terms of subject matter and business initiatives.[10] The Fascist cinema policy was in some ways contradictory, reflecting the uncertainty of the government in realizing the institutionalisation of a cultural form whose role and space in Italian society were at that time in a difficult period of transition, neither completely central nor peripheral.

With the consolidation of Fascist power in 1925, one of the objectives of the regime was to take control of the various communication systems, radio, cinema and newspapers. The birth of the Istituto Luce in November 1925 was supported personally by Mussolini. From that moment, propaganda, control, censorship and incentives are constantly intertwined, making the cinema an industry to which the regime paid special attention, above all in virtue of the power of images and the awareness that cinema was a key instrument in organizing consent and propaganda. With the beginning of the autarchic period, in the 1930s, the measures taken to relaunch and expand the sector followed one another thick and fast and went in two main directions: measures to encourage private national production and the direct participation by the state in cinematographic activity, by setting up bodies and firms under its control. Fascism had as models both American and Soviet cinema. American cinema was despised for its aggressiveness and its market laws, but admired for the kind of perfect and efficient industry it had been able to build. Soviet cinema was appreciated above all for its educational role, not only during the Fascist regime but also after 1945, when the possibility of entrusting cinema to the Ministry of Education was subject to speculation

Italian cinema was censored and controlled—in some cases at the service of political propaganda—but was backed both by the Fascist regime and the democratic government. In the post–Second World War period, people involved in the cinema often invoked the need to free the sector from the close ties with political power. Nevertheless, when there was a legal vacuum (it was 1955) there was an equally pressing request that the state should not abandon the cinema to a poverty-stricken fate, but provide support and protection. Equally ambivalent were the goals that ANICA, the most important cinema association, founded in 1944, wanted to achieve in the short and medium term. It appealed to the free market—also to prove it had broken with the past—but at the same time asked for public financial support to further the revival of business initiatives.

It proved difficult to dismantle the complex system of incentives, protection and support set up by Fascism. The new democratic government inaugurated its relationship with the national cinema industry, claiming that "the practice of film production is free" and for the whole of the reconstruction period the cinema seemed to be an economic sector that operated in a kind of no man's land. Far more serious problems linked to the reconstruction of a country devastated by the Second World War had priority on the government and allies' political and economic agenda. In this first phase, the industrial prerogatives seemed to have become once again separated from those of the state, unlike what happened in the Fascist period. Just a year after the end of the war, producers made their voice heard and asked for the direct action of the state, both with protective measures (compulsory times of showing) and with financial backing. Increasingly, the government began once more to take an interest in cinema, and the way they acted does not seem to point to significant discontinuity with the past. Compulsory times of showing, subsidies, government loans, awards, a prior control of subject matter and scripts helped Italian cinema to take the difficult step towards renewal, until the cinema boom in the 1960s made its mark.

The difficulty in analysing the relationship between cinema and state, especially as far as legislation is concerned, is closely connected not only to the complexity of the subject studied, but also to the ambiguity of the term cinema policy. As cinema is not only a product, but also a form of expression with an extraordinary communicative power, cinema policy includes measures both of an economic and of a cultural nature. Generally, these measures are the result of negotiation between different stakeholders; they respond to different objectives and have specific instruments that vary from screen-time quotas to public subsidies, low interest loans, quotas on foreign films imported, the establishment of schools to train technical staff and academies for actors, and the organisation of film festivals (Zagarrio 2002, de Grazia 1981, Tannenbaum 1972).

The aim of economic policy is to strengthen the productive system in order to develop and consolidate a sector able to generate economic wealth. Cultural policy instead aims at nurturing the sense of national identity, encouraging, for example, art houses, guaranteeing the survival of a sector able to be promoter and vehicle of the culture and of the specific value system of a country.

Whether the emphasis is placed more on the economic than on the cultural aspects of the cinema or vice versa influences the type of choices that a particular government decides to make. In Italy, the state has often taken on the role of a stopgap for development (Gerschenkron 1962), and this has been done in various fields of the national economy. However, clearly public policies in the automobile industry have not affected the type of cars turned out. The case of cinema is different—and its specific characteristics depend on this—where government decisions affect also the end product, the film, modifying and sometimes compromising the producer's and director's creativity.

This ongoing tension between the economic and cultural grounds for public intervention has generated a historiography debate with contradictory aspects. Some publications seem to suggest that cinema policy, above all after the Second World War, was directed at defending the interests of the industry but humiliated the interests of art. The debate on the relationship between state and cinema has often been approached with a prescriptive analysis, which has led to judging choices made by the government of the time with hindsight, without considering that political proposals could prove to be unconnected with the existing productive and cultural structures. The efficacy of legislation cannot be only, and exclusively, evaluated on the basis of the interests of art. Even though, for example, the measures providing protection and support after the Second World War seemed to favour a more commercial production, they actually did help Italian cinema to bridge the gap that separated it from the American movie industry.

Given its own non-material nature, cinema requires a framework encouraging exchanges and the circulation of ideas and technologies, so that innovation can be constantly sustained. Italian cinema history shows that this happens when cinema has found its place within the broader social, cultural and economic context. This means, when cinema has been institutionalised as an independent field: "everyone is for the shorter path, however the only possibility is the longer way. If we want to make a competitive industry, we need authentic film-makers. People who feel the cinema with the same gravity as other artistic fields".[11]

## Notes

1 Ottavi, Nino 30 November 1937, "Organizzazione della produzione", *Bianco e Nero: quaderni del Centro Sperimentale di Cinematografia*, Vol.11, quoted in Miccichè, Lino et al. 2006 (eds.), *Storia del cinema italiano: 1934*, Rome-Venice: Bianco e Nero/Marsilio, p. 680.
2 *Costruire*, in "La Cinematografia", 1–15 giugno 1929.
3 Quoted in the Italian professional journal *Reset. La via del cinema*, September-October 2005, n. 91.

4 The cultural and economic dominance of American films has been widely documented academically. See de Grazia 2005, Trumpbour 2002, Higson and Maltby 1999, Thompson 1985.
5 See Douglas (1986), North (1990), Streeck (1992) on institutions.
6 Fofi, Goffredo 1978, Introduction to Pellizari, Lorenzo (ed.), *Cineromanzo: il cinema italiano 1945–1953*, Milan: Longanesi.
7 Guido Gozzano 2008, "Il nastro di celluloide e i serpi di Laocoonte", reprinted in *Poesie e Prose*, edited by Alberto De Marchi, Milan: Garzanti, 1966, pp. 1167–1175.
8 It was only in 1948 in an article published in the cinema magazine "Bianco e Nero" called *Il cinematografia e la teoria estetica* that Benedetto Croce clarified his view of the cinema and conceded that it was possible to consider it an artistic form, like poetry, music and theatre.
9 Montanelli, Indro 14 June 1956, "I film costano troppo in confronto a quello che rendono", *Il Corriere della Sera*, quoted in Aprà, Adriano, 1978 (eds.), materiali sul cinema italiano degli anni '50, vol. II, Pesaro: Mostra internazionale del Nuovo Cinema.
10 Ricci, Steven 2008, *Cinema and Fascism: Italian Film and Society, 1922–1943*, Berkeley: University of California Press.
11 Margadonna, Ettore 25 febbraio 1933, "Lettera aperta sul cinema italiano", *Cine-convegno*, 1: 13.

## Bibliography

BURCH, Noel 2001, *Il lucernario dell'infinito. Nascita del linguaggio cinematografico*, Milan: Il Castoro
_____. 1973, *Theory of Film Practice*, New York: Praeger Publishers
CASETTI, Francesco 2005, *L'occhio del Novecento*, Milan: Bompiani
_____. 2002, *Communicative Negotiation in Cinema and Television*, Milan: Vita&Pensiero
CONTALDO, Francescio, FANELLI, Franco 1986, "10.000 km. Ad est di Hollywood. Sviluppo e sottosviluppo dell'industria del cinema in Italia", in Magrelli, Enrico et al. (eds.), *Sull'industria cinematografia italiana*, Venice: Marsilio, pp. 15–26
DE GRAZIA, Victoria 1981, *The Culture of Consent: Mass Organization of Leisure in Fascist Italy*, Cambridge: Cambridge University Press
ELSAESSER, Thomas, BARKER, Adam (eds.) 1990, *Early cinema: space, frame, narrative*, London: BFI
GAUDREAULT, André 2004, *Cinema delle origin o della "cinematografia-attrazione"*, Milan: Il Castoro
GAUDREAULT, André, MICHEL, Marie 1989, *Histoire du cinema. Nouvelles approches*, Paris: Sorbonne/Colloque de Cerisy
GERSCHENKRON, Alexander 1962, *Economic Backwardness in Historical Perspective, a Book of Essays*, Cambridge, MA: Belknap Press
GRIEVSON, Lee, KRAMER, Peter (eds.) 2004, *The Silent Cinema Reader*, London-New York: Routledge
HESMONDHALGH, David 2002, *The Cultural Industries*, London: Sage
HOSKINS, Colin, McFADYEN, Stuart, FINN, Adam 1997, *Global television and film: An introduction to the economics of the business*, Oxford: Oxford University Press
ODIN, Roger 2004, *Della finzione*, Milan: Vita & Pensiero

SEDGWICK, John, POKORNY Michael 2010, "Consumers as risk takers: evidence from the film industry during the 1930s", *Business History*, 52, 1: pp. 74–99

TANNENBAUM, Edward 1972, *The Fascist Experience: Italian Society and Culture, 1922–1945*, New York: Basic Books

TOWSE, Ruth (ed.) 2003a, *A Handbook of Cultural Economics*, Cheltenham, UK/ Northampton, MA: Edwar Elgar

WILDMAN, Steven 1995, "Trade liberalization and policy for media industries: A theoretical examination of media flows", *Canadian Journal of Communication*, 20, 3: pp. 367–388

ZAGARRIO, Vito 2002, *Non c'è pace tra gli ulivi*, Rome: Fondazione Scuola Nazionale di Cinema

# Index